Law, Orientalism and Postcolonialism

Focusing on the 'problem' of pleasure, *Law, Orientalism and Postcolonialism* seeks to uncover the organizing principles by which the legal subject was colonized. That Occidental law was complicit in colonial expansion is obvious. What remains to be addressed, however, is the manner in which law and legal discourse sought to colonize individual subjects as subjects of law. It was through the permission of pleasure that modern subjects were refined and domesticated. Legally sanctioned outlets for private and social enjoyment instilled and continue to instil within the individual tight self control over behaviour. There are, however, states of behaviour considered to be repugnant to, and in excess of, modern codes of civility. Drawing on a broad range of literature (including classical jurisprudence, eighteenth century Orientalist scholarship, early travel literature, and nineteenth century debates surrounding the rule of law), yet concentrating on the experience of British India, the argument here is that such excesses were deemed to be an Oriental phenomenon. Through the encounter with the Orient and with the fantasy of its excess, Piyel Haldar concludes, the relationship between the subject and the law was transformed, and must therefore be re-assessed.

Dr Piyel Haldar, LLB (Mddx), PhD (Lond) is a Lecturer in Law at Birkbeck, London.

Discourses of Law
This successful and exciting series seeks to publish the most innovative scholarship at the intersection of law, philosophy and social theory. The books published in the series are distinctive by virtue of exploring the boundaries of legal thought. The work that this series seeks to promote is marked most strongly by the drive to open up new perspectives on the relation between law and other disciplines. The series has also been unique in its commitment to international and comparative perspectives upon an increasingly global legal order. Of particular interest in a contemporary context, the series has concentrated upon the introduction and translation of continental traditions of theory and law.

The original impetus for the series came from the paradoxical merger and confrontation of East and West. Globalization and the internationalization of the rule of law has had many dramatic and often unforeseen and ironic consequences. An understanding of differing legal cultures, particularly different patterns of legal thought, can contribute, often strongly and starkly, to an appreciation if not always a resolution of international legal disputes. The rule of law is tied to social and philosophical underpinnings that the series has sought to excoriate and illuminate.

Nietzsche and Legal Theory: Half-Written Laws
Edited by Peter Goodrich and Mariana Valverde

Law, Orientalism and Postcolonialism: The Jurisdiction of the Lotus Eaters
Piyel Haldar

Forthcoming:
Identity of the Constitutional Subject: Selfhood, Citizenship, Culture and Community
Michel Rosenfeld

Endowed: Regulating the Male Sexed Body
Michael Thomson

The publisher gratefully acknowledges the support of the Jacob Burns Institute for Advanced Legal Studies of the Benjamin N. Cardozo School of Law to the series *Discourses of Law.*

Law, Orientalism and Postcolonialism

The Jurisdiction of the Lotus Eaters

Piyel Haldar

Routledge
Taylor & Francis Group
LONDON AND NEW YORK

First published 2007 by Routledge-Cavendish

Published 2023 by Routledge
4 Park Square, Milton Park, Abingdon, Oxon OX14 4RN
605 Third Avenue, New York, NY 10017

Routledge-Cavendish is an imprint of the Taylor & Francis Group, an Informa business

Typeset in Minion by
RefineCatch Limited, Bungay, Suffolk

British Library Cataloguing in Publication Data
A catalogue record for this book is available from the British Library

Library of Congress Cataloging-in-Publication Data

Haldar, Piyel.
Law, orientalism and postcolonialism: the jurisdiction of the lotus eaters / Piyel Haldar.—1st ed.
p. cm.
Simultaneously published in the USA and Canada.
ISBN 13: 978–0–415–96224–7
ISBN10: 0–415–96224–2
ISBN 13: 978–0–415–96223–0
ISBN10: 0–415–96223–4
1. Law.—Psychological aspects. 2. Crime. 3. Colonization—Psychological aspects.
4. Orientalism. 5. Postcolonialism. I. Title.
K346.H35 2007
340′.19–dc22

2007024900

ISBN13: 978–0–415–96224–7 (pbk)
ISBN13: 978–0–415–96223–0 (hbk)
ISBN13: 978–0–203–93792–1 (ebk)

Contents

Acknowledgements

First, and by no means least, I owe a debt of thanks to those of my colleagues at Birkbeck College who helped me in various ways, whether by providing cover, easing administrative burdens, pouring coffee, withholding sage advice, or patiently witnessing existence; Carly Cooper, Peter Fitzpatrick, Valerie Hoare, Matthew Weaitt, Nathan Moore, Oscar Guardiola Riviera, Lindsay Farmer, Fiona Macmillan, Daniel Monk, Michelle Everson, Imelda Maher, Linda Mulcahey, Victoria Goodyear, Sue Baines, Shannon Osbourne, Adam Gearey, Christine Weber, Emma Sandon, Joanna Bourke, Sue Wiseman, Patricia Tuitt, Victoria Ridler, Thanos Zartoloudis, Helen Reece, Amanda Perry-Kassaris, Pat Costall, Clare Grant, Charles Stephens, Penny McKenna, Eugene Macnamee, Sarah Ramshaw, Paul Raffield and Pat Costall.

More often than not the formulation of academic ideas and arguments occurs away from the more formal platforms of institutional life, such as conferences or seminars. They seem to emerge from corridor conversations, during a quick lunch, over a much needed cup of tea (tea with friends is seldom innocent). There were those profoundly playful friends whose conversation, and care of words, magnetized daily life at Birkbeck; Maria Aristodemou, Leila Dajani, Patrick Hanafin, Elena Loizidou and Les Moran. Costas Douzinas and Anton Schutz continue to make me see things otherwise ignored. I can make no comment about these friendships that isn't already known or felt.

Versions of some of the chapters in this book were tested out on a number of good friends and colleagues in a number of settings.

Challenges, comments and encouragement came from Bill MacNeil, Julia Chrysostalis, Grahame Orr, Brad Sherman, Shaun McVeigh, Jodie Dean, Paul Passavant, Tim Murphy, Beverely Brown, Angus Macdonald, Adam Tiompkin, Peter Gay, Peter Rush, Alison Young, Nasser Hussein, Ravit Reichman, Eliane Glaser, Andy Gordon, Cornelia Vismann and Maureen Spencer. Dipan Das looked after me in Calcutta when I first began this research. In particular, Rhodri Hayward and Peter Goodrich never failed to provide a wealth of ideas—often in moments when I had run dry.

I received an enormous amount of encouragement and motivation from friends outside of academia. I must mention Crispin Bending on whose recommendation I read J.G. Farrell, *The Seige of Krishnapur.* How was he to know that the pleasure of reading would result in dry academic inquiry? Tom Walker acted as a good sounding board while detouring around Queen's Park with the kids. Suk and Billy Bains were always on hand to help out with the laughs. Proper acknowledgement must be made of my friend Michael Caswell. Michael passed away in 1999. He was my English teacher for only four years of our twenty-year friendship. He liked to play down this fact. But it was as a teacher that he first gave me the taste for academic inquiry. As a friend he also encouraged me to write this book. I'm not sure he would have approved of the argument, but he would have been vain enough to share some of the pleasures that arise out of publication.

My parents and my brother Neil spurred me on in the way that only the close can.

This book might well be dedicated to any of the above but for the existence and love of Amrik and Lila. Lila (whose name means 'play') has just turned two and has already discovered that complex alchemical formula for turning words into something approaching gold. With them life is exhilarating.

Preface

What happens when legal civilization happens upon a very different way of thinking about subjectivity? What happens to the notion of subjectivity when a culture, emerging towards secular modernity and already sent neurotic by its own capacity for wealth and pleasure, meets a culture that far exceeds the norms of mercantile greed? The impact of colonialism and Empire has had its obvious impact on the status of those directly subjected to its laws. Such an impact has been the focus of postcolonial and subaltern studies. However, the impression left on the West by other cultures through the colonial encounter seems to provide a set of jolts that shock Western subjectivity into different ways of existing. There is contained, in the long term of this historical encounter between the two halves of the globe, a phase in the evolution of the Legal subject that has never been told.

Western subjectivity might be defined by its critical urge to delve into the particularity of itself as a created being. In our post-Christian and liberal minded times, that is to say, as heirs to a Christian tradition, the subject takes pride and interest in the diversity of things, in the individuality of personhood, and in the interior microcosm of selves. Everything interior must be colonized so as to be understood and mined for resources. But such self-reflection does not indicate that the Western subject is a parochially defined entity. Far otherwise, the modern subject seeks some sort of universal validity that, in fact, only emerges when different legally defined civilizations clash. Moreover, the urge to colonize subjectivity becomes clearer when Occidental legal cultures seek to assimilate those who are initially outside its jurisdictional reach.

The history of the Empire is often written as a history of random and accidental stratagems; it is often set against a geography made up of piecemeal acquisitions and accretions. Nevertheless, the capture of the hearts and souls of colonized peoples unearths within the legal institution a structural capacity for colonizing subjects that is far from accidental. The aim of this book is to examine the Western urge to colonize subjectivity by examining the impact of colonialism and Empire. The history of colonialism is not here being used merely as an example to illustrate the process of colonization. In fact the historical fact of colonialism brings about a particular way of thinking about the subject.

This is a historically saturated work of legal theory, and some prefatory remarks about the long historical term of its focus (indeed, fascination) are necessary. Such remarks might well be made through a synoptic outline of the book which by chance follows a historical trajectory of sorts. The first point to state is that the focus is much narrower than a wide-angle view of the Occident and the Orient. The book is preoccupied with the manner in which the common law only really uncovers its own peculiar theory of the subject in its attempt to set up camp in India. The reasons for the choice are mainly historical. India provided early travellers, from the fifteenth century onwards, fertile ground on which to compare different styles of government and different styles of behaviour. By the eighteenth century, East India Company officials were concerned with the establishment and application of common law principles in the relevant parts of India. The difficulty was of applying one legal institution onto another culture with very different ways of understanding subjectivity. Finally, the nineteenth century sought to establish in India bonds between state and subjectivity that were on a par with those established in England; bonds that were effected through the principle of the rule of law. The particular problems occasioned in India, not least of which is the emptiness of the phrase 'rule of law' exposes a common law way of thinking about subjectivity that exceeds provincial and Occidental concerns. The concluding argument of the book suggests an Orient already incorporated within the body of the common law.

The first chapter sets up the theory that the common law stakes its authority in the field of Western civilization. It colonizes both the social and the subjective domains through seemingly extra legal means of inscribing behaviour and a range of affects. Key to this analysis is therefore the notion that the common law is an institution characterized by codes of normative pleasure. The statement that pleasure is key to the institution of legal subjectivity is one that will be explored and contested in general terms before establishing the limits of this theory. What will be proposed is that pleasure is determined according to its opposite—namely that which exceeds it. Pleasure and civilization can only properly be assessed in relation to an excess of enjoyment,

Chapter Two adds flesh to the bones. The importance of pleasure and its relationship to excess is given prominent place in Western jurisprudence. In this respect, the works of Plato are instructive. It will be argued, however, that Plato's theory of pleasure is Orientalist. Excess needs to be expelled from the art and craft of state legalism. Such excess is characteristic of Eastern forms of government and excess. It lies in the form of luxury, evil, indolence and appetites. That Plato differentiates good pleasure from bad excess is a theme repeated over again in a number of works that share a jurisprudential concern over the correct identity of a legitimate state.

By Chapter Three, we seem better equipped to follow a set of early travellers from England to India. The journals and narratives of these early travellers set about demonstrating, through the language of fantasy, the excesses of the East.[1] The main purpose of this chapter is unashamedly expository. It is to demonstrate the influence of Plato's descriptions of Eastern excess on Western travellers, and the manner in which the fantastic descriptions of excess serve to shape an emerging sense of post-medieval subjectivity. Nevertheless, a more theoretical point is to be made concerning the language of describing excess. It is through fantasy, rather than through any verifiable narrative, that the East becomes the scene of excess. It may be argued that fantasies have always pervaded the study of legal methodology. However, it is the Orientalist fantasy that becomes an unacknowledged technique in measuring the jurisprudential distance between West and East: between pleasure and its excess. Whichever way he faces, the legal subject is positioned only in relationship to the Orient.

The subject matter of both Chapters Three and Four is predominantly the Moghul court of India. Through these travel adventures, the denigration of excess is firmly linked to despotic government. Much of the material used for these chapters has been collected from a number of sources. They date from the end of the sixteenth century through to the eighteenth century. The journeys were undertaken by a number of adventurers and East India Company men seeking to trade with merchants in the East. Additionally, ambassadors and envoys were sent to the Moghul court by James I, in order to secure more formal treaties of trade. Many of these set up the first factories of the East India Company in Surat, Madras and Bengal. The records of these early navigations are contained in two principal collections. Richard Haklyut's *Principle Navigations* of 1584 was the first series to collect these individual records concerning voyages from

Cabot onwards and was designed to bolster national pride in England's maritime achievements. As influential was Samuel Purchas' collection which incorporated that of Haklyut. Key to my analysis are the journals of Sir Thomas Roe, written during his time spent as the first English ambassador to the Moghul court (1615–1619). The court was then ruled by the Emperor Jahangir. Roe's journals are obsessed with the detail of courtly life, the rituals, the adornments, the peculiarities of behaviour. But these descriptions are written with stern morality. His tent mate was the chaplain to Roe's entourage, the Reverend Edward Terry. His journal provided valuable material on the question of Eastern femininity and luxury. Other voyages undertaken by Tom Coryate, William Hawkins, William Finch and later James Forbes were also useful in describing the difficulty of setting up domestic arrangements. What also emerges from these descriptions are the first seeds of ethnography and the first attempts to record a history of India.

Of course these travel narratives, while disapproving, also betray a deep rooted envy for the excesses of courtly and quotidian life in Moghul India. Denigration and envy, attack and seduction. These are twin characteristics that can only really be separated in the most mischievous and fictitious manner. Largely out of necessity I have preferred to analyze the suspicion that these travellers also displayed envy in a chapter apart. Chapter Four attempts to provide a theoretical account of these travel narratives by asking the question; 'what is it that these travellers really want out of excess?' Of course the attraction to an indulgent lifestyle, the satisfaction of appetites, the access to mineral resources are always to be coveted. But there is more to envy that exposes and imperils the limits and desires of a legally fabricated subjectivity. The conclusion revolves around the position of civilized subjects in relation to an excess that he presumes he once had. The East, India in particular, thus becomes a land that through fantasy might hold the key to pre-civilized existence.

It might be argued then that this envy for Oriental excess sows the seeds for the growth of Indophile literature in the eighteenth century. The relationship between subjectivity and the suspicion of Eastern pre-origins is given fuller treatment in Chapter Five. This chapter will examine the scholarly works of Sir William Jones. Formally a *puisne* judge in the Supreme Court of Calcutta, Jones pursued a rabid interest in the history, linguistics, arts, literary culture and religions of India. He set up the Asiatic Society based on the same institutional privileges of the Royal Society. More pertinent to the theme of this book, he theorized the phantasm of Oriental excess as the Oriental sublime. This category of the sublime, he claimed, was not an aesthetic category in the strict Burkean sense. Rather, a sense that law derived from a sublime source is what invigorated the (Hindu) laws of India and established bonds of reverence between the legal subject and the codes he was taught to follow. What emerged from Jones's scholarship was a sophisticated sense of legal subjectivity through which obedience is borne of affect. Such sublimity, he argued, is what raises the level of Hindu laws to a level comparable to the common law. So much so that in Jones's version of the fantasy of Oriental excess, the two jurisdictions must have, in some immemorial past, emerged from the same source. The practical applications in the context of colonialism were convenient. The eighteenth century marked a period of transition in British India. British presence in India was now paramount in many areas and was more than just economic in purpose. The factories themselves became communities that had to be ordered (criminal courts were established by Royal charters in 1727 and 1753). The employment of natives presented its own peculiar legal problems. Once made, the argument, that common law and Hindu law (or indeed other laws), shared a common sublime origin, lead easily to a proposition that established the universality of law according to which all are subject.

Connecting the Oriental sublime to the common law seems therefore to mark a new relationship with Eastern excess. It is the first step towards assimilation, towards incorporating excess within the structural and institutional fabric of the common law. Such a process continued throughout the nineteenth century and was not ignored by the spirit of utilitarianism. Chapter Six examines the utilitarian reforms in India as an exemplary moment in the establishment of a modern state defined in relation to the rule of law. Utilitarianism, as is so often argued, did not eradicate Orientalism from its theoretical or structural framework. Rather it found a use for Oriental formulary based on excess and extravagance. This chapter activates the argument at two levels. At the level of abstract theory, the writings of key utilitarians such as Jeremy Bentham, John Stuart Mill and James Fitzjames Stephen (then a member of the Indian Legislative Council) were stuck in a paradoxical relationship to Oriental excess and despotism. They were obviously opposed to all forms of Orientalism by predisposition. Nevertheless, the extrication of Orientalism from its theory meant that utilitarianism can be shown to have structural links to Oriental forms of government. Such a link is made obvious when the utilitarians came to consider how best to forge links between subject and state. What happens when your theory, however well considered, is so dry that it seems empty? The utilitarians had no easy answer to the problem of affectivity and subjecthood. The problem in India was urgent. The memories of the wars of annexation, the cruel and arbitrary occupation of lands and resources, and the Sepoy uprisings were still fresh. Bonds of loyalty between the Indian population and the British Imperial government had to be forged if the new bureaucratic system were to be of any use. The answer was to set up a ritual in which to announce the idea and effects of a rule of law and to establish bonds of loyalty and trust with the Indian population. Such a ritual was structured around the very set of Orientalist formula that was derided as being symptoms of unimaginable excess. This chapter thus follows the contemporaneous debates surrounding the grand rituals (Durbars, or Imperial Assemblages) and their importance as a platform for utilitarian ideals. Such a relationship between utilitarianism and Oriental ritualism is characteristic of every attempt to link the state to legal subjectivity.

The clear counter argument that can be made against this book is that its concerns are limited to a number of historical moments that are key to understanding the evolution of the modern legal subject. Excess, however, ceases to become an important factor in post-utilitarian legal cultures. Certainly, the fantasy of excess is one that seems to be indulged only by the neo-conservative administrators keen to raise the level of threat to World Order posed by Saddam Hussein. Beyond that, the fantasy of excess seems to have lost its value in any juridical or jurisprudential manner. Nevertheless, and the concluding chapter will attempt to argue this point more fully, the fantasy of excess against which the relationship between East and West is organized still exists through a sense of nostalgia. The idea of the just and reasonable man, the man who embodies the principles of the rule of law, is one that pervades a number of works of literature and film nostalgic for the days of the Raj. These cultural artefacts clamour for the days when reasonableness can be measured against a real enemy of excess. Put differently, the fantasy of excess is now incorporated into the language of nostalgia.

CHAPTER 1

Introduction: the Colonization of the Legal Subject

Freudian and post-Freudian theories have structured themselves largely around the notion that the law has a double life. On the surface of existence lies the most obvious and posited forms of legality; consciousness, morality, civic obligation, rights, rationes and statute. Below this surface lies the underlay that really does the uncredited work of holding together social existence. A whole circuitry of buried codes—the unconscious, the transgressive, the obscene, surplus enjoyment—wriggles away, invisible to the eyes of cognitive or behavioural scientists. Consider the work of Slavoj Zizek as one of the latest in a long line of theorists to adhere to this double-life, or schizoid theory of legality. For Zizek, it is acts of transgression, of illicit enjoyment, that exert pressure on individuals to comply with the spirit of community. We, as members of a tribe, identify not with the public law, but with specific forms of transgression which seems to suspend the law. But such forms, however they look and however they are felt, always lie below some surface, they 'remain undercover of the night, unacknowledged, unutterable'.[1]

Depending on one's standpoint, everything is considered either in terms of depth or height.

Is it not the case that the transgressive lies on the same surface of a horizontal plateaux? And, could it not be that this superficial plateaux is geographically and historically constituted? That is to say, that East and West share a surface according to which it is the East that suffers all the characteristics of surplus enjoyment and transgressive *jouissance* as a result of Orientalism and colonialism. The argument that runs throughout this book is that the status of the East has been fabricated, fantasized, and sometimes envied as being the other side to law. The relationship between East and West has been structurally maintained so that the East performs a transgressive function necessary to the constitution of Occidental legality and subjectivity. Indeed, a suspicion that arises is that the East prototypically took on all the characteristics of the unconscious and that it is only with the discovery of psychoanalysis that the East's 'legalistic' function begins to diminish.

But why is it necessary to have this Eastern side to law? The question becomes easier to explore once we examine the relationship between law and subjectivity. Such a relationship focuses on the manner in which law inhabits the subject (or, colonizes the subject) as a site of civilized and civic pleasure as distinct from the supposed Oriental forms of surplus enjoyment. Colonialism offers us a history—a history of a legally instituted subjectivity. The place of the subjects pleasures have to be delineated more carefully and slowly. This chapter will set the Occidental background, examine the way in which social existence and subjectivity are colonized, and spell out the relevance of pleasure. It will be left to subsequent chapters to explore the East as the structurally fabricated other side of law.

Occidental Legality

Colonialism offers us an observable process by which law organizes, rationalizes and assimilates that which is, or those who are, initially outside its imperial jurisdiction. It exposes the manner in which the law weaves these historically hitherto unconnected peculiarities into its own theoretically all-encompassing textual order. It exposes a process of subjection and uncovers an interlacing range of mechanisms employed in justifying its universality and grip. What occurs in the specific context of colonialism, in other words, is indicative of the very structure of Occidental juridical thought.

That is not to say that this study is directed solely at legal/political theorists and thereby bypassing or ignoring the industry of post-colonial scholars within other disciplines. In spite of the title of this book, I would not regard this as a work of post-colonial scholarship. The colonizing grip of legality has yet to be relinquished and does not allow us to lay claim to a post-colonial condition. Nevertheless, the arguments proposed here are intended for an audience and a claim is made for post-colonial studies to take more seriously the manner in which Occidental law takes over social existence and the juridical position of subjectivity; they need to take into account the range of juridical and institutional mechanisms that are involved in this process of colonizing the social sphere and the individual subject. In this sense, it will be argued that the post-colonial condition is more than political and economic post-exploitation. While the geographical location of the structure of domination might change and has to be reconnoitered, the colonization of the subject by law describes a universal predicament, a way of being shared by all; colonialism, in short, describes a global form of existence colonized by, and subject to, the universalizing propensity of law. One need mention only briefly that orthodox studies into the history and theory of colonialism, and in particular those studies that attempt to account for the place of law in cultural imperialism, remain silent about the question of the subject. According to such studies, colonialism is taken to be a geographically specific and historically located phenomenon. Colonialism thus emerges quite narrowly as cultural imperialism in which institutions from one culture are replaced with those of another (sometimes at the risk of violating constitutional notions of Western state theory).[2] Building blocks are exported and are used to prepare the institutional substructure of the modern world. And yet, even if there is a more radical tendency among colonial historians to emphasize the violent shaping of new social spheres by powerful/corrupt/benign regimes, the posts of subjectivity remain unaccounted for and lie dormant.

There again, even if such studies do investigate the task of law, the colonial relationship with questions of legality tends to be based upon legal positivism. Law, in other words, assumes a limited character either as an occupation or as an object issuing a set of rules applicable to, yet estranged from, the domain of subjectivity. The place of law remains under-theorized even in more recent scholarship devoted to the question of post-colonial subjectivity. There are, of course, numerous studies that place the colonial subject as having been constituted through discursive strategies and technologies of power.[3] Current scholarship, extant across a number of disciplines, is concerned with the processes through which the subject of whatever race is colonized and held riveted to structures of governmentality. According to such studies law is often afforded some degree of analysis and assumed to be a key factor in a wide range of subjectifying colonial discourses.[4] To be sure, there can be no denying that law was an important instrument of colonial regulation. Researchers have studied the various surveillance techniques that placed, or placated the colonial body. The legal protection afforded to widows by criminalizing self-immolation, or the passing of the 1835 English Education Act in India provide two examples in which recent critics have unmasked seemingly liberal policies of colonial rule.[5] However, juridical concerns within colonial studies are usually specifically located and, as a result, law, while recognized as being a key factor, is inclined to be treated as nothing more than a secondary symptom of civility, morality or governmentality. The tendency has been to regard discourse as a wider complex served by a number of occupational disciplines of which law is but one. In any case, whatever the place or part law has within these discourses, the subject still emerges as an effect of an essentially positivist set of rules and institutions.

Instead, law must be understood as being rather more foundational to discourse. This primary place of law and its colonizing effects are more discernable if we examine a particular theoretical cul-de-sac that emerges from the number of studies concerned with recuperating and restoring the subject as a site of agency and resistance. Typically such studies examine property relations, first nation rights, aboriginal interests and the legal recognition of different and dignified 'subjectivities'. The question, or paradox, that initiates these studies and always, inevitably, remains unresolved is 'how can agency, autonomy, independence, sovereignty or self-rule be granted by an institution that is inextricably linked with a Colonial regime from which a proposed body seeks independence'? A minimum amount of reliance by one party upon another is required, and, as with all gifts, there are expectations of gratitude, timidity and other conditions of subservience from the donee. The dignity of man starts to look questionable. But there is a trickier Gordian knot than this requisite reliance upon the generosity and comity of law. Even if the recognition of 'full sovereign rights' were possible, the question remains as to how such rights might be granted to an exploited group without taking into account what determines their drives and desires in the first place, or, to put it only slightly differently, without taking into account their own radical self-alienation? The subject who objects to a form of government asserts his right to object by giving *reasons* within a juridically shaped social structure rather like the prayers of a groaning suppliant. Such reasons give form to his desires to remove the incumbent authority, and such a burning sense of injustice is pre-shaped. Both reason and desire operate within the tight limits of legal discourse. Pierre Legendre argues that the right to object is a subjective power of self-inscription into forms of inquiry and rational argumentation.[6] The argument could be expanded. Even in its less formal manifestations (violent uprising; fasting; salt marches) objection is seen, felt, rationalized and justified as a right. Such a right, such *ius*, does no more than fuel the subject. The subject alienates herself as soon as she stakes her claim as an autonomous subject. What emerges is a sense of 'self' measured against the law, and what remains is a radical failure to rise above this legal existence. Complaint is predicated upon an inextricable compliancy to law. So that a side effect of any success in bringing down a form of political rule is that Law remains intact, emerges triumphant, and even, perhaps, replenished.

That the 'subaltern' is always already a conditioned subject is widely recognized.[7] However, a failure to account fully for the manner in which political agency is *legally* established remains. Taking our cue from a range of authors such as F.W. Maitland, Marcel Mauss and Pierre Legendre, the subject lives both according to and through the law. If accepted, the argument has profound repercussions in the field of post-colonial theory. For, it is law rather than race or nationality that lies at the origins of all social institutions concerned with the subject. The status of personhood, as Mauss described it, is defined by the rule of law, by rights and duties as well as by genealogy, family, role and rank.[8] Or, as Maitland argued in a lecture on the possible sharing of interests between jurisprudentialists and moral philosophers, the law commandeers personhood as a fictional 'right-and-duty bearing unit'. The person, in other words, has to be thought of as a subject endowed with institutional meaning and not as an anthropological agent. In this respect an individual is as much a unit subjected to the law as the state, the church, a university, or a corporation. All are species of the same genus and are to be treated equally as *persona ficta*. It follows that with respect to individuals, the specific variants of territory, nationality or ethnicity (or indeed, gender, or biological vitality) are left out, or at least disguised, in the colonization of (an ideally obedient) subjectivity. All subjects must be stripped down or 'de-epidermalized' (to alter a term from Franz Fanon) in order to be brought in line. They must be treated only as legal subjects.

The spread of modern Occidental legal systems and their institutions over larger areas, and the administration of laws to greater numbers of people propound the gradual demise of local laws and crystallize the disregard for individual differences. The principle that the law should be applied neutrally and without consideration of local variants was basic even to Roman colonization and is a point of Roman law (the *ius gentium*) that still survives as a characteristic of Western legal systems.[9] Vital as it is in the current climate of political paranoia, an account of bias is, therefore, a concern for analysts of the decision-making process and of specific laws. Indeed, the racism inherent within the legal process must be attributed to its structural blindness and impartiality that leaves open a means of engendering an emotional bias at the level of decisions. Such abstraction in which *all* subjects are anticipated by and attributed to the law necessarily supports the dream of law to acquire a universal, trans-national appeal.

Having said all of this, it is still unclear as to how the question of the subject (as opposed to the jurisprudential fiction of legal personhood) might be assigned to the study of law. Legal studies has traditionally suffocated such questions or recognized them only as belonging to other disciplines, other subjects. After all, the rational legal order is cool, impersonal and uninterested in matters of being. Subjectivity necessitates an aggravating set of concerns that are treated by lawyers as properly falling to the inquiry of those scholars interested in the affective scheme of being rather than in the province of reasonable behaviour. Historically, and most obviously, the 'fight for mansoul'—to use the title of an early church poem by the lawyer Prudentius—is staged as a specifically un-secular Christian production. The control of the drives and desires of the subject is a matter of distinguishing Christian virtues from pagan vices. Within temporal modernity one is tempted to suggest that the poor subject is left emotionally and spiritually flustered in looking for its proper place, seeking refuge among philosophers, psychologists and psychoanalysts (or, perversely, the subject might well dispatch himself back to the church gesturing fanatically).[10]

Indeed, it might be objected, that what I mean by subject is in fact nothing other than legal personhood and that this category is simply a fiction relevant to Courts and a select band of juristically minded thinkers; that it simply aids the courts to think of 'right-and-duty bearing units' in order to equiparate individual people and corporations as rationalized neutral units; that it simply ignores, or treats as irrelevant philosophical considerations such as 'essence', 'substance', or indeed 'difference'. It might be objected that such metaphysical considerations are to be considered far more important in defining the character of man well before the law grants him his rights and imposes obligations. The philosophic character of man, according to such an objection, must surely be the precondition of bearing rights and obligations. This introductory essay, however, endeavours to show how, through colonization, the law reaches, informs and constitutes all lived experience so that any philosophical formulation as to the essence of subjectivity must surely have to take into account the idea of the *persona ficta* as the condition of existence. And so too must any account of the colonial or post-colonial subject.

We need not necessarily move away from the focus of traditional legal theory or methodology in order to account for the colonization of subjectivity. There have been a number of calls to 're-think' and broaden the understanding of law. According to these, such a 're-thinking' of law demands a move away from the analysis of traditional legal institutions.[11] More recently, more urgently and certainly more critically, Douzinas and Gearey have argued that any account of the 'ways in which subjectivity is created as a site of freedom and subjection' requires a move from a restricted jurisprudence in which law interrogates its discipline in order to fix itself as the province of reason. In its place, the authors argue for a (return to) general jurisprudence that uncovers the philosophical, psychoanalytical and literary dimensions of law that always threaten to explode the institutional legal order. The proposition made here is that by examining the very principle of reason that is used to close off law's empire and to deny the relevance of subjectivity, one is already forced into uncovering the operation of a 'general [juristic] economy'. What the following analysis makes clear is that legal rationalization, by its very nature is a broad and far reaching process. Reason disguises the manner in which law is engaged with the question of subjectivity. But the very moment and act of concealment alerts us to law's foundational and programmatic status. We have come to expect that the terms 'reason' and 'rationalization' are precarious chimera used mainly by judges to express an abstract ideal. Even advocates, based on years of enforced empirical research, question the possibility of ever meeting a reasonable man. Like the London routemaster, the Clapham omnibus is now a museum piece and its most famous ex-passenger/ghost—the 'reasonable man'—seems to have lost himself in the crowds! Nevertheless, legal rationalization becomes and remains the key juridical motif used in gaining entry to and assimilating both the social sphere and those more subjective terrains that lie beyond the border. Rationalization accounts for the manner in which law storms the bastions of life, taking life over, and camping upon its alien territories.

What follows, in other words, is an attempt to account both for the socio-genetic and the psycho-genetic structures of life by focusing on the trope of rationalization. Such an account will hopefully show how a sociogenetic explanation of colonialism inevitably gives way to one of psychogenesis. Consequently, as shall be shown in the final sections of this chapter, the definition of law breaks down into the pedagogic micro-forms of rationalizing and taming the behavior of the civilized subject. The resulting fiction of the subject is a legally constituted entity with a supposed set of noetic abilities and affective orders; it has will, capacity, emotions and desires. Above all, it lives life within a circumscribed sphere of pleasure. It is at this point that the main theme of the book can be introduced. Pleasure, it will be argued, must be treated as a jurisprudential trope and as a means of colonizing the rational subject. This helps us to introduce and locate the predominant theme of the book that examines what happens when aspects of the Orient interrupt the exact constitution of the legal subject as a well-behaved entity. Or, put differently, it allows us to examine the emergence of a structural relationship between pleasure and fantasies of Oriental excess. At this point, considerations regarding the subjects pleasures and desires that are nominally excluded from law and legality are revealed (thus a proviso—while sticking to an examination of legal science one cannot help but defer and refer to the language of psychoanalysis and cultural theory as it illuminates the shadow area of legal subjectivity).

Rationalizing the Social Sphere

The impulse to colonize, to commandeer and to replicate is quite obvious within the rational legal agenda (in this respect the history of colonization is not shorter than the history of law). According to Weber, for example, the logic of capital, which is itself 'pre-conditioned by a specific kind of legal order',[12] is that it imposes its laws on all potentially non-capital cultures and civilizations co-opting them to sub-serve hegemonic interests while simultaneously protecting them from the state through the grant of rights and entitlements.[13] But the argument can be read as one that invests law with far more foundation and pervasive powers. For the medieval West, whose political and legal arrangement is dependent on the Christian theology of domination, the imposition of law upon society is based upon and supervised by the idea of an absent Other, or what Freud calls 'the enormously exalted father'.[14] The colonization of the social sphere by law depends first upon Divine Reason. It is Reason that guides the medieval subject and his status. Reason defines the hierarchy of the medieval West and the idea of a mystical source of authority is replicated in the factual power held by patriarchal, magisterial or princely power. Indeed the whole hierarchical structure of society depends upon the actualization of such Reason.

Modern law, on the other hand, is characterized by a more theoretical rationality; it is an abstract, learnable and calculable set of norms with a particular efficiency. The modern application of the word 'rational' describes a state of affairs and the end product of an efficient process of rationalization.[15] It is in invoking the latter sense of *process* that rationality still carries with it the sense of spread and infiltration. Modern secular rationality, like its medieval predecessor, attempts to occupy all conceivable space. This secularization of what was once a theological motif is peculiar and paradoxical. Rational law is reasonable; it is a principle of moderation in so far as it limits theological reason (or any form of absolute rule) as a condition of existence and justice. Yet, it is also used as a way of characterizing the triumph of Western law as the embodiment of an objective and universal set of principles.

Thus, like its medieval avatar, modern rationalization continues to structure the class and rank of subjects within the social sphere. That legal order, based upon the power of property, pre-conditions the social division of class is, of course, so well commented upon by scholars of Marx and Weber that little here needs to be added. But as Weber also notes, modern European legal systems continue to support and stratify a complex system of status and honor. Property ownership is therefore both an indicator of class and of social estimation; 'in the so called pure modern "democracy" it may be that only families coming under approximately the same tax class dance with one another'.[16] The process of legal rationalization thus increases its hold, for the social estimation of honor also gives rise to further entitlements and material monopolies supported by the legal order.

It might be noted, since it is pertinent to the colonial enterprise of bureaucratizing the world, the position that lawyers as a particular class have in shaping the hierarchical structure of the social sphere. The full realization of legal order (as well as particular rules) according to policy and in conformity to reason is formulated and applied by a class of professional lawyers. Forms of juridification and rationalization have been developed through 'intra-juristic' conditions appropriate to the mixed bag of legal professionals. The role of legislators, judges, legal *honoratiores*, academics, and all those with *puisne* expediential decision-making and rule-shaping powers have aided the spread and purchase of law. But this model of the legal profession, rendered hierarchal according to degrees of authority and specialties, is replicated across the full range of public institutions. Law establishes a complex range of hierarchies and a pattern of different interweaving administrative discourses emerges in which each is taken over by, and invested with, the full force of law. What spreads across the field of public institutions is a regulated 'way of doing things'. Decision-making, or rule defining, powers designated to different officials are similarly rationalized and ranked whether in the legal field, in hospitals, factories or the civil service.

This rationalized 'way of doing things' might now be specifically regulated by administrative law, but its effect is certainly not limited to questions of *ultra vires* or natural justice. It is through the rationalization of hierarchies that individual characters and mentalities are shaped; it is through these hierarchies and the process of subinfeudation that law percolates its way into the professional mentality of each office. The point is strikingly, and less tritely, illustrated by Rudyard Kipling in a short and reactionary story called 'The Conversion of Aurelian McGoggin'. Clever, well-educated and self-opinionated McGoggin arrives in India. Having read the theories and 'isms' of Compte, Spencer and Clifford ('they deal with peoples insides from the point of view of men with no stomachs'), he commences work as a civilian armed with ideas about secular humanism (it should be noted that Kipling never labels this particular 'ism,' and is content merely to surrender McGoggin's belief system to the whole theologically differentiated history of *ismos*). According to McGoggin's beliefs, there could be no one person higher than another, least of all himself. And so his 'rarefied religion' is clearly at odds with the structure of command and obedience required of his office. Kipling scoffs. McGoggin soon learns. The bureaucratic heat of the Indian office gets to him and it is soon clear the institution was no place to stick to his creed. In any case 'not a soul was interested in McGoggin's soul'. The tension between his 'isms' and his duty produces more than an obstinate neurotic personality. He suffers a spectacular breakdown and is sent away to a hill station for recuperation. Following his recovery, he returns, faith broken and chastened, to work. The lesson is straightforward. The civil servant must both obey and give orders. He must take up, as his own, the legalistic mentality of office life; he must shape his character and adapt to the simple rational chain of obedience . . . or die. Whether in India or England, such a reactionary outlook on life survives and underpins industrial progress; India simply makes clear what is fogged by the effluvium, the 'machinery and asphalt', of London.

> Life, in India, is not long enough to waste in proving that there is no one in particular at the head of affairs. The Deputy is above the Assistant, the Commissioner above the Deputy, the Lieutenant-Governor above the Commissioner, and the Viceroy above all four, under the orders of the Secretary of State, who is responsible to the Empress. If the Empress be not responsible to her Maker—if there is no Maker for her to be responsible to—the entire system of Our administration must be wrong. Which is manifestly impossible.[17]

A number of further points might be made. First, Kipling stresses that the behavior required of a good professional civilian is a 'way of doing things' both in and out of the office. His subservience is a matter to be acted out in his social life, at his club as well as at work. Indeed, in another short story, 'Her Majesty's Servants', Kipling extends the chain of command to include those outside the payroll of the Indian Civil Service. The structural design even applies to, and absorbs animals; mules, elephants, horses, and bullocks. Second, the symptom suffered by McGoggin during his breakdown was aphasia: 'something had wiped his lips of speech'.[18] Secular humanism, or any similar effort to live outside the rationalized structure of institutional life, or to break the bond between responsibility and loyalty interferes in the wires of speech and memory that make up the bureaucratic subject. Life outside the law is life as a non-speaking being, life without memory. But, as Kipling might have said: 'that is another story' to which we shall return briefly.

Legal Pluralism and the Rationalization of Everyday Life

There is a more horizontal effect to this spread of legal rationalism that stretches out across the social field. And, it is here that we might begin to use colonialism as an illustration of the process of legal colonization in which that which was previously outside is reigned in. The effect of rationalization, as law inches its way across social life occupying every available space, is that indigenous custom has to surrender to the logic of reason. The history of modern law across Europe charts the expulsion of customary law from the borders of what constitutes legality and legitimate forms of governance. In civil law jurisdictions, the great codifications and written constitutions of the eighteenth and nineteenth century marginalized custom as a source of law. Law ceased to be rooted and cultivated in regional soils and folk understanding. The organization of law, and the identification of substantive laws, thus became a matter for state institutions, for civilian authority rather than popular spirit, or for textual codes rather than oral transmission. In short, centralized legal systems begin to colonize and occupy all territories left vacant by the exile of customary law.

Can the same description of the colonization of everyday life be applied to the common law? The answer is not so straightforward. From the isolated and insular perspective of the English legal tradition, the links between custom and common law have always been more complicated. For the expulsion of customary law takes the paradoxical form of its assimilation into formal doctrine. This process of gathering, or colonizing, pastoral customs into the fold of the English legal system, as has often been pointed out, provides the common law with its own distinguished tribal identity. The *legis non scripta* that forms the basis of the doctrine of *stare decisis* marks the common law as being specifically and peculiarly English. It is a law for the English, and above all, it derives from the English since an immemorial time. From the herd of early common lawyers, Fortesque, Hale and Blackstone were all keen to point out that the common source of the origins of law, which had lain with the people over the centuries, was the very basis for its authority. It is a law that, since before the beginning of legal memory, has developed with the slow accretions of 'wisdom' that evolve from the spirit of English existence. Notwithstanding parliamentary legislation, the basis of the law is to be found in what Savigny called the *volkgeist*, the spirit of the ancient people.

The same apparent reverence for customary law is expressed in Colonial expansion. In India, it was the work of Mountstuart Elphinstone that contributed to the idea that good government was to be promoted through the continued existence of customary law. Away from the metropolitan centres of Company activity (Bombay, Madras, and Calcutta), Elphinstone realized the practical difficulty in enforcing English laws in remote rural areas. Whether in the courts of the *Pesva* of Poona, and the *Raja* of Nagpur, or in the heat and dust of local village disputes, Elphinstone was convinced that the West should avoid grafting its own legal system on to a set of indigenous orders. But these practical difficulties in creating hybrid systems do not explain why official policy did not seek to change the customary law of those areas wholly within British control. It ought to be remembered that as far back as 1608 the common law courts had stated that 'if a Christian king should conquer the Kingdom of an infidel . . . the laws of that infidel are abrogated'.[19] Why then would a proud and muscular national legal system not attempt to replace those of the villages?

One answer points out an exclusion clause in the contract between colonizer and colonized. Local custom could not supercede the principles of natural justice laid down by the British. Resident customs and rituals associated with the resolution of disputes were permissible insofar as they were not repugnant to 'universal' values of humanity—principles that were determined, of course, according to the Occidental standards of the colonizers. While the principles of natural justice were, of course, vague, the idea that they had priority over local custom was clearly articulated in numerous pieces of legislation during the late nineteenth century. Another answer would seem to be that beneath, or apart from, the concerned rhetoric of Orientalists and the prudent policies of official residents, common law ways of thought did in fact penetrate the interior provinces of colonized culture. In so doing, and according to different tactics, much was done to reduce and erode village customary life. It was largely through the missionary zeal of Victorian reformers (once the East India Company had surrendered to Crown rule) that the colonies were to witness the severe erosion of customary law. The reformatory work of the pedagogically unchallenged Thomas Babington Macauley became an example used throughout the former British Empire. For, it was largely through

Macauley's insistence that a code of laws was instituted across the whole of British India thereby fixing what Peter Fitzpatrick has termed the 'once-protean identities' of pre-colonial existence and custom.[20]

Mention must also be made of the quasi-legal mechanisms that were employed. Customary law was open to the keen gaze of anthropologists and lawyers to isolate, collect, and tabulate. The bare bones of village life and customs were exposed to a harsh northern light. Law became a central and potent mechanism in collating information from remote areas. The governance of these areas depended upon such knowledge of local custom. In the British courts, whenever the issue arose, the existence of indigenous customs became a question of fact rather than one of law.[21] The problems inherent in such evidential practices are obvious. On one level, the process required the reduction of ancient systems of thought to translatable and translated versions of an ungraspable and enigmatic original. The knowledge of local customs gained by British courts became something other than the supposed 'pre-discursive' reality of those customs. On another level, Elias notes that the ascertainment of native customary law had as much to do with establishing (Western) principles of certainty and transposing them onto the 'awkward and wayward' oral systems found in villages.[22] The process of ascertainment can be seen to be part of the universalization of Occidental civilization.

In short, while customary law existed and continues to exist as a formal and recognizable system within many postcolonial nation states, its validity and purpose may be defined only in the shadows cast by the official legal systems of those states. In other words, colonial forms of common law legality rationalized and determined the customs arising from everyday life. The implications of this observation are profound. What is more disturbing is the power of Occidental legal systems that continue long after Western empires have ceased their administrative duties. Having physically left their protectorates and colonies, colonial power still affects those independent states, but it does so from the very local levels of village life, from the *panchayats*, and the *kgotla*. Customs no longer emerge from the everyday. Rather customs, and indeed everyday life, become the product of Imperial forms of law.

Colonization and Civilization

The rationalization of custom and everyday life is in fact a reassemblage of a much more virulent aspect of Occidental legality. The extension of rules and legal systems across the non-European world is in itself a matter of extending the values of civilization, imposing those values across different customs and cultures. Norbert Elias puts it: '[the West] works in a direction which sooner or later leads to a reduction in the differences both of social power and of conduct between colonists and colonized'.[23] In other words, notwithstanding the fact that progress is measured according to the political, economic, religious, technical, moral or social axioms of the West, the aim of civilization is to transcend national and cultural characteristics. 'Civilization' states Braudel, 'is the grandfather, the patriarch of world history.'[24] It is what permits social and economic development, trans-nationally, from the lowest levels of material life to the grandest commercial institutions. Unlike 'culture', which might refer to the characteristics, self-image or endeavours of a particular nationality, civilization collects an assemblage of qualities applicable across humankind. It binds together individuals, even foreigners, into a single joint community and provides for them a common pasture.

However, the relationship between law and civilization may be stated in stronger terms. The concept of civilization is not confined to the social manners of a hyper-refined and technologically advanced society.[25] All such claims to progress from the West are open to counter-claims from traditions that are quite obviously rich in social codes, community values, literary and scientific endeavours. What was/is needed is one element of Western civilization that might be used to lord it over all other claims from elsewhere. Indeed, it is the chimera of legal rationality that measures which of the competing civilizations is more advanced. According to the Weberian analysis, the rational interpretation of Western forms of law stands opposed to the idea of law found in sacred and/or custom-based traditions. What these other communities are reckoned to lack is modern theoretical reason. As Weber puts it: 'Kadi knows no reasoned judgment whatever.'[26] Decisions based on thaumaturgic forms of justice, such as revelations, prophetic dicta, and sacrifice, those based on patrimony, hereditary charisma or on the most informal of procedures, reveal the structure of both institutions and communities to be primitive and lacking in progress. As the measure of what is perceived to be a superior and advanced civilization, 'reasoned judgement' (even if issued by a common law judge) and just rule become the yardsticks against which other cultures and civilizations are measured. Indeed to become subject one has to enter civilization, just as under Roman law a person could be manumitted into the *civitas*.

It is at this level of analysis, that colonial expansion is legitimated. Rationality must necessarily claim a condition of universality. From the precepts of Roman law onwards, legal rationality applies across peoples and across territories.[27] It cannot, by definition, co-exist with any other system of thought; to do so would risk contamination by the irrational. The universality of rational (secular) law is therefore based on the debasement and eradication of a whole range of heteronomies that belong to, and determine the laws of, other 'inferior' cultures: carnal desire, theological determinism, clairvoyancy, magic.

Thus just as Edward Said claims that Western civilization defines itself against the East, so too does Occidental legality. In terms of the early history of modern law, Orientalism is a key concept in fixing or providing the finishing touches to 'whatever it is' that constitutes Western legal rationality. In its encounter with the East, law develops a seemingly more defined system (non-thaumatolatrous, non-charismatic, non-carnal) with the apparition of universality.

Civilization and Repression

The superimposition of Occidental legal rationality upon other cultures suggests more than the triumph of one civilization (self-perceived to be rational) over others (suspected to be based on irrational, or underdeveloped forms of reasoning). For, it is at this level of analysis that the post-colonial condition of subjectivity starts to become apparent. Civilization itself takes hold of the individual subject as much as it does culture; it legislates and coheres the rational subject. As Norbert Elias is keen to point out in his exploration of the antithesis between civilization and *kulture*, civility applies a cosmetic make-up; it fabricates the *persona*, the social mask. Elias's own account of the 'civilizing process' thus explicitly moves from a socio-genetic account of the civilizing process to an account that requires an appreciation of the specific psychological process of development and growing up. We are born into a social order shaped by the civilizing process and which in turn colonizes and shapes the emotional range of existence as a means of inhabiting the legal subject.

The history of civilization sets up a kingdom forever reserved for man; a kingdom set apart from those of cats and dogs etc. At one level, the effort of human labour, the use of tools and the manufacture of objects, transform a natural world into a specifically human world. The list of differences is endless. The evolution of *homo-sapiens* as a distinct civilized species is also a question of knowledge, writing and the exercise of higher mental activities; it is also a question of manners, of shame and of sumptuary expenditure (or 'accesorizing'). According to Derrida, it is also a question of the 'technicity' of clothes: 'he would only be a man to the extent that he was able to be naked, that is to say to be ashamed'.[28] Perhaps man's evolution is also a question of listing differences. Whatever the case, all these demarcation points share one feature which is man's negation of nature, even his own nature: 'man negates himself; he trains himself'.[29] The point has been taken up most recently in legal and political theory by Martha Nussbaum arguing that a disgust of our own humanity informs the passing of particular laws, judgments and punishment; law legislates for a dignified life free from shame and all that might disgust.[30] Out of such negation develops civilized man. Thus for example, the horror of *excreta* (which Bataille reminds us, 'is a uniquely human trait') leads not only to disgust but also to the cultivation of taste, discernment, refinement and ultimately of judgement.

On another level, civilization might be described as a set of prohibitions colonizing the affective domain of man in order to check its more carnal aspect. The negation of nature is in effect a restraint upon the satisfaction of animal impulses; a strangulation of the power of carnal desire and primal urges. The shaping of emotional life sorts out the appropriate from the non-appropriate, the licit from the illicit. To put it in more Freudian terms, civilization is linked to the scientific management of instinctual needs and performs the 'great common task of preserving mankind against the superior power of nature'.[31] According to this analysis, civilization undertakes the position of the *carnifex* and the function of prohibition in a performance that has at its heart the welfare (the humanity) of individual subjectivity.

Elias has already famously shown that this analysis of civilization links the province of manners to the emergence of the modern state and to the place of the individual therein. In literature, the character of the late nineteenth century upper class Englishman in the colonies being described as the incarnation of the rule of law, is perhaps the most famous representation of the link between manners and law.[32] For Elias, social propriety, decency and fair dealings between individuals (initially all forms of flattery to be used in court circles) are to be regarded as methods of prohibiting primal instincts and clamping down on inter-feudal violence. Any warring tendencies between factions had to be placated by the State through the formalities and refinements of courtly life. Indeed, the State was to reserve for itself the monopoly on violence. Thus, the formality required in order to turn turbulent nations into peaceful ones stands opposed to ideas of honest feeling. Honest opinions, true virtue and gut instincts are linked, in other words, to non-State inter-subjective violence. Conformity to the law was a stance, a pose, a requisite form of decency necessary for the overall civilization of humankind. Whatever the citizen might truly believe, and in whichever direction he might feel his 'inner moral compass' to point, his subjectivity was defined only through this bourgeois façade. Such sacrifice in favour of conformity became a condition of existence and of State organization. As Elias, quoting the Marquis de Condorcet, points out: 'despite the barbarity of some laws, despite the faults of the administrative principles . . . one may observe that the peoples within the realm lived in peace under the protection of the law'.[33]

But the civilizing programme of legal rationality inhabits and structures more than the consciously, if profoundly, polite subject. Indeed, the full occupying force of law is felt once we move away from the social to the psychic structures of life. We are no longer in the province of consciously compliant, or non-compliant individuals such as represented by Kipling's character of Aurelian McGoggin. In shaping the modern legal subject, civilization leaves its imprint; it is more than cosmetic. Civilization might well arise from dogmatic prohibition rather than reason. However, its ambit lies precisely in the process of rationalizing the subject, as a means of disguising man's own nature and the supporting structure of unreason. For Elias, 'rationalization itself, and with it the more rational shaping and explanation of social taboos transforms and affects the *whole* personality, the level of drives and affects no less than the level of consciousness and reflection'.[34] Those honest opinions, those dirty tendencies and aggressive inclinations become sublimated, deeply submerged in the unconscious; what replaces this jumbled primordial mess is the figure of rational man.

Pleasure

The mechanics of this conversion and colonization of the subject require more detail before its fuller implications for legal theory might be ascertained. For Freud, the conversion of man into the theoretically rational and coherent subject depends upon the relationship between two basic principles. The pleasure principle that incorporates the primitive domain and instinctual life of man, is kept in check by the reality principle. According to the latter principle, man develops inter-subjective skills, rational choice and conscious understanding if only to cope with the scarcity of materials that his desires might otherwise cause him to plunder. There is only so much 'stuff' in the world, only a finite amount of 'objects' to go round, and so by necessity man's desire for, and pleasure of, them must be restricted. The immediate gratification of desires, or the power of untrammelled *eros*, have to be sacrificed in favour of a civilized order of labour, utility, productivity and security. The reality principle sounds like the dull condition of our civilized existence. Nevertheless, it accounts for the regulation and satisfaction of our drives. Civilization, legal rationality, provides a range of substitutes (Freud uses a range of terms such as 'repressive modification', 'economic compensation', or 'substitutive satisfactions' interchangeably) in order to redeem and satisfy that which is otherwise insatiable. In this respect, the subject's individual psyche reflects the social scene and *vice versa.*

Jacques Lacan turns these primitive urges into a desire for something that cannot be achieved let alone calculated. Less empirical than Freud, the object of desire is unyielding and cannot be named. But our desire for them are nevertheless to be choked by the law, never to be activated. 'The law and repressed desire are one and the same thing.'[35] postulates Lacan, invoking the wider sense of law as a set of principles propelling the course of civilization and governing social existence as well as the order of language. However, the sense of law also boils down to a more specific relationship between interdiction and repressed desire that indicates the specific civilizational mechanism at stake. The law is to be identified with and inseparable from pleasure; it collapses into pleasure as it were. It is pleasure itself that is the *sine qua non* of civilization and which substitutes for the unnamed and unattainable object of desire, it keeps us out of reach of the *objet petit a.* Pleasure, in other words, provides the repressive modification of the primal urge, and provides the sense of satiety for the otherwise insatiable appetites of man. The Lacanian surprise is that in fact the thing that represses carnality looks more like the thing repressed than it does the law, or at least the law understood in its narrow sense. The law of pleasure asks us to enjoy but not to excess: 'a little bit of what you fancy . . . but no more than your just desserts'. It permits and denies in the same breath of its command. Moreover, pleasure, while certainly a prescript that aims to prevent the subject overreaching himself and therefore to avoid unpleasure, is not to be understood strictly in the sense of Freud's pleasure principle. The types of permissible behaviour are of a refined and tamed nature that become internalized and structurally linked to a symbolic order. Pleasure thus describes a range of permissible forms of behaviour and, following the lines of argument pursued by Kant, Schiller, Huzinga, Callois and Bahktin, is to be seen as an indication of how non-repressive and liberated civilization has become.

The place of 'pleasure' as a specific juridical trope in the colonization of subjectivity has a long history. It comes to be the juridical placebo, or even the *pabulum* that nourishes the subject. The jurisprudence of pleasure and the nature of its place within legal theory deserves a separate and more patient analysis and will be dealt with in the next chapter; here the broad theoretical gist of the argument should suffice.

It cannot be readily assumed that pleasure is antithetical to the process of Western legal rationality. That the subject is one who enjoys himself should not be taken as a biological predicate; pleasure is to be differentiated from need (for warmth, food etc.) so that our organization must be considered more plastic than animal. Rather, Lacan places pleasure within the register of ethics. Indeed, Lacan's principle of pleasure might be considered a radical revolution in the history of ethics. Traditional schools of ethics given to apolaustic questioning (including utilitarianism and modern legality) place pleasure as an end; the pledge of redemption, or, more basically, the promise of a happy and successful future, organizes the social life of the individual. Everything is arranged around the ultimate achievement of peace, equity, and happiness (for individuals and for the greatest number). For Lacan, such pleasures in blocking the path of desire for the *objet petit a*, actually constitute subjective life (in theological terms, for example, the promise of heavenly pleasures diverts the Christian subject from a life of sin and so constitutes the subject as Christian *ab initio*).

Pleasure then is to be distinguished from the torrid zone of violent, burning and carnal excess. Its connection with the enterprise of rationality stems from the fact that it is duller than excess. It is lepid and pleasant and thus constitutes civilization as it progresses away from the animal kingdom. It is through pleasure that the subject learns how to conduct itself in a civilized manner thus negating and outlawing his animal desires. Pleasure is what endows the human subject with a sense of rationality made obvious in the rational decision-making process that allows us to differentiate between acceptable and non-acceptable behaviour (pain, sin, crime, excess). What emerges is the figure of the rational man who is able to choose in order to resist impulses (it matters not that in the worst case scenario that there is no choice and that the pursuit of absolute carnal excess has been deactivated). Pleasure becomes the emotional conduit that allows law to take hold of the subject and provides the raw material for reason. Here, the link between law and pleasure in the colonization of subjectivity strengthens its grip. Pleasure, for Lacan, operates as a mode of legal rationality; a process of sorting out the subject, rendering it coherent and stripping the subject down to its civilized, universal ideal. Thus pleasure is the method by which the subject comes to know, or rather feel, the law. But, more forcefully, it is also the process by which the law colonizes and inhabits the subject; the law abides in me through pleasure. We want our pleasures, we want our law. Organizing our sentient surfaces and the internal perception of our own bodies, we feel, rather than know, the law. Only by dint of pleasure (even at the level of rights and liberties) does the law become profoundly necessary, compulsive and irresistible.

Pleasure, then, is the institutional cause and fate of subjectivity. As Lacan puts it 'we do not know what it means to be alive except for the following fact, that a body is something that enjoys itself (or can be enjoyed)'. It is through the process of being colonized by law that the subject is *made to feel* as subject; the subject feels, and imagines, himself to be more or less like a rational unit of subjectivity (like an object). To be sure, such an affect may be misplaced and misunderstood, it is after all fictional. Yet, the *model* of the individual and autonomous subject still informs us and directs our manners. Even if subjectivity is a fiction, such a fiction is legislated and maintained so that the subject experiences and feels himself to be alive as himself (the problem may be posed in more Lacanian terms; within the symbolic register the subject is always already alienated from himself. Only in the imaginary domain, however, does he take himself to be whole).

Pleasure also disguises the idea that rational subjectivity is the product of a process of subjection and subjugation. It disguises cause and genealogy and replaces the subject with the figure of the citizen or the human with rights. A sense of autonomy is borne out of pleasure. It saturates us with 'the confidence that it is a do-able task for me to speak in no-one's name but mine [and] functions as the founding device of the shaping of the Western legal structure . . . it is this confidence that gives rise to a *Western-nomos*, a nomos cast in the specifically Western figure of the *auto-nomos*'.[36] Schutz elaborates. Such confidence does not have its origins in classical political philosophy of civic autonomia. Rather it is a matter of discipline, of cleansing the self-understanding of genealogy. In Schutz's analysis, it is this modern disciplinary confidence trick of autonomy that distinguishes the Western canon from other legal orders, other civilizations. Autonomy is the meta-legal yardstick that measures competing civilizations: 'what the western pattern is incompatible with, is the possibility of a *nomos* not predicated on an *autos*'.[37]

The argument pursued here posits the idea that the confidence to claim oneself to be an autonomous entity is an affective condition borne of pleasure (global consumerism provides the perfect example. What is sold to a non-Western audience is not the taste of coke, or the comfort of jeans, or the facility of technology, but the image of a Western subject seen to be enjoying these goods as part of his confidence and autonomy). Moreover, the sense of pleasure itself, whatever the manner of its cause, takes us out of any sense of heteronomy. The moment of pleasure does not fuse with the social field, and suffers no mixture with history. Pleasure is situated in my body and no-one else's. Which might explain why the younger generation always thinks it has invented sex—'how can anyone have been here before'? The Western subject at play becomes the cause of subjectivity and the very idea that the subject has been colonized must be camouflaged.

The lack is excessive

What is it that pleasure prevents the subject gaining access to? Why should Lacan invoke the name of the law with its implications of force and authority? Desire, according to Lacan, is always for something lacking (the ideal, the *agalma*, or the *objet petit a*). But this *manque*, this lack that cannot be named or calculated is in fact an excess. On one hand, such excess describes all that exceeds that which is required for the fabrication of the modern civilized legal subject. It 'exists' (or is fantasized as existing) somewhere beyond the fringe, or, above the meniscus of our own spheres of being. While, on the other hand, excess points to the savage animal energy that the primal pre-subject might otherwise have enjoyed. This latter energy, or *excess enjoyment,* is not simply surplus to requirement; rather this is an unimaginable excess that the modern subject has no way of apprehending or calculating. Excess enjoyment is not simply juridically disqualified. However aberrant the non-libertarians among us perceive the term to be, the term 'excess enjoyment' does not correspond to any pathology such as lust, desire, lasciviousness or licentiousness. It is not a form of illicit behaviour that might fall foul of criminal codes. It is not a form of unreason such as madness; such excess is even more radically intractable and unrecordable. The unthinkable nature stems from the fact that excess enjoyment structurally belongs to another juridical order.

Western political theory has always suspected the possibility of excess within its own territory. Perhaps the most consistent theorist of this excess enjoyment within Western juridical and political structures is Slavoj Zizek. For Zizek, what transgresses normal codes is not necessarily antithetical to the law; enjoyment might suspend the code of law, but it nevertheless 'binds the community' and pressurizes the individual to comply with its mandate of group identification.[38] The law is split. The topside of law (the register of positive laws) may not acknowledge this unwritten, secret, mode of transgression, nevertheless the underbelly (excessive, corpulent, sinful) performs a necessary function of creating solidarity through a shared guilt in the obscene. But in Zizek's work, the status of enjoyment itself undergoes transformation. The 'metastasis of enjoyment' (as Zizek titles one of his key works), seems to imply an ethical standard (even becoming the 'sublime object of ideology') that differentiates it from the unutterable excess that this work is here concerned with. Take for example, the various tales of Faust as the paradigmatic literary example of transgression. Is his really a life lived to excess of the law? Is he not completely subject to the law? Is his dilemma not borne out of a *contract* with the Devil who in turn has his own ethical pact with God? In more sociological terms, we might also begin to question where obscenity exists these days? Pornography (if it were ever truly transgressive) has become commodified and incorporated in high street retail; do it, see the film, buy the t-shirt. Surely excess lies elsewhere than in the domestic arena.

Indeed, there are moments in Zizek's *The Metastases of Enjoyment*, where surplus enjoyment indicates the order of dumb pleasures that we have just analyzed as being essential to the civilizing process of subjectivity. Thus, the very subjection and subordination to a political order brings about a specific enjoyment (or, rather pleasure); 'not only an enjoyment provided by an awareness that people were living in a universe absolved of uncertainty, since the system possessed an answer to everything, but above all the enjoyment of the very stupidity of the system—a relish in the emptiness of official ritual'.[39] The dangers of this empty space are emphasized as a lethal possibility inherent in any juridico-political system to do what it wants. In other words, the subjects enjoyment of the stupidity of the system is symptomatic of an excess of power enjoyed by the political system; 'the public message of responsibility is supplemented by the obscene message of the unconditional exercise of power: "Laws do not really bind me, I can do to you whatever I want, I can treat you as guilty if I decide to do so, I can destroy you on a whim" '.[40] Such an observation seems as if it merely reiterates classic liberal concerns expressed by Montesquieu or Voltaire. But Zizek's point is that the possibility that the state *might* exercise excess power is, in fact, what actually terrifies the subject into obedience.

It is the claim of this thesis that the covering up of excess enjoyment is a much more cunning process in which the subject takes centre stage. In colonizing subjectivity as a mode of pleasurable existence, the subject is led to believe in the ethical and civilized parameters of his own political system in spite, or indeed because, of any evidence to the contrary. Indeed, any excess that the West might discover lurking in its own vaults (either as potential or as an obscene supporting mechanism) is but a shadow of the excess that arises from the perceived home of excessive enjoyment and despotism, namely the East (in all its generality). Recent developments in what Nasser Hussein calls the 'Jurisprudence of Emergency' draws attention to the ease with which the law can suspend itself in 'exceptional' circumstances.[41] The use of Bagram air base, or Guantanamo Bay provides the West with examples of places of exception in which political systems can tap into their surplus obscene energy. Yet, in spite or because of the exercise of this excess that is always presented as a necessity, the East is consequently presented in an even more heinous light. The 'War on Terror' might result in Western states negotiating the suspension of laws, and the sacrifice of civil liberties, but this is sold to us as 'nothing' compared to the alternative possibility of the most lethal terror flying in from outside. Even in drawing from the surplusage, or from the underbelly of the juridical scheme of things, there remains a phantasm of excess that haunts the West and that seems to emanate from and attach elsewhere.

The observation of potential threat within Western legal statecraft, however accurate, also blinds us temporarily to the manner in which excess is much more than the idea of political violence held in reserve and it elides one of the most significant methods in which Western legal and political theory has attempted to hide its dark secret from its own subjects. In other words, a significant feature in the metastasis of enjoyment is that it belongs somewhere other than in the domestic arena. In its need to remember the dangers of excess, the West pretends it is elsewhere, beyond the grey ditchwater of its coasts, and then much further. Excess is always placed elsewhere. Pre-subjective, carnal, uncivilized, demonic, absolute chaos are the non-things that are theoretically jettisoned from the overall pleasurable scheme of things but they are re-situated and re-assigned around different parts of the globe. What will be argued in subsequent chapters is that Orientalism manages to shift the *mise-en-scene* of excess to the East. All these excesses are *fantasized* as belonging in that non-place east of the Sublime Porte. Like the Arabian Phoenix in Mozart's *Cosi Fan Tute*, excess cannot be said to 'exist'. It has (paradoxically by definition), no *ipseity*. The colonization of subjectivity according to pleasure and civilization means that we have no capacity to think of this excess; it is beyond any systemization, beyond assimilation, beyond ethics. Fantasy thus comes to be the only language in which the East is exaggerated. Through fantasy, the Orient comes to be regarded as the historical repository of excess; it comes to be suspected as the place of 'excessive lack'. The mechanics of fantasy will be analyzed in a separate chapter, but suffice it to say, such fantasies place under investigation whole systems of Oriental thought, behaviour, aesthetics and so forth that might seem only incidental to juridical and political concerns. It may be that, in some existence beyond this fantasy, Eastern and Western modes of subjective existence are not so very different, that excess enjoyment (either as a potential threat or as a hidden kinetic support) lurks globally in all institutional spheres. Nevertheless, as shall also be examined in later chapters, these Orientalist fantasies, even in focusing on mere description of surfaces, stage the juridical process of instituting subjectivity.

To claim that the law needs to externalize and then fantasize about this excess in order to shape its own contours is also to claim that the fantasy of excess is necessary in order to codify civilized pleasures as civilized. The institution of subjectivity relies on what it is not and the juridical motif of colonization means that attention is paid to the negated. Excess becomes an ethical non-standard. Or, to change metaphors, the East becomes some kind of ghostly landfill site that eventually needs to be sifted through for evidence, each potentially dangerous element bagged up and archived for clues as to what constitutes excess. It is in this sense that the lawyer as archivist of the Orient and as guardian of Western civilization assembles the Western subject as something that remains after everything else has been excluded. What gives law its force, what gives it orientation, is in fact this deterritorialized excess that is fantasized as existing east of its own jurisdiction. Excess has to instruct pleasure. It is not enough to say (as Zizek does) that pleasure does the work of law. Excess (or, the fantasy of it) has an imperial and tutelary function as a necessary part of legal rationality.

Conclusion

A more corpulent and productive theory of colonialism emerges once the factor of legal subjectivity is fed in and once the manner in which the subject comes to be rationalized is analyzed in more detail. Such an analysis needs to pay close attention to two interconnected devices and these are the themes that will be explored during the course of the next chapters. First, there is a need to detail the juridical role that pleasure has played as a civilizing force and as an integral part of the theory and practice of contemporary organization. Second, such pleasure exists only in the strangest of relationships with these phantasms of excess. That relationship based upon fantasy allows us to explore further the colonizing impulse at the heart of Western legality.

This is not to suggest that we are able to return to an authentic pre-colonized subjectivity or locate the true pre-colonial Oriental. Libertines and ascetics are united with some branches of liberal theory in proposing that legislated pleasures, conferred rights and alternate seductions keep us away from authentic freedom. In the nineteenth century civilization is seen as destructive of harmony. Engels, for example saw in the anti-natural aspect of civilization, the very means by which lower classes are exploited. Freud, following a number of precedents, highlights our discontents with civilization. And, much more recently, critics of Edward Said have found fault with him for failing to address the pre-discursive Orient and resuscitate a pre-colonized Oriental subjectivity.

Of course, a worrying price has to be paid for inhabiting our pleasures and addictions. For Freud, civilization makes necessary the suffering of individuals by sacrificing pleasures in the face of reality. We become boiling bags of trouble and torment, walking packets of Prozac. For Hubert Marcuse, the role of pleasure even represses the need for liberation. Such are the psychical neurotic consequences of having to adapt to the reality principle.

However, no theory can manage to undo the structure of domination. Nor can theorists, however Shamanic their position within the academy, uncover intact, let alone release, these lost worlds and subjectivities. The breaking of the bond between liberty and civilization that leads to repression remains a source of anxiety. Obviously, we are no longer in a position to reclaim the purity of instinctual life. Nor, of course would we want to go back to a position in which life, like the fictional Daleks from the television series Dr Who, obeys only the imperative to exterminate! Freud recognized this at the very inauguration of his thesis on civilization:

> If one imagines prohibitions lifted . . . how splendid, what a string of satisfactions one's life would be! True, one soon comes across the first difficulty: everyone else has exactly the same wishes as I have and will treat me with no more consideration than I treat him. And so in reality only one person could be made unrestrictedly happy by such a removal of the restrictions of civilization, and he would be a tyrant, a dictator, who had seized all the means to power. And even he would have at least one cultural commandment: 'thou shalt not kill'.[42]

But theory can inquire into the jurisdictional efficacy over the subject and the manner in which the requisites for an obedient subject are introjected. And the structural/genealogical relationship between the fantasy of these lost worlds and our subjectivity can at least be mapped. We might then explore part of the riddle of our being that seems to emerge in the fraught encounter between East and West.

Moreover theory can at least alert us to the phantasmatic potentialities—or, 'larval possibilities' (as Artaud was fond of calling them)—that have been repressed in the name of colonization. What alternative forms of progress and living have been lost? Are there potentialities left discarded in the realms of excess that might yet enable the subaltern to speak? The impossibility of the subaltern speaking is a condition endemic to all questions of subjectivity in so far as the subject becomes colonized by law. It is only the law that permits the sayable. Outside of this lies the realm of potentialities and these potentialities can only be fantasized about.

We have yet to argue that pleasure has had any place in the history of Western jurisprudence. This will be dealt with in the next chapter. The difficulty of exploring, or fantasizing about, what lies outside the realms of Western legal thought will then be highlighted in Chapters Three and Four. Chapters Five and Six will then examine the consequent demise of excess as the East is tamed and brought into a universalized jurisdiction. In all cases the history of colonialism will be used to observe the juridical process of colonizing the subject.

CHAPTER 2

Plato and Orientalism

Continual pleasure is no pleasure.[1]

Introduction

The aim of this chapter is to analyze in more explicit fashion the jurisprudential relationship between law and pleasure. The last chapter provided a cursory glance at broader theoretical examinations by Lacan and Zizek regarding the role of pleasure in colonizing subjectivity. However, what remains to be uncovered is how the manner in which the legal subject as a site of pleasure comes to be inhabited by law has been the topic of jurisprudence itself. Moreover, the argument pursued in this chapter will be that this 'minor tradition' of jurisprudence uncovers a virulent strand of Orientalism. That is to say, the question of legally sanctioned pleasures, the permission granted by the state to indulge in a range of pleasurable activities, as we shall see, enables the legal subject to act in an ideally civilized manner. But it does so by measuring sanctioned pleasures against uncivilized codes of conduct; an excess form of pleasure (which, for the purposes of this argument we shall call excessive enjoyment) has to be expelled from the legal subject. What becomes clear in examining these texts is that, rather than burying it, such excess seems to be transformed into an Eastern phenomena (although 'phenomena' is too strong a word for what are in effect phantasms). A form of Orientalism is inaugurated as soon as the West starts to consider the problem of pleasure.

Put differently then, the problem of excessive enjoyment is not therefore foreign to dry legal inquiry. Questions about enjoyment slip easily and obviously into a history of fundamental jurisprudential concerns that attempt to distinguish between behaviour that should be permitted, regulated or forbidden. In both *The Laws* and *The Republic*, Plato recommends that the nocturnal council of state draw up a register of different forms of enjoyment differentiating between those which are, and those which are not, compatible with wisdom and virtue. The immediate problem, particularly in *The Laws*, lies in the practical framing of a model of legislation that also pertains to an ethical ideal. The legislator has to calculate which of the pleasures are essential and useful with respect to full virtue, and which of them should be excluded. In attending to these differences, however, juristic wisdom places under interrogation different types of behaviour, character and the reputation of different systems of interdiction and styles of government.

The comparison between prohibited and permitted forms of enjoyment and the link between these to the idea of a legislative state is not new. There have been numerous studies that connect the juridical problem of enjoyment to the political one of tyrannical or despotic rule. Most, or, nearly all of these studies place the origins of this relationship either in the works of Hegel, or in those of Aristotle. In both, excessive enjoyment characterizes the exercise of a master's rule over his own household servants, or slaves. We will return to analyze the Aristotelian and dialectical or Hegelian versions of the relationship between master and servant later in this chapter. The claim made here, however, is that there are other specific traditions of thinking or, as will be claimed, *fantasizing*, about excessive enjoyment. The one pursued throughout the course of this work may be discerned through a reading of a number of Plato's works, all of which, in contrast to those of Aristotle or Hegel, emphasize the extra-territorial otherness of excessive enjoyment. That is to say, pure despotic enjoyment belongs elsewhere than at the domestic scene. It means something more than a 'lack of legitimacy' as it does in Montesquieu. Rather, despotic and excessive enjoyment is, for Plato, unimaginable and excluded from all social purpose. In this sense, as I hope will be made clear, the Platonic doctrine of pleasure might be described as a more rigorous defence of Occidental systems of statecraft than those Aristotelian or Hegelian counterparts which allow for the possibility that tyranny and excess lurks within all political systems.

This chapter will therefore compare the Platonic Orientalism of excessive enjoyment to the Aristotelian/Hegelian tradition of despotism.

What is to be concluded is that Plato, in linking excessive enjoyment to despotism and expelling it outside of the domestic arena, inaugurates a minor tradition of thinking about excess and despotism. Plato, the 'father' of philosophy thus breeds an orphan line of thought in which excess enjoyment is a state so hostile to filiation itself that it has to become Orientalized.

Plato's Doctrine of Pleasures

What pleasures are permitted? In book two of *The Laws*, Plato writes of the educational benefits of drinking parties which, he tells us, do not necessarily stimulate us into 'bacchic frenzies'. On the contrary, the ideal legislator has to permit among his people a degree of pleasure essential to their happiness. The art of enjoying oneself is essential to the moral salvation of society and pleasure ends up doing the work of law. Transgression is encouraged.[2] For the Athenian, the primary goal of legislation should be to promote and enable self control which is basic to the management of friendship and larger social groupings. A degree of inebriation is valuable since resisting temptation when mildly drunk enables men to acquire the self control necessary for the moral well being of the soul and the community. Control trains and directs the soul towards an idea of the 'good that is beyond essence' (conceived in philosophical terms as *agathon*).[3] 'The individuals attitude towards himself . . . and, the form of supremacy he maintained over himself were a contributing element to the well-being and good order of the city.'[4]

An additional argument concerns the physical state of happiness. The animal 'man', he says, is born with essential and profound gymnastic energy: 'born into the world completely mad: it bawls uncontrollably, and as soon as it can get on its feet it jumps with equal abandon'.[5] When Dionysus presented the world with wine his intention was not to seek revenge by driving men insane, but to provide us with a medicinal cure. By drinking wine the body is reminded of its natural gymnastics and is incited to sing and dance! Drink awakens the natural rhythm and harmonies with which man was born. The child and the drunk thus indulge in the same pleasure which might be described as the pleasure of self-discovery, self-control and prudence. The gymnastic torsions common to both is simply indicative of the process of getting to know one's own self. The body becomes its own object that must be known, appropriated, colonized.

The ability to master the correct forms of singing and dancing during these drinking parties not only leads to physical fitness (an essential feature of self control), but leads to a well developed sense of judgement through which the individual may distinguish between the merits and demerits of musical form or the rectitude of tradition. Furthermore, it aligns us with the harmonious forces of nature. Even in its cultic form, Dionysian energy educates, harmonizes and cures. This 'pharmaceutical' side of Dionysus is given stronger expression by Euripides:

> His powers are manifold;
> But chiefly, as I hear, he gave to men the vine
> To cure their sorrows; and without wine, neither love
> Nor any pleasure would be left for us.[6]

For Euripides, it should be noted, Dionysus helps man reconcile the two opposing sides to his nature (the specifics of gender are important and relate to a discussion of feminization of Oriental jouissance in Chapter Three). On the one side exists the rational and civil qualities that stabilize communities. On the other side lies *daimon* life; the life of spirit and instincts that liberates man from tedious responsibility. Both are essential qualities, both exist as 'undeniable fact'. The wages of failing to recognize this are high. The *Maenads*, those women possessed of the Bacchic spirit, become repulsive and bestial only when we ignore the life of pleasures, when we concentrate solely on the conventional, and when we assume the sovereignty of civility:

> Bulls, which one moment felt proud rage hot in their horns
> The next were thrown bodily to the ground, dragged down
> By hands of girls in thousands; and they stripped the flesh
> From the bodies faster than you could wink your royal eyes.[7]

Such cultic considerations are not lost on Plato. Throughout the corpus of Plato's work pleasures provide a theory and a practice of ethical conduct and an essential element of social order. The *Philebus*, for example, provides the most sustained philosophical engagement with the question of pleasure, by employing a dialectical method in order to synthesize pleasure and knowledge into the ingredients of a good life and a life of dignity. In the *Symposium*, the pleasures afforded by the drinking party sets the backdrop against which the discourse on friendship emerges. Pleasures are not, therefore, antithetical to the law.[8] Justice does not wrestle Eros into defeat and so, in this respect, it would be wrong to characterize law as being 'dead from the waist down'. For Plato, law neither exists in a state in which passions are absent (*apatheia*), nor in a state of indifference towards them (*adiaphora*). All that remains is for the nocturnal council to draw up a category of approved acts (*kathekonta*).

Moreover, the treatment of pleasure as an essential social energy does not dry up even in invectives directed against hedonism. Cicero, for example, famously barks at the egoism inherent in the Epicurean pursuit of pleasures. Yet, in *De Finibus*, he cannot help but recognize a fundamental relationship between justice and pleasure:

> [Affection] which, coming into existence immediately upon our birth, owing to the fact that children are loved by their parents and the family as a whole . . . gradually spreads to influence beyond the home, first by blood relations, then by connections through marriage, later by friendships, afterwards by the bonds of neighbourhood, then to fellow citizens and political allies and friends, and lastly by embracing the whole of the human race. This sentiment . . . is termed justice.[9]

The role such pleasures continue to have in cultivating and regulating the subject's relationships to himself, to others and to the general well-being of society, can be traced across the broad range of literature that deals with the place of pleasure and entertainment within modern society. Stephen Orgel's examination of the importance of the spectacle during the English renaissance claims that the illusion of theatre had a specific impact on audiences by exemplifying the princely virtues of magnificence and munificence.[10] The pleasures associated with masques and balls expressed both power and the principle of magnanimity as a political virtue. These were images of the good to which participants and spectators should aspire. In terms of the project of colonialism, the range of pleasures attached to Imperial rule merely should be noted. Riding, polo, pig sticking, hunting, shooting etc., were diversions that both constituted British social life in India and helped to vest the participants with authority and qualities of bravery, power and heroism.[11] The importance of the Hill stations as a location where power and entertainment mixed should not be underestimated. These were cool summer retreats, restorative areas of leisure, which nevertheless, re-invented the idea of a colonial ruling class with all the attached privileges.

Such pleasures, however, are embedded even deeper into the social strata of existence, and the idea that they are essential to the governance of social order has been pursued most famously by Mikhael Bakhtin.[12] For Bakhtin, the carnival is a vestige of pre-modern urges which nevertheless survive modernizing programmes. Yet again, the carnival is not antithetical to the law. On the one hand, it provides a social safety-valve in order to release a build-up of tensions between those in authority and those subject to that authority. The carnival creates an illusion of freedom by permitting an enunciative platform from which to criticize or satirize wrong-headed authority. Thus, on the other hand, carnivals might simply propose an alternative social structure by calling for the re-ordering of wealth according to fairer principles of equity. The power of the quotidian to effect reform and their potential to reorganize the 'republic' for the better have been well analyzed. Furthermore, these licensed festivities, that are always in danger of 'kicking-off', regenerate power and authority in order to re-legitimize them. Or, as Stallybrass and White argue, the energies of the carnival have become sublimated, turned into a spectacle providing 'voyeuristic glimpses of a promiscuous loss of status and decorum which the bourgeoisie had had to deny as abhorrent in order to emerge as a distinct and "proper" class'.[13] In this sense modern carnivals share, with the more carnivalesque rituals of early modern Europe, the staging of a symbolic fight between desires and thought, between appetites and temperance. Such carnivals typically render extra-vulgar the desires associated with the lower body; belly, food, genitals, cod-pieces.[14]

We see similar ideas to those expressed above, behind the medieval office known as the 'King of Misrule', more tellingly known in Scotland as the 'Abbot of Unreason'. These mock dignitaries were appointed in all royal and mayoral courts, and, often, in houses of noblemen along with a retinue of officers and musicians. Their duties, which were to direct festivities and symbolically ritualized horseplay, derived from the ancient Roman saturnalia where public businesses, the law courts and the schools closed for the duration of the holiday. These festivities, encouraged and sanctioned in all rule-based societies and communities, such as universities, schools, the inns of court and modern offices, provided more than freedom from restraint. These revelries should not be thought of merely as a release from the pressures of work. They were designed to the opposite effect in order to re-establish moral and social bonds and in order to give meaning to prohibitions and interdictions: 'the excess consecrates and contemplates an order of things based on rules'.[15] Indeed, from an anthropological and somewhat trans-historical perspective, ritual licence makes obvious the human horror of nature and the carnality of birth. Rituals, lend themselves to repetition. They give communities a sense of history. They thus mark a distance from animal life: that is to say from a 'life without history'.[16] What is celebrated is man's entry into a civilized, legislated and symbolic order in which he emerges as autonomous and independent from the filth of the bestial.

In addition to these legislative functions, the idea of a doctrine of pleasures has had more obvious impact on the numerous theories of capitalist economy. As Bataille argues, while it may seem that pleasurable indulgences are useless and deprive the worker of his ability to participate in the production of labour, it nevertheless produces satisfaction and 'this satisfaction in its collective form, determines the value of wealth, and thus the nature of economy'.[17] Whatever the theory, the carnival and other licensed forms of pleasurable activity, survive as an authorized form of transgression with specific legislative and social functions and effects.

All in all, pleasure gathers together a number of activities that cohere social life so that at least one commentator (Huizinga) has designated man as *Homo Ludens.*[18] Aside from the anthropological connotations of this term, the collection of mischief makers, carnival characters and so forth are *bona fide* legal figures; law's darlings. They are deficient, they insult, provoke, fuss and bother, but they possess a productive efficiency, accidentally discovering things, inventing fire, re-inventing reason, determining rules or provoking the most essential of decisions. Above all, like a proud parent overlooking his cheeky daughter, these forms of transgression are in fact nothing more than the emergence of a sometimes fiercely independent autonomous subject trying to forget her genealogy and do things for herself.

In this sense, the court jester, the office fool, or, indeed, the mischievous child belong to a group of institutional favourites in a tradition that dates back to Plato. In embodying specific pleasures, around which whole communities play, they become the very personification of the law. Indeed it is obvious that for Plato (or, at least to the Plato who wrote *The Laws* rather than *The Republic*), the moral and social benefits of pleasure are not made available simply through partying. The pleasure offered by a work of art, for example, affects moral character since individuals are fixed by a desire to imitate the good represented in plastic forms. The pleasure of art is the pleasure of the virtuous. The artist becomes a law-giver, and as law-giver, must take pains to ensure that injustice is never portrayed as a means toward happiness. What binds the community spirit, establishes friendship, and trains good judgement, are not the positive forms of regulation, but those forms of almost innocent misconduct sanctioned and carefully managed by the law. Inculcating prudence and self control, as the primary aim of legislation, is achieved neither through repression nor censorship, but through the cultivation of moderate indulgence and harmless pleasures. The specific pleasures to be enjoyed when, temporarily, the law *seems* to suspend itself is what enables a sense of autonomy and self control.[19]

The Despotism of False and Unlimited Pleasures

Nevertheless, for Plato, the danger of exceeding the normative limits of pleasure persists, and such over-indulgence is in danger of contributing to the demise of social stability. Plato's sense of enjoyment is one which by necessity has to be limited and a moderate, if not austere, economy of pleasures soon emerges. If the ideal citizen has to exercise self control (via the use of pleasures), the question arises as to what constitutes the normative zone and what constitutes an excess. He concludes book two of *The Laws* by warning future legislators against treating drink as 'recreation pure and simple [where] anybody who wants to can go drinking and please himself when and with whom he does it, and do whatever he likes at the same time'.[20] Drinking must be directed towards social justice and the happiness of all. It cannot become an unfettered and useless means of recreation.

Similarly, in the *Republic*, Socrates warns his interlocutors that the use of pleasure has to be moderated: 'The drone-type will, as we said, be swayed by a mass of such unnecessary pleasures and desires, gets a taste of the drones' honey and gets into brutal and dangerous company, where he can be provided with every variety and refinement of pleasure'.[21] On the one hand, an excess of pleasure is both physically and psychologically harmful: 'pleasures that exceed by their force and intensity [drive] foolish people to near madness and to shrieks of frenzy'.[22] A fierce bestial nature takes over when the reasonable part of us is asleep and relaxed, when we are completely unaware of sense and shame. A man possessed by animal nature, for example, does not 'shrink from attempting intercourse (as it supposes) with a mother or anyone else, man, beast or God, or from murder or eating forbidden fruit'.[23] On the other hand, therefore, what Plato finds so offensive about extreme hedonism is not simply the manner in which it corrupts natural bodies, but the manner in which it distances human action from the sphere of reality. Thus, in *Philebus* the enjoyment of a presumed state of affairs are profoundly misjudged since such forms of enjoyment are illusory and directed at appearances and deceptions. They are described as *phantasmata*, and properly belong to the Platonic class of the unlimited and to the series of simulacra; those bad copies that falsely claim affiliation to the ideal. As we shall see, the paradigm figure who indulges in these phantasmatic pleasures is that of the tyrant: 'The philosopher's pleasures are the most real of all pleasures: all others are to some extent mixed with pain and therefore illusory, particularly the pleasures of the tyrant.'[24]

A distinction has to be drawn between pleasure and enjoyment. Where pleasure is essential to the composition of the legal subject (who is self aware, able to control himself, able to conduct himself in social gatherings, and able to live in friendship with others), enjoyment is simply and profoundly useless. Where one is innocent and moderate, the other is dangerous and extreme. Where one performs a law-like function, the other exceeds the law. Thus, the democratic character is one who 'restrains himself from those pleasures that lead to expense rather than profit'.[25] And, in the more philosophical terms set out in *Philebus,* pleasure must always be in the process of becoming, 'it comes to be for the sake of some being'. Enjoyment, on the other hand, is absurd since it is pleasure that exists for its own sake.[26] But, the type of enjoyment we are concerned with here is not simply an aberrant criminal energy that can be put right. It is not the notion of civic vice as the opposite of civic virtue. Rather, these are phantasms and deliriums that haunt Plato from beyond any comprehension.

Even the Epicureans who admitted to the primordiality of particle chaos as the condition of all life, and celebrated friction as the cause of fires and galaxies, recognized the dangers of excess. For Lucretius, a man satiated with sex would be thwarted in love. The violence of excessive passion 'destroys the normal gentleness of what we find pleasing; it destroys what is ordinary, regular and domestic'.[27] By extending the bodily sensations beyond the confines of sanctioned pleasure, enjoyment explodes and disrupts the norms characteristic of liberalism. Enjoyment marks out an illicit domain where everything is in excess, where there is too much excitement and stimulation, where the superabundant vitality of individuals marks the collapse of society.[28] And, its illusory quality threatens identity.

The prohibition of excessive enjoyment is, therefore, not simply one which is designed to maintain a healthy body (whether the body natural or the body politic). It is necessary for the very faith and respect required for laws to work in the first place. Since Plato, institutional life and the legislative state, cannot help but rest on this fundamental interdiction. The same is implied in Freud's analysis of the myth of totem and taboo, which he uses to show the emergence of guilt, 'of social organization, of moral restrictions and of religion'.[29] The murderous behaviour of the 'primal horde' is a reaction against what they perceive to be the excessive polygamous enjoyments of the *urvater.* It is only once prohibitions are installed to prevent the horde gaining access to the wives of the murdered father and therefore to their own enjoyment, that order re-establishes itself. The respect shown for the law is subsequently played out in annual rituals honouring the dead father (thus, in Freudian terms, phantasies of what is forbidden are essential in positing a focal point around which identity is established).

A further theme has yet to emerge and, in this sense, Freud's assertion that the *urvater* is a tyrannical and violent father figure alerts us to a key factor in the interdictions against excess. For Plato, it is not merely the citizenry who should be forbidden a life of excessive indulgence. It is more important, in fact, that government officials, political leaders, legislators and monarchs should abstain from such behaviour. Moderation is associated with justice. And so, since Plato, the idea of excessive enjoyment has become inextricably linked to the mischief of unqualified authority and to the political concepts of tyranny and despotism. For Plato, the tyrannical character is one who is superficially similar to the criminal type insofar as he 'combines the characteristics of drunkenness, lust and madness. Life is a round of extravagant feasts and orgies'.[30] But madness and criminality are merely subsidiary passions ('an extra crop of desires') that he has to employ in order to 'plunder from all available sources [or else] his life will be torment and agony'. The tyrant is in fact subject to a greater force, and he has to feed his 'master passion' with all the pleasures of a dissolute life.

It ought to be noted then that for Plato, the tyrant is neither one who breaks nor rises above the law, but one who obeys another law. He may be an unconstitutional sovereign, or an absolute power unlimited by the law, but he is nevertheless one who has surrendered himself to a different supremacy. Tyranny cannot be judged according to specific acts. The extreme enjoyment being described here is not, as some classical scholars would claim, an aberrant erotic energy that can be re-educated towards civic virtue.[31] Rather, it is phantasmatic enjoyment itself that is tyrannical and that characterizes tyranny and that compels an individual to tyrannize others. This as a 'master passion' is therefore another more extreme version of the law-like function performed by pleasure. 'His [master passion] tyrannizes over him, a despot without restraint or law, and drives him (as a tyrant drives a state) into any venture that will profit itself.'[32] To indulge in extreme enjoyment means to be possessed by another law of a completely different (xeno)genesis, and this in itself puts into question the very idea of law.

The theme of self-control inculcated through Plato's drinking parties, is therefore, paradoxically characterized as a freedom. The practice of innocent pleasures helps save man from acting in servitude to *aphrodisia* and the more excessive forms of desire. In mastering the base appetites, the citizen avoids being tyrannized by excess desires and the leader avoids the exercise of tyrannical government. As Foucault puts it: 'in order not to be excessive, not to do violence, in order to avoid the trap of tyrannical authority over others, the exercise of political power required, as its own, principles of internal regulation, power over oneself'.[33] A state of 'ethical negativity' exists in being passive to base and dangerous appetites.

The argument may be pursued upon more psychoanalytical grounds. If institutions inscribe pleasures as a means of self-regulation, they do so at the level of the unconscious. As Pierre Legendre argues, our desires are determined by our subjection to the law. Consequently, studies of transgression are to be located 'at the level of the relationship between enjoyment and law'.[34] Transgression, art, the poetics of rebellion, non-violent protest and the efficacy of the subaltern voice—all these forms of defiance are conditioned by law and contained within a pre-established zone of pleasure. It is unclear from reading Legendre what price there is to pay for exceeding this limit of pleasure. At times, he suggests there is no possibility of excess. Elsewhere any excess release of energy is 'paid for dearly in the currency of guilt'.[35] And yet, further on, he claims what lies beyond the zone is madness: 'a basic maxim of the western tradition suggests that the enemies of the faith are both mad and delirious (*dementes vesanosque*)'.[36]

The Jurisdiction of the Lotus-Eaters

What is clear, however, is that as a consequence of legal subjectivity, the sensation of extreme enjoyment is unimaginable and, as we have already noted, illusory. Or, to use Plato's own terminology, extreme enjoyment is *phantasmatic*. One cannot think about the idea of enjoyment that disrupts conventions without succumbing to those conventions circumscribed by language and the law. It is beyond experience, language and law and this is precisely why it is phantasmatic and beyond the 'correct' apprehension of reality. Indeed, an excess of enjoyment is what we can only imagine and fantasize to be had by others. The importance of this last observation is that enjoyment is something that happens to others elsewhere than at home. In Plato's case, those others turn out to be the Persians. In book three of *The Laws*, Plato has the Athenian characterize the Persian monarchs as tyrannical since they lived a riot of debauchery and unbridled pleasure.[37] While they granted liberties to their subjects, allowed free speech, and listened to opinion on policy matters, the monarchs never considered the benefits of correct education and handed their children over to a 'womanish education' conducted by the royal harem. This education was one of extreme luxury and unsuitable in acquiring traditional Persian skills required to produce hardy shepherds and soldiers. So that, when these children succeeded to the throne, driven out of their senses on liquor and lacking self-control, all they knew was how to live a life of unrestrained debauchery. It was through a lack of education in the delicate art of pleasure and abstinence, that the Persian monarchy was to fall from grace:

> So, when [his children] succeeded to their inheritance on the death of [King] Cyrus, they were living in a riot of unrestrained debauchery. First, unwilling to tolerate an equal, one of them killed the other; next, he himself, driven out of his senses by liquor and lack of self control, was deprived of his dominions by the Medes and the Eunuch.[38]

In this respect, it is interesting to note how the Persian monarchy continued to be demonized by the early Christian church, in terms of excessive enjoyment. The early church fathers, Tertullian and Minucius Felix, both express their shock that 'the Persians consort with their mothers . . . [and laugh] at the tragedy of *Oedipus*'.[39] It is around such fantasies that classical Orientalism revolves.

The theme of de-territorializing and locating excess enjoyment elsewhere is one that is repeated again and again throughout the history of what might be termed 'minor jurisprudential' works on pleasure and enjoyment. What Freud's myth of Totem and Taboo shares with Plato's doctrine is the idea that such enjoyments belong to other communities, and other, usually Eastern, cultures. It is always primitive, or foreign communities such as Persia which mark the domain of illicit enjoyment. On the surface of it, this observation may be contradicted by pointing out that in *The Republic* even democratic governments, in their thirst for liberty, may produce prohibited and anti-social behaviour since the democratic character is one for whom all types of pleasures hold equal value:

> If anyone tells him that some pleasures, because they spring from good desires, are to be encouraged and approved, and others, springing from evil desires, to be disciplined and repressed, he . . . says all pleasures are equal and should have equal rights . . . one day it's wine, women and song, the next water to drink and a strict diet; one day it's hard physical training, the next indolence and careless ease.[40]

However, (in spite of Plato's anti-democratic sentiments) the democratic character is not yet on a par with the licentious and libidinous tyrant: 'when he was still democratically minded and under the influence of the laws and his father, [this swarm of pleasures] only appeared in his dreams'.[41] His vice is corrupted by virtue. To be purely licentious, he has first to mix with brutal and dangerous company and *then to leave home.* He has to cut the paternal tie, and become a foreigner. Such characters, Plato emphasizes, 'will emigrate and take service with a tyrant elsewhere'[42] and 'the young man of unnecessary pleasure goes off to live with the lotus eaters'.[43] The accusation of an excessive life lived elsewhere is here given the sanction of myth. The lotus-eaters, it ought to be remembered, feature briefly in Homer's *Odyssey.* Living in a 'state of dreamy forgetfulness and luxurious ease' they enticed visitors to their Island. Having fed on the 'honey-sweet' *lotos* plant, even Odysseus's men had cause to forget their friends and homes, preferring 'to dwell for ever with the lotos-eating me, feeding upon lotos and letting fade from their minds all memory of home'.[44] The fantasy of excess has a location but only on what Tennyson in his poetic adaptation of the myth of the lotus-eaters calls the 'alien shores' where 'slumber is more sweet than toil'.[45]

At the risk of merely compiling a dossier on this aspect of classical Orientalism, it need only be noted how this theme of the 'location-elsewhere' of enjoyment is repeated in, and structures, the works of both Pliny and Quintillian. As George Didi-Huberman has shown, for Pliny, unproductive expenditure, excess or transgression is linked to the aesthetic concept of *luxuria. Luxuria* threatens 'the immemorial quality of an autochthonous juridical world but also the theoretical model of a genealogically conceived resemblance'.[46] The origins of this heinous threat to the juridical and familial order lies, again, somewhere in Asia. It was 'the conquest of Asia that first introduced luxury into Italy'.[47] A similar contra-distinction between acceptable and unacceptable uses of ornament, or embellishment, in speech is made by Quintilian. Asian rhetoric is exuberant, frivolous, degraded, effeminate and excessive. It exceeds the pleasures afforded by the beauty of a properly measured rhetoric. By overindulging in the use of ornament, Asian rhetoric lacks any function or cognitive value. Attic rhetoric, on the other hand, is virile and noble.[48]

To suggest that there is a strand of juridical or philosophical thought that seeks to establish excess enjoyment as belonging elsewhere, and as having no place here at home, may seem a little trite. Is this after all, not the same distinction that distinguishes between sinful heathens and Christians, between savages and those who are more civilized? I hope, however, that at least two reasons have presented themselves. First, immorality, or sin, however problematic as concepts, belong to the philosophically, religious and criminologically defined category of 'experience'. These are instances of behaviour that lend themselves, at least in theory, to empirical measure. Excess, on the other hand, is characterized as breaking away from the juridical order of genealogy, and of being phantasmatic. As phantasy, excessive enjoyment belongs to an area closed off to inquiry. It is foreign both to 'our' way of thinking and to thought itself. Second, all this contradicts received thinking about the place of enjoyment. So far a number of themes have emerged which will help us differentiate Plato's concerns from those of both Aristotle and Hegel. Despotism is linked to enjoyment but in such a way that enjoyment becomes the master, it forces the subject to break the paternal link so that despotism has no place in the domestic. It is to this latter aspect that we can now turn.

Aristotle's Domestication of the Despot

One of the consequences, listed by Plato, of the effects of excessive enjoyment, is that those who find themselves surrendering to the phantasmatic law of excess enjoyment are forced to plunder their fathers wealth. In terms of the law, the repercussions are profound. This is no ordinary crime of theft. What is at stake in following the imperative of despotic enjoyment is the interruption to the principle of paternity. Roman law would eventually install a dogmatic logic of reproduction according to which paternity itself would determine the very cycle of life in terms of subjectivity, power, ownership and rights. Law, by regarding itself as the progenitor of subjective life, claims the status of paternity. To steal from the father would be to confound the juristic order of genealogy.[49]

The essential differences between the Platonic and Aristotelian formulations of despotic enjoyment can be summarized as follows. Where, Plato has the despot cutting the familial and paternal ties, Aristotle has the despot actually occupying the place of fatherhood. It is paternity itself which, for Aristotle, raises the very possibility of despotism. It is the father figure that determines the zone of pleasure, and as such, it is capable of defining the contours of licit pleasures far too widely. Indeed, for Aristotle, the despot is the head of the domestic household. Despotic enjoyment is treated as a domestic problem, and is located, in the first instance, at the level of household management. It characterizes the relationship between master and slave, husband and wife, or fathers and children. The exercise of rule over the domestic slave is despotic in so far as it exists only for the benefit of the master and not for the good of the community or the *polis*. The father rules over slaves and not free men.[50] Despotism, the relation between master and servant, is based on force and, the tyrant rules 'without any form of accountability, and with a view to his own advantage rather than that of his subjects'.[51] Yet, the enjoyment of despotic power for

Aristotle is not transgressive; the tyrant is still capable of attaining a state of 'half goodness'.[52] And, of the master-slave relationship, Aristotle maintains that it is possible to exist in 'a community of interest, and a relation of friendship'.[53] Indeed, just as the King is prone to tyranny, so the tyrant is capable of honour and aiming (however partially) at what is good.

By analogy, this corrupt form of mastery over slaves, might be used to describe a tyrannical government that exercised power without considering the good of the community. But this power need not break the law. It is a form of government that 'is conducted in obedience to the law'.[54] It is also a form of government that can be exercised over consenting subjects. For, it is always possible to rule over consenting subjects as a master rules over his slaves if that rule is exercised with a view to personal advantage. Kingship and tyranny overlap. Where a King aims at what is good, the despot grasps at wealth. But, Kings are subject to passions and so are prone to tyranny. All forms of sovereignty are capable of despotic injustice. For Aristotle, it is unnecessary to seek examples away from the Greeks. The tyrants of *Politics*, like Pisistratus, all reside at home. In this Aristotelian sense, the surplus enjoyment of the *Politics* may be equivalent to the surplus-value determined by the law of capitalism.[55] Here excess may be described as a surplus that can be commodified and exchanged, stolen and retrieved.

This form of enjoyment however is markedly different to the transgressive enjoyment of Plato's fantasies of the Persian monarchs, or Homer's lotus-eaters. It already obeys a recognizable law and is both a measured and a measurable excess; 'one could know in principle, if Ajax, Antigone, or Creon, Caesar or Brutus surpassed the measure and one could know which measure was being exceeded'.[56] This enjoyment is already something different to the phantasmatic and unimaginable fantasy of enjoyment that Plato uses to distance other cultures.

The point is worth stressing since it is from this Aristotelian starting point that a whole tradition of engaging with despotism develops. Take as a highly pertinent example Alain Grosrichard's *The Sultan's Court*, which takes as its point of entry Book I of Aristotle's *Politics*, and adopts a Lacanian framework of analysis in order to examine the writings of Montesquieu, Voltaire and travellers to the East. At one level, Grosrichard's beautiful analysis clearly pursues the idea of alien enjoyment. This idea of enjoyment, expressed in the excessive cruelty and lust of Oriental leaders, is revealed as constitutive of eighteenth century political discourse. In much the same way as Plato contrasts liberal democracy and Persian monarchy, enlightenment philosophers signalled the triumphs of Western over Eastern forms of government through comparisons designed to condemn the excessive enjoyments had by the latter. A sort of planetary discourse emerges, in which philosophers roamed an imaginary East looking for any slight divergences and variations that would cast the West in a fairer light. The examination of Eastern governments provided a useful counterpoint at the time when social and political structures were being re-thought in the West and formed the distant background against which Western power gained legitimacy. More than any other political type, it was the Eastern leader who was depicted as an arch-despot unbounded by law. It is in the East alone where the consent of the people is sacrificed for the pure enjoyment and excessive liberties of the monarch. The grand commercial and maritime powers of the West, on the other hand, gain legitimacy from the idea of permission. In England, for example, it was the law, common to all, that granted licence to accumulate wealth. The East India Company, so often challenged over its greed and corruption, was chartered and, therefore, accountable to Parliament. Despotism, on the other hand, was to be distinguished and extricated from the typology of Western political orders; as the ultimate symbol of political evil, it becomes a wholly Eastern phenomenon.

In his intense intellectual reworking of the concept of despotism, however, Grosrichard is more concerned to expose the way in which Western political theory *misrecognizes*[57] the nature of its own institutions and, in so doing, 'betrays the secrets of [all] political domination'.[58] It is at this point that Grosrichard confuses Platonic with Aristotelian versions of arbitrary rule. Enlightenment political writing about Eastern government, according to Grosrichard, in fact exposes the Western anxiety that despotism might well lurk within the boundaries of its own states. The frenetic anatomization of other forms of life betrays a specific paranoiac complex. The fear is that an acknowledgement of any authority through consent may well be no different to an unconditional subjection to power: 'What the concept of despotism enables us to think about, what is given form by it, is less the reality of a political regime than the ineradicable measure of the imaginary by which all political power is maintained.'[59] Eastern despotism simply makes visible that which, in the West, remains secreted behind the facade of consent and beneath the bureaucracy of political institutions. It makes manifest the nature of *all* political power and of its processes of subjectification.

The Aristotelian model informs the philosophical discussion that underlies modern approaches to despotism. Montesquieu, to take one example, locates the evils of despotism in its opposition to the goals of human development. Despotism is rooted in the laws of nature and invokes a natural fear that weakens the bonds between members of society.

Montesquieu's *Persian Letters*, which mocks the reign of Louis XIV takes as its basis a comparison between Asian rule and the French monarchy. In letter 103, for example, the Persian traveller, Usbek, claims the Asian subject is 'governed by a succession of phantoms'.[60] Those phantoms are the enigmatic rulers who remain hidden away inside their seraglios. Power remains identical irrespective of the charisma of the individual ruler:

> [e]ven if a dozen kings were to slaughter each other in turn they [the Asian subject] would not be aware of any difference . . . their methods are tyrannical and atrocious . . . the king has no desire to make [changes], because, with power as extensive as his, he has everything that it is possible to have; if he changed anything, it would only be to his prejudice.[61]

Only by turning to an analysis of Eastern despotism, is Montesquieu able to launch his disrespectful and iconoclastic criticism of European monarchies. In letter 136, Montesquieu notes the potential of royal authority (the 'sovereign perched unsteadily on an unshakeable throne') to grow into absolute power.[62] The powers of European monarchs is as great as those of the Sultans of Persia 'but' says Usbek to Ibben, 'they do not use it to the same extent as our sultans'.[63] Yet, despotism is more than a potential lurking within the French monarchy. Its kinetic energy is felt in powers related to the distribution and enjoyment of wealth 'where a few private individuals possess all the wealth, while all the others languish in the depths of poverty'.[64] Moreover, what the French and Persian monarchy share is the ability to plunder the emotions and desires of their subjects. Both systems, however different in political theory, rely on a similar structure of power based on affect and attachment. In letter 24, Rica, the second Persian traveller, describes the King of France as 'the most powerful in Europe. He has no goldmines like the King of Spain, his neighbour, but his riches are greater, because he extracts them from his subjects' vanity'. As he continues in the same letter, 'this king [of France] is a great magician. He exerts authority even over the minds of his subjects; he makes them think what he wants'.[65]

However, this Aristotelian tradition of thinking about despotism, and the post-Aristotelian tradition of confusing despotism with absolutism blinds us to some essential differences some of which are at least highlighted by Montesquieu himself. Indeed what distinguishes East from West is both a set of corrective mechanisms and a difference in theories of subjectivity.

Despotism, for Montesquieu may be characterized as force without such restraint. And so, corrective mechanisms have to be put in place. More importantly, in the West unlike the East, they *can* be put into place. Such mechanisms would prevent monarchies, even absolute monarchies, descending into arbitrary rule and would encourage the principle of liberty. More specifically, in the *Persian Letters*, it is honour that operates as a cultural restraint. Later, in the *Spirit of the Laws*, the solution is found in the specific devices and fragmentation of government. The point is not unique to Montesquieu. For Pascal, Tyranny is famously characterized as force without justice. As Louis Marin points out, for Pascal there are three flaws inherent in the tyrannical attitude towards greatness. First, the despot places himself at the centre of everything; a narcissistic illusion maintains his position within all property and inter-subjective relations. Second, by virtue of this 'narcissistic illusion', all others become potential or actual enemies, threatening the illegitimate order of power. Finally, the aspect of force without justice that attaches to tyrannical power entails a negation of tenderness.[66] For Pascal, legitimate power must be defined as one which recognizes subjects and treats them with tenderness.[67]

The second point of difference between absolutism and despotism revolves around the status of subjectivity. Absolutism does not eradicate the status of subjectivity. To be sure, under absolute monarchies, subjects have diminished freedoms, but these are freedoms nonetheless. Subjectivity remains an institutional form.[68] Under the Occidental theory (or suspicion) of despotism, it is assumed that the subject is completely and profoundly lacking. Indeed the subject under despotism is thought to be nothing other than an object, a *res*, a play thing.

It might be objected that without honour, constitutional devices or Pascalian tenderness, the Occidental state nevertheless holds in reserve a terrifying and silent power. The West cannot escape the spectre of despotism and all its possibilities. However, it seems to me that what Grosrichard has so beautifully pointed to is not so much the despotic secret of Western statecraft but rather the possibility of totalitarianism. If this is the case, a whole new thesis on the differences between totalitarian regimes and despotic regimes opens up. The terror of totalitariansim lies not in treating its subjects as things to be destroyed. Rather subjectivity is to be preserved over other forms of subjectivities. Neither is totalitarianism characterized by the phantasms of useless expenditure. The pleasure it derives is from the mixture of destruction (of those it sees as aberrations of subjectivity) and self-preservation. Indeed it might be argued that totalitarianism has more in common with the Platonic phantasms of the East than with any characteristics of the Aristotelian father.

Hegel's Master-Servant Dialectic: Enjoyment, Despotism and Postcolonial Theory

In this respect, the Platonic phantasm of distant enjoyments also pitches askew the dialectic of enjoyment found in Hegel's account of the relationship between lord and bondsman. Enjoyment for Hegel is that which resides either in the state of mastery, or in the state of bondage. In this sense, it cannot be compared to the excessive abandon of the Persian monarchy. For Hegel, or at least, for the different forms of postcolonial criticism still characterized according to the dialectic, enjoyment *exists* as a tangible benefit that accrues to Imperial power (whether domestic or foreign), or in the form of a certain satisfaction enjoyed by the servant (colonial slave, domestic subject, company officer etc). In occupying a position of mastery, the former colonial powers are assumed to have derived an excess of enjoyment (in terms of surplus wealth, or the luxury of living conditions) over colonized nations. While the slave may consequently enjoy the master's protection, it is the master who is able to transgress the forces of *imperium* or *dominium* often rising above the rule of law with emergency or military powers.[69] On the 'dunghill of servility', the slave does not even own his own life, his lot is 'labour and renunciation', and is regarded as an expendable part of the bargain. In these terms even the introduction of the rule of law to the colonies cannot be seen simply as an act of emancipation but as one more mechanism in ensuring and legitimating mastery over countries that continued to produce and work for the (excessive) pleasure of the Empire.

Take for example, the company drawing for a Calcutta resident depicting his house, servants and pets (see book cover illustration). The relationship between master and servant seems illustrated all too clearly. The wealthy resident is not even represented and his carriage remains unoccupied, for these are objects of his possession and, as their owner, he rises above representation. His enjoyment is represented through his absence. Were he to be portrayed among his possessions—in the carriage perhaps—these objects would have acquired different significance and valued for their use and function. Here, instead, is a collection of all the master's possessions which, in not being used or in being surplus to use, simply manifest his social distinction. Among them the servant is one other item, perhaps one to which or whom is attached the least value. The servant seems docile; his shoulders are lax, his legs are at ease, his face seems nervous and he clutches a fly whisk with extra tension. Where the servant seems weak, the horse is masterful, upright and strong. Its muscles are painted with solidity and it has the correct posture acquired through both breeding and training. There is a crucial disparity between the well bred horse and the lowly servant. There is a disproportion in size between the two figures that emphasizes the lowly status of serfdom.

It is important to note that the painting would have been executed by an Indian artist in order to satisfy the Orientalist desires of company officials. Key to this analysis in which the East is presented as docile to the pleasure of the West is the place of Orientalism as theorized by Edward Said. According to Said's analysis, this largely literary and artistic discourse, inspired by the works of those such as Antequil, Jones and Colebrook, crafted a world which was exotic yet manageable. It converted the 'mysterious' East into 'plain' fact. The Orient was made easier to rule once it had been reconnoitred and subjected to scholarly description. The cultural documents of Orientalism of which exist numerous novels, narratives, poems, plays, maps, paintings, photographs and works of translation, are what made Imperialism possible. The exotic nature of life—the flora and fauna, the peoples and the deities which ordered everyday life—were all tabulated, listed and objectified. Surveys conducted in the eighteenth and nineteenth centuries sought to map and transform a land of 'incomprehensible spectacle into an Empire of Knowledge'. Photography presented a view of what to many British was a mysterious inaccessible land they nevertheless possessed. Said's criticism thus extends to the tasks undertaken by those such as William Jones: 'whose official work was the law, an occupation with symbolic significance for the history of Orientalism'.[70] Jones's knowledge, particularly of the law, and his attempts at translating and codifying those laws was filtered through a select and interested class of Indian pandits who were no more objective in their appraisal of Hindu works than Western Orientalists. Through scholarly observation, came knowledge and therefore power. The East was initially owned by those who studied it and, we may add, by those who took great pleasure in studying it.

Additionally, Orientalism provided Europe with fodder for the consolidation, regeneration and expansion of its own history. Mastering Oriental languages not only provided a tool for facilitating Imperialism, but it provided links between European and Indian languages at a time when the former needed desperately the legitimating force of antiquity. Through the strategies of what Said calls 'historical confrontationism' and 'sympathy' comparisons between East and West established a sense of commonality through hidden elements of kinship.[71] Even through the seeming humanism of these strands of scholarship, what the East loses, Said argues, is not simply control over its own politics, but its very identity. In translating the esoteric knowledge of Oriental cultures, in making it plain for domestic consumption and enjoyment, the Orientalist scholar produces a representation far removed from the truth of the Orient: 'He is never concerned with the Orient except as the first cause of what he says.'[72] For Said then, the Orientalist is detached and removed from the world he seeks to portray. 'At most', he says 'the real Orient provoked a writer to his vision; it very rarely guided it.' The geographical use of the term 'Orient' itself, flattens a vast and varied terrain into flat cartographic dimensions. Lost in its folds are the thousands of different cultures which have at one time or another made up the different lands of Asia and the Middle East. Everything distant and exotic, everything different and singular was buried beneath the term 'Orient'. Similarly, the singularity of the other falls within an entire system of thought that operates according to (often contradictory) stereotypes.[73] All Orientals are weak, yet despotic, sensual yet licentious, stupid yet cunning. For Said, Orientalism constructs a biologically inferior race of unintelligent backward individuals all waiting for the European enlightenment to reach their land and for the enlightened visitors to breathe life into them.

At this crude level of explication, it is easy to see how Said produces a binary opposition between the enjoyment of power and its lack, which conforms to the opposition between colonizer and colonized or master and servant. In excising the East which had informed medieval Europe, the West attempted to become more assured of itself and of the universal values of its enlightenment. The problems with Said's analysis, for many post colonial critics (with the notable exception of Homi Bhabha), rest upon this binary structure which reproduces the idea of a monolithic Western power in opposition to the homogenous, docile and powerless East. The problem is that it sets up a divide between master and servant where former colonized nations seem condemned to a life of servitude.

Enjoyment, however, is not attached solely to the ankles of mastery. Far otherwise. In accordance with the rules of logical dialectics, it switches place from master to servant and back again. In this sense, the master cannot be a pure despot. Lordship requires recognition but this recognition comes from the degraded consciousness of the servant in bondage. The master's enjoyment of power is limited because he is recognized as master only through the eyes of a slave (an animal/a non-person). His enjoyment passes through a stage of unpleasant corruption that necessarily dilutes the effect and prevents full satiety (satisfaction 'lacks the side of permanence and objectivity').[74] The self-consciousness of the master as master is necessarily alienated from itself and far from absolute: 'In this recognition the unessential consciousness is for the lord the object, which constitutes the *truth* of his certainty of himself . . . his truth is in reality the unessential consciousness and its inessential action.'[75]

Moreover, the fate of history lies not with the master but with the servant: 'discipline and service are more essential than mastery over the thing. It is what is essential to consciousness'.[76] The servant, in other words, is given the task of handling and shaping the object of the Master's desire. This relation to the object is what gives man its history. The work of the subaltern studies group, by implication, has also reiterated the argument that historical progress in the colonial context is the product of the exploited worker rather than the colonial master. By focusing on the counter-narratives of peasant insurgencies they claim that mastery only came about when 'natives' were obliged to domesticate the alien as master.

Conversely, the slave himself is not bereft of all pleasure since, in abdicating all responsibility, he believes that he lets his master determine his fate. The master serves the servant and what the latter enjoys is the satisfaction derived from this belief that an omnipotent is in command: 'All you need is to assume that the master, the despot, the collective receptacle or master of power, is simultaneously also the master of possibilities and . . . in effective command of what happens, of history.'[77] For Lacan this enjoyment is the reason for his servitude in the world. Work and enjoyment are not opposed to each other.

This side of the dialectic, the one which reveals the servants' enjoyment as being logically connected to his relationship with the master, has resulted in two broad theoretical repercussions. First, the idea that the servant derives pleasure from his position within the dialectic underpins a broad range of literature arguing the benefits of colonial rule and, it should be added, contemporary forms of globalization. As Findlay, in his analysis of Hegel's phenomenology makes clear: 'it would seem that imperialism and colonialism at certain stages of development are given justification'.[78] For Hegel, bondage does not prevent the servant from rising above the primitive state of nature and participating in the progress of civilization. Similarly, it is argued that, in spite of its savage brutality, colonialism gathers the hard working colonized subject into the fold and 'common wealth' of the civilized world.

Strategies of government were announced in terms of the goals and benefits of social protection and modernization.[79] Educators, missionaries and civil servants in the nineteenth century firmly believed that their subjects would find revelation and exaltation through the civilising benefits of their missions. Previous governments had steered India away from the path of progress and into an inert state of ignorance. Emancipation from torpidity, according to reformers such as Trevelyan, could only be achieved through an Anglican education.[80] And for Lord Macauley, knowledge gained from such an Anglican education would give Indians 'ready access to a vast intellectual wealth'. The enjoyment felt by the servant was the joy of accepting Christianity, or the rule of law, of being accepted into the evolutionary progress of civilization and a joy often fanatically expressed in gratitude. The *Autobiography of an Unknown Indian*, for example, was dedicated to the memory of the British Empire: 'All that was good and living within us was made, shaped and quickened by the same British rule.' Even Marx had argued that, in spite of the horrors of imperialism and the 'profound hypocrisy and inherent barbarism of bourgeois civilisation', India would derive future benefit from colonialism and that, at least, its workers had been delivered from their own dark ages of feudalism:

> The native army, organised and trained by the British drill-sergeant, was the *sine qua non* of Indian self-emancipation, and of India ceasing to be the prey of the first foreign intruder. The free press, introduced for the first time into Asiatic society, and managed principally by the common offspring of Hindus and Europeans, is a new and powerful agent of reconstruction. From the Indian natives, reluctantly and sparingly educated at Calcutta, under European superintendence, a fresh class is springing up, endowed with the requirements for government and imbued with European science. Steam has brought India into regular and rapid communication with Europe, has connected its chief ports with those of the whole south-eastern ocean, and has revindicated it from the isolated position which was the prime law of its stagnation.[81]

The problems are obvious. The benefits that the servant gains from his relationship with the master are benefits only insofar as they have been calibrated so by the master. The contours and contents of civilization, to which the servant will eventually gain admittance, is determined according to a master culture. This argument applies even to a society such as the Asiatic Society founded by William Jones in 1784 in order to conduct inquiries into the 'arts, sciences, literature, history and antiquity' of the Orient. The society would eventually open its doors to Asian as well as European academics. Yet, the field of inquiry, the limits of Orientalist discourse and the very topics deemed worthy of academic interest are measured and determined according to Western methods of study.

At a deeper structural level Spivak has argued that the dialectic itself, within which the position of the servant is placed in his movement towards self knowledge, progresses according to the laws of an

Occidentalized history which subsumes the complexity and fragmentation of experience into a smooth unilinear flow of time.[82] Hegel, in other words, adopts a chronotype that functions only by ignoring non-Western, or Oriental methods (as illustrated in the *Srinad Bhagavadgita*) of simultaneously measuring time *and* the diversity of experience.

The second repercussion of the way in which enjoyment is described in Hegel's dialectic is that it is often conflated with mere pleasure. The enjoyment linked to the position of Lordship is not absolute enjoyment and cannot approach the phantasmatic nature of despotic or savage enjoyment. Enjoyment cannot be reduced to an actual state of affairs. If enjoyment is able to pass between master and servant then it is a sensation that can be limited, that can be economized, that it is something with substance that is able to flow from point a to point b and in so doing may be put into use. To reiterate and labour the point, this is not the fantasy of excess without limits that troubles and informs Plato's theories of pleasure. Because enjoyment is not pleasure it cannot be assimilated into the dialectic in this manner.

Enjoyment as fantasy places a far more sinister aspect to alien cultures. In this sense, and returning to the company portrait, it is not the absent master who has surrendered his freedom to the excesses of a forbidden life. Rather, the fantasy of enjoyment has been projected onto the body of the servant. The portrayal of the servants body is that of an unashamed body. His slouch is the slouch of non-conformity and defiance. Here, the weak body absent of sinew (*atonia*), implies a weak character. It is at odds with the Western notion of proper deportment which is represented by the horse. As Vigarello argues, an ethic of comportment underlies Western notions of civility and manners.[83] What is celebrated is activity, strength, distinction and self preservation. Correct posture reflects a moral attitude. Or, in the terms set out by classical philosophy, a character of good sinew (*eutonia*) is one possessed of ethical virtue. Physical rectitude mirrors moral rectitude. In this portrait, it is the upright stiff body of the horse that implies obedience. The servant does not merely represent serfdom and the lowly status of manual labour. Far otherwise, his body is a sign that the impulses of flesh and heart have not been tamed into submission. What is absent is precisely the look of recognition that would place him on a par with Hegel's bonded servant. There is something about his comportment that defies recognition, and that escapes the dialectical game. This then is not a docile body. It is soiled, disgusting and ignominious, but it is a body that escapes emasculation. Rather this is a body upon which the fantasy of excess has been imposed. The absent body of the master is all too recognizable. The unknowable body is the one which has been portrayed.

In Hegelian terms, the servant is not a slave to the dialectic. This is one who pre-exists and exceeds the relationship. What Plato does is to reverse the positions so that an excess of enjoyment lies not with the colonizers but with those who will eventually come to be colonized.

Conclusion

Once the nocturnal councils are made aware of the ethical premises of pleasure, Plato launches into the next set of problems. What happens when philosophy is institutionalized? What would the ideal society of pleasures look like? To illustrate, Plato sets up his own mythical utopian colony of Magnesia. Yet, it cannot be assumed Magnesia is vacant, characterless ground upon which an ideal community can be built. Plato decides to locate the mythical colony in the East. There is already the prejudice of territory and the weight of fantasy implicit in this otherwise seemingly innocent geographical decision. This is the same East of the Persian monarchs and of the *confabulatores nocturni*, those whose tales were told and whose laws enacted only during the night. This is the same East that, for Hegel, will be the place where the rising sun blinds man to his individuality and where the natural will of subjects and leaders is uncontrolled.

At a basic level, the arguments that follow rest on the implications of this classical form of Orientalist fantasy. The Platonic fantasy of excessive enjoyment is one which reverberates throughout the history of imperialism and colonialism. The jurisprudential distinction, in other words, between state-sanctioned pleasure and illicit enjoyment has been crucial in colonizing and measuring the political distance and relationship between one ground and another, between Greece and Persia, or, between Europe and Asia.

CHAPTER 3

The Sultan's Enjoyment

> The men who grow angry with corruption, and impatient at injustice, and through those sentiments favour the abettor of revolution, have an obvious apology to palliate their error; theirs is the excess of a virtuous feeling. At the same time, however amiable may be the source of their error, the error itself is probably fraught with consequences pernicious to mankind. (Godwin, *Enquiry Concerning Political Justice*, 1793)

> There certainly however, some may say, are some advantages peculiar to despotic governments: they have fewer lawyers, and fewer law-suits, and those few are more speedily decided. (Bernier, *Travels in the Mughal Empire*, 1671)

Introduction

A paragraph from the journal of Vasco da Gama, written during his travels late in the fifteenth century, describes his impressions on visiting a King's palace in India for the first time:

> It was a large Hall, with many benches artificially wrought one above another, in the forme of a Theatre. The floor was covered

> with Silke, the walls hanged with curtaines of Silke, embroidered with Golde. The king lay in a rich bed, with a Tyre on his head set with Stones and wrought with Gold, clothed with Silke, having many golden Claspes on the Brest. On his Eares hung jewels of great value: his Toes and fingers, with Rings and Gemmes made a glorious splendour: His personage was comely, tall majesticall.[1]

It is difficult not to enjoy such rich descriptions of the grand imperial courts of the East. Whatever the purpose of their visits, travellers such as da Gama, became spectators to a set of extraordinary, and often spectacular, scenes set in the royal pavilions. Yet, this is not a unique eye-witness account and its power to fascinate does not derive from its singular perspective. Indeed, da Gama's report of the Indian seraglio was not the first and could have been written by any one of a number of other travellers between the fifteenth and eighteenth century. Similarities in detail, or in the choice of vocabulary, serve as an index which makes of these reports more than a mere bundle of facts with no moral, social or philosophical purpose. Oriental commonplaces were left to ferment in a series of travel accounts which succeeded that of da Gama. In each of these journals, descriptions moved around a stock set of images that included moonlit seraglios, armies of horses burdened with saddles of gold, elephants caparisoned in battle armour and imperious sultans dressed in silks, pearl chains, ruby broaches, diamond aigrettes and emerald encrusted slippers. Seductive as they are, the tone of these accounts betrays a complex set of desires and prejudices that were, and, to some significant extent, remain, characteristic of the Occidental encounter with the East. Later memoirs of journeys made to India during the seventeenth and eighteenth centuries, while still obsessed with the same limited stock of commonplaces as those of da Gama or Mandeville, demonstrate less awe and more obvious distaste with the Oriental court. It becomes apparent that the question of taste is indistinguishable from a stern moral odium which has the effect of discrediting the very structure of Moghul imperialism.

Common academic assumption has sometimes been prone to suggesting that the East represented a kind of dark-realm, or dream-world, through which early merchant travellers somnambulated.[2] More specifically, Stephen Greenblatt's majestic disquisition into similar reports of the New World during the 'Age of Discovery', views early encounters with non-Europeans as if they were 'first encounters' that arrested the travel reporter with a sense of wonder: 'Wonder—thrilling, potentially dangerous, momentarily immobilizing, charged at once with desire, ignorance, and fear—is the quintessential human response to what Descartes calls a "first encounter".'[3]

However, the very repetition of common themes, topoi, motifs and descriptions contained in this genre of literature, suggests that the West was neither asleep during this period nor was it suddenly or rudely awoken by a completely strange entity. Strictly speaking, these encounters were not 'first encounters' but were fastidiously informed by literary precedents (from Megasthenes onwards) and by a whole army of near contemporaneous peers. It may be that the Orient, having already been subject to classical Attic accusations, differed from Africa or the Americas in this respect. Lanterns had been lit in the East on previous encounters and, as a result of this half light, there is an even more disturbing quality than that of blinding wonder. A hallucinatory effect develops from the repetition of detail in which the usual temporal and spatial determinants of veracity or falsity are lost.

This is not to suggest that the East did not have, or, through the force of repetition, come to have, a strange quality. The common themes that emerge from these reports, as we shall examine here, all 'point to' the suspicion of Oriental excess. But such strangeness is borne of language. Indeed, the repetition of these themes seem to represent the struggle of language to express excess. Travel narratives perfectly exemplify the Peircean semiotic trope of indexicality. The exact nature of excess cannot be thought and escapes language. Nothing seems to be more closed off to inquiry. Language can only point to something that is elsewhere than in the words used. Perhaps the question raised by Montaigne, quoting Cicero, best illustrates the difficulty: 'the Cyreniacs ... maintain that nothing external to themselves is perceptible, and that the only things they do perceive are the sensations due to internal contact, for example pain and pleasure'. The problem is that if there is something that exceeds the subject, then it must necessarily lie outside legal thought in some inconceivable non-zone beyond the capacity of sense and perception. How can law or language know of it? Can there really be a limit to the jurisdiction of law? Is there an end to the colonizing impulse that resides in the process of legal rationalization? Or, is there the tiniest of apertures through which the excess might be scoped and therefore contained?

The claim made here is that these irreconcilable excesses that are resistant to ordinary forms of knowledge can only be fantasized about. One might say that the authors of travel narratives are merely guessing at what might exist in this inaccessible Oriental world where 'anything goes'. However, to use mental categories such as 'guesswork' and 'suspicion' would infer that a world of excess might exist or might have existed *a priori*, and that eventually some wilful (or accidental) excursion of the body, or intellect, might take us there. Fantasy, on the other hand, connotes a different 'logic'. In psychoanalytic terminology, the non existent object of Orientalist discourse cannot be known apart from through fantasy and such fantasies have an effect. That is, they create and narrate and manipulate the object; whether or not the object (the excess) ever actually existed is both an impossible question to answer and a redundant one to ask. Fantasies fabulate the world, and in this sense, they are not antithetical to the grand legal projects of rationalizing the world.

So that on one level, fantasy becomes the means by which the perceived excesses of the East might be staged as a mark of difference, and of uncivility. Travel accounts written by English merchant adventurers, particularly during the early years of the East India Company, evinced a commonly held fantasy that Eastern leaders, along with government and legal officials, were immersed in an excess of enjoyment that was (in strict theory) unavailable to their Western counterparts. Immoderate and extreme, the manner of their conduct would have constituted transgressive behaviour in the Western. East of the 'Sublime Port', however, excessive enjoyment was exactly what was supposed to be permitted. In this sense, it is important to note that the 'superabundant vitality'[4] of individual despots could not be described simply as a pathological impulse. The despot is not simply a criminal lunatic, he must be wicked for other, more structural, reasons. This is what distinguishes the fantasy of Oriental excess from aberrations in Western behaviour. The excesses of Oriental enjoyment are not equivalent in any way whatsoever, to criminality, madness, psychosis, or even aristocracy and so forth. These pathologies are aberrations within the Western symbolic order. Oriental excess enjoyment, on the other hand, is all the more disturbing and unthinkable because it derives from a completely separate system with its own corrupt structure, its own corrupt set of duties, its own corrupt symbolic order. Thus, it cannot even correspond to what Zizek calls the obscene supplement of Western public law (that is, obscene enjoyment that looks to be transgressive but which nevertheless holds together the idea of community). Both problem and solution were classically Platonic; if evil is deemed good by and for the unjust, it is because the whole system, foundations and all, must be fantasized as being corrupt. Corruption becomes the meaning given to excess, it becomes, in itself, a matter of duty, a matter of law. Indeed, following Lacan's observations about the Marquis de Sade, the evils of despotism might even be considered ethical in so far as individual evil acts suspend egotistical interests in favour of a (im)moral law. In the East, so it is perceived, evil becomes the law: 'the supreme being is restored in Maleficence'.[5] And, as such it is radically unthinkable and from the perspective of Western vocabularies, without any corresponding meaning.

On another level, therefore, the very word 'fantasy' manages to give a frock coat to the formless excesses of the East.[6] Fantasy establishes for the East a common law based on evil and corruption. Fantasies, even in the very act of rendering some behaviour meaningless, require that this strange world is given meaning. In effect the grammar of fantasy ('it is strange but true . . . unbelievable, but believe it . . .') is created in order to fulfil the function of description and to overcome the impasse of ordinary language; it is through this fantasy of excess that the whole machinery of interdiction in the East is given meaning and rendered corrupt. What is interesting is the manner in which the 'whole system' comes to be regarded as corrupt through fantasy. Everything in the East would seem to have been infected. The luxurious arrangements and formal rituals of the Indian state-rooms had been the source of anxiety for the British since the early seventeenth century and came to be regarded as signs of an extravagant, capricious and whimsical government which degraded and tortured the Asian subject for the pure enjoyment of the Sultan. The Orient seemed to be an unpatterned world of appearances which reflected the assumption that boundaries between licit and illicit behaviour ceased to exist. The Western fantasy thus saturates the Orient by presenting it at an aesthetic level in order to designate it as the unwanted. The lavish seraglios and *mahals* of the East became an essential backdrop against which both the figure of the despot, and the theory of despotism emerge. Early modern and modern (as opposed to Platonic or Aristotelian) descriptions of despotism were always set within these state rooms and harems, or else emerged from opiate fuelled ceremonies and banquets. The Sultan was almost always depicted in these accounts as a politically insane animal who luxuriated in a paradise designed solely for his own enjoyment while exercising unlimited and arbitrary power. Unconcerned with the economic or moral well being of his kingdom, this figure was rarely pictured in any state other than those of obese laziness, indulgent effeminacy, or selfish cruelty. The effect of fabulation contained in the fantasy of the East thus renders what was necessarily unimaginable into a range of aesthetic signs. Or, to put it differently, the focus on particular and material aesthetic signs supported the fantasy of unimaginable excess; the over-repetition of these descriptions and semiotica assures the strangeness of what is being described. Excess enjoyment cannot be articulated unless channelled through 'something'. Descriptions of despotism never venture accurate definitions but illustrate the excess by focusing on rituals, splendour and pomp. The aesthetic exuberance of the Imperial seraglio and the dark forces of despotic power became inextricably linked.

The question arises as to why travel narratives might be used to uncover this form of Orientalist jurisprudence? Enlightenment philosophers concerned with political theory seemed equally concerned with a fantasy of the Imperial Orient. Such transgression is described in much more virulent and specific detail by travellers than by later philosophers such as Montesquieu who links the corruption of despotism to a lack of honour vital to monarchies.[7] What makes travel narratives so compelling is in fact this focus on detail and description establishes a reflection of the common law in which what is common across the Orient is this evil, corrupt excess. All the tricks of attempting to verify discourse are employed. As a result, travel narratives are purely descriptions of the East and the East alone. More effectively, and with longer lasting consequences, they disguise the underside of Western sophistication by shifting the theatrical backdrop of excess to the East. Occidental philosophers, on the other hand have less Orientalist concerns. For them the Imperial Orient simply reflects all that the West is not.

The second point to note is that these reports of the East were ways of understanding a potential market place. Travel narratives, as Michel de Certeau has argued, are therefore 'interdisciplinary laboratories'. While still inchoate, early versions of modern disciplines might be discerned jostling next to each other. Ethnography, linguistics, modern political philosophy. A jurisprudence emerges from travel narratives that is based on a need to record, tabulate and colonize the world. What makes the traveller such an exemplary jurisprudentialist? It is not simply that the traveller wishes to place interdictions upon forms of excessive behaviour; that falls under the narrower function of political philosophy. Instead, the traveller wishes, through fantasy, to rationalize such behaviour. He wishes to assign such behaviour to a scheme of things lacking in reason, where judgement is never based on deliberation, where institutions are primitive, and where needs are left uncontrolled.

Fabulating the Forms of Oriental Corruption

Excessive enjoyment is established, through the pages of these travel journals, as a form of Oriental common law. Just as the English common law was rooted in the law of the land, in the unwritten customs and manners peculiar to the English mentality, so too does its Oriental counterpart derive its energy from the excesses of nature, from the effeminate temperament of the people, or simply from the climate of the East. Where the English common law was defined in relation to the genteel pastoral customs of a mythical golden age, the Indian system of interdiction was related to wild orgiastic excess.

Nature

The descriptions of Oriental nature not only illustrate a realm of uncivility, but link that realm to a whole legal political way of describing things in terms of rationality. Nature became the backdrop, emblem and cause of wasteful expenditure. That is, it marked a state of no pleasure where there was no renunciation of pure instinct.[8] From the jungle to the seraglio, the whole of the East, or so it was imagined, was absorbed in the sort of behaviour which transgressed European codes of civility. Early narratives of journeys to India were fond of describing the Oriental jungle in which vegetation spreads occupying all available space. The accounts of Marco Polo, Vasco da Gama and John Mandeville not only described the seductive profusion of exotic fauna, flora, and precious commodities that were to be found throughout the East, but they also reported diabolical aberrations of nature. Descriptions of rhinos, pythons, ostriches, and giraffes, were exaggerated and metamorphosed into colossal beasts. Elephants were so large that locals were able to 'fix castles on their backs, from which eight or ten men fight with javelins, bows, and those weapons which we call cross bows'.[9] Every aspect of nature was reported as being in excess of normality. Nicolo di Conti, for instance, asserts that he saw among the men of India 'one who was three hundred years old'. These accounts of the aberrations of Oriental nature have a long history. Megasthenes reports that:

> They [Indians] get the gold from ants. These creatures are larger than foxes, but are in other respects like the ants of our own country. They dig holes in the earth like other ants. The heap which they throw up consists of gold the purest and brightest in all the world. The mounds are piled up close to each other in regular order like hillocks of gold dust. The people who are next neighbours to the ants, with a view to plunder these heaps, cross the intervening dessert, which is of no great extent, mounted on wagons to which they have yoked the swiftest horses. They arrive at noon, a time when the ants have gone underground, and at once seizing the booty make off at full speed. The ants on learning what has been done, pursue the natives, and overtaking them fight with them till they conquer or die, for of all the animals they are the most courageous. It hence appears that they

> understand the worth of gold, and that they will sacrifice their lives rather than part with it.[10]

Of course, it was not only the profusion and size of species, but also the unpredictability of their behaviour, that was regarded as aberrant and transgressive. The land, described as being populated by people 'eating carrion, wearing the guts of sheep about their necks for health and rubbing their heads with dung of beasts and dirt',[11] was also a hunting ground for animals who killed for a pleasure beyond utility. In the eighteenth century, James Forbes, based in India for sixteen years as a clerk to the East India Company, comments of the tiger that: 'he will eat nothing but what he destroys himself'.[12] His description of a man killed by an animal during a hunting party turns from simple report to horrific narrative in order to emphasize the unnecessary nature of the murder: 'his hands and feet sucked, and chewed to a perfect pulp, the teguments of the limb in general drawn from under the skin, and the skull mostly laid bare; the skin of it hanging down in strips, obviously effected by the talons'.[13] Forbes's writing employs the narrative device of adding more detail than absolutely necessary not only to depict horror, but to suggest that this was no simple efficient killing for the sake of hunger. Gratuitous detail mirrors a gratuitous motive and the addition of extra detail attempts to recreate a sense of the tiger's frenzy.

While the passage conveys the unfathomable pointlessness of the animal's behaviour, there was more to the danger inherent in nature than the immediate threat of physical harm. The external image of Indian nature, often regarded as luxurious, was all the more evil for being deceptive:

> Aromatic gales and spicy groves; trees adorned by flora and Pomona; pellucid lakes and murmuring fountains; charm in poetical descriptions; we wish to dwell in such delightful scenes; a residence in the torrid zone *convinces us of their fallacy*; hot winds and arid plains, unrefreshed by a cooling breeze or living spring annoy the Asiatic traveller; and admitting the existence of such pleasures in the temperate climate and fertile provinces of Hindustan, we know from experience, that a constant possession of the loveliest objects, often renders them insipid; the revolving seasons and variety of Europe seem more congenial to an Englishman than the luxurious monotony of India, even in its most pleasing form.[14]

The venality of 'pleasing forms' and 'delightful scenes' which disguised the monotony of Oriental life is a theme repeated again and again in order to link together the paradisaic setting of rural India to a state of sin and corruption. It is a point made by Forbes in the following description of the dangers of bathing in Oriental gardens:

> One morning [a] young lady in the state of Musidora, was alarmed by a rustling among the palmyra leaves which covered her bath; and looking up, beheld one of the garden genii, with brilliant eyes under the expanded hood of a large *cobra de capello*, pushing through the thatch, and ready to dart on the fountain.

As if the allusion were not already obvious, Forbes continues the biblical reference in more explicit terms: 'Pure and unadorned as Eve when her reflected beauties first met her eyes, the lady and her handmaids made a precipitate retreat through the grove.'[15] At one level, the moral of the tale may simply be to abstain from bathing in dangerous places. But it is obviously more than this. The scene in which the drama is set—the paradisaic garden, and the proto-diabolical figure of the serpent—institutes an immediate relationship between the fertility of nature and its allure into the ways of death or sin. The princess never stood a chance. Faced with the choice of certain death, or dishonour, she chooses the latter and runs naked through the garden before 'gazers, whether in the form of gardeners, snakes or monkeys'. In the Biblical tradition, of course, paradise was always-already linked to the corrupt excesses of nature which writhed beneath each leaf.[16] The idea of a land of fabulous wealth, (this 'earthly paradise') was destroyed by an endless profusion and abundance of diabolical aberrations and natural dangers. However, the scene reported here is not a fall from paradise. This state is non-lapsarian rather than post-lapsarian. No fatal act of disobedience needed to be committed, no choice needed to be made between good and evil, for nature had already immersed everything (everyone) in death or shame.

The function of describing the peculiarities of Oriental nature was not simply to tabulate, name, and colonize that which needed to be tamed. These descriptions of nature also set the backdrop against which ideas of Oriental despotism could emerge as natural disposition. For, what these descriptions of nature allow travellers to do is to characterize despotism as being something more than the product of individual corruption, so that despotism is seen to be fixed as part of an overall structure of life and behaviour peculiar to the East. India becomes nothing other than a field of slaughter, where both animals and tyrants are able to squander and extinguish life. Excess, cruelty and deception were instituted as intrinsic both to the nature of the Orient and to the Oriental character. The passion with which the Sultan exercises justice is of the same dangerous and frenzied order of behaviour to be found in nature. Here there are no subjects, only animals.

Consequently, there are many examples related by these travellers of the manner in which the exercise of the Sultan's powers of punishment reflect the unfathomable evil of Oriental nature. It is during the infliction of pain that the despot appears as an insane animal, a 'mad dog', or a cunning serpent who takes pleasure in the suffering of others. Hawkins relates the incident of an official whose duty it was to guard and protect the wardrobe of the Great Moghul. Once, having accidentally broken a 'faire china dish' the keeper of the Kings wardrobe sent a trusted servant to 'China-Machina over land' to find a replacement dish. When the servant failed to return after two years, news of the damaged dish eventually reached the King. The wardrobe keeper was ordered to be whipped by two men. After a hundred and twenty lashes, the King commanded his porters to beat the man with small cudgels: 'at the least twenty men were beating of him, till the poore man was thought to bee dead, and then he was haled out by his heels . . . and carried unto perpetual prison'.[17] A particular pleasure accompanies these descriptions of cruelty which, like the descriptions of animal behaviour, goes beyond comprehension and the utility of punishment. One ventures into the inner sanctum of the harem as if entering into the jungle. Servants live in fear of the Sultan who, very often titled himself after a particular animal. Much was made of the fact that Tipoo Sultan had decided to call himself the 'Tiger of Mysore', and that his bed chambers were guarded by four Royal Tigers. Even daily meals are turned into bloody rituals in which the Sultan enjoys to excess the product of his cruelty: 'Hyder Ali and his son Tipoo were *regaled* at breakfast with a vesselful of the ears and noses of our poor sepoys who fell into their hands.'[18] Where the descriptions of despotism reaches maximum intensity is in the frenzied and remorseless behaviour of the Sultan which mimics the dangers and force of Oriental nature. It is little wonder that those such as Locke and Montesquieu, in their own different ways, relate despotism to a state of nature and in opposition, therefore, to the goals and ambitions of human nature.

Religion

The very existence of earlier travel narratives may well be sufficient evidence that travellers had discovered not only a land of commodities, but had entered the dark territories of sin. These journals, richly informative though they are, may be read as a form of confession through which the author attempted to purge himself of any moral infection he may have caught during his time abroad. The case of Nicolo di Conti, a Venetian nobleman and merchant explorer who set out in 1419 with his wife to travel East, is instructive. Joining a caravan of 600 other merchants in Arabia, and learning Persian on the way, di Conti arrived in India at the port of Cambay from where he began his exploration of the subcontinent. There is nothing to render di Conti's account of his journey any more remarkable than those of other explorers of the time. Descriptions of Oriental forms of nature are as detailed and as exaggerated as any other account from this period. On his return journey, however, he and his family happened to be captured by 'a band of infidels', and, in order to save his wife and children from certain execution, Conti was forced by his captors to renounce Christianity. Five years after he had returned home, the Venetian decided to seek absolution from Pope Eugene IV, whose proscribed penance was to make Conti recount his adventures to the Papal secretary and his scribe, Pasggio Bracchiolini. The *Travels of Nicolo di Conti*, was a result not of a desire to describe mere observations, however exotic, but of a desire to atone.[19]

Not only does the very fact of the Orient breach the law, but its religions also link the tradition of superstition to a cynical imperialism. There are many images which present the Indian religions in a violent and obscene light and it is sufficient to take one example of sacrifices made to an idol of Juggernaut. What was designed to impress the reader was the sheer colossal scale of the ritual. The throne of 'this lascivious God' is described as having been at least 60 feet high and placed on a 'stupendous car'. Attached were six long cables by which the crowd drew the chariot along. The idol itself is described in details which bear semiotic association with Christian depictions of the Devil. The impropriety and deformity of Asian images of angels who almost always fitted the description of the Christian Devil was a persistent and relevant theme in Elizabethan and Jacobean travel literature. Take, for example, the description given by the merchant explorer William Finch (1608–11), who describes the Hindu deities as: 'divells, intermixte in most ugly shape, with long hornes, staring eyes, shagge hair, ugly pawes, long tailes, with such deformity and difformity, that I wonder the poore women are not frightened therewith'.[20] These descriptions alerted the reader, during the post-reformation, to the idolatrous zest for images.

Once we have a sense of the magnitude of the idolatrous ceremony at Juggernaut, Forbes introduces to his account dramatic images of perversity and violence. A high priest having pronounced 'his obscene stanzas' made way for 'an aged minister of the idol who then stood up, with a long rod in his hand, which he moved with indecent action, and completed the variety of this disgusting exhibition'. More disturbing are the vivid descriptions of those pilgrims who would offer themselves in sacrifice to the idol by lying down before the wheels of the moving tower. These victims of their own sacrifice 'were left to view a considerable time, and were then carried by the hurries to the Golgotha, the place of skulls'.[21]

What was denigrated was not simply another faith, but the hostile forces of uncontrollable excess and the manner in which the ceremony undercut the Christian code of manners and civilization. The self immolation of the followers of Juggernaut indicated the barely fathomable idea of a type of enjoyment reached only at the point of death, the point at which the individual abandons himself to annihilation.[22] The profusion of gods and cults, the mingled confusion and the group ecstasy in which individuality was submerged became cause for antagonism. All that which exceeded the civilized norms of monotheism was to be found in India attached to the different forms of heathen worship.

Observations of religious excess, and the fatal lure of its excitement, were inevitably made in the first journal to be written by an ecclesiastic in India. Edward Terry, chaplain to the first English embassy in Agra (1616–1619) compares the 'Mohammedans' at the court of Jahangir to the 'priests of Baal' and to 'mis-led Papists, who seeme to regard the number rather than the weight of prayers'.[23] The attack was levelled both at a religious attitude which mistook form for content and at one in which multiplicity and duplicity could only be regarded as symptoms of evil. Continuing the mathematical bent of his observation that Hinduism in particular was divided into a number of different sects, Terry declares 'but I know Satan (the father of division) to be the seducer of them all'.[24] The difference between Christianity and Hinduism was based simply on the opposition of monotheism to an unlimited polytheism but this divergence was felt in the stark contrast made between order and excess. Poly-dissemination was a common enough cause of Christian anxiety which warned against the incarnation of the Devil in the multiplicity of forms. Where Christianity had only the one Devil, paganism bred an infinite hoard of demons, and where Christian authority was unlimited, paternal (despotic) and contained in the single figure of God, a religion such as Hinduism vested its authority among any number of mothers and fathers. Where the theocratic legal order of Western legal institutions relied on a singular cause of causes, the polytheocracy of Hinduism suggested the anarchy of cause. The paradoxical conclusion which escaped the notice of these travel writers was that the Christian God, with His unlimited and jealously guarded power, must surely have been a more despotic God than one who had to share power with others.

Evidence of diabolical forces was not restricted to these religious displays. The Devil infiltrated the whole of the Moghul government. The point was made by Thomas Roe, the ambassador to James I at the court of the Moghul Emperor Jahangir, who writes that: 'All cunning that the Divell can teach us is frequent eaven in the cort where is wanting noe arte nor wicked subtilty to bee or doe evil.'[25] The examples of such evil activity, during Roe's embassy, saturate life in the Imperial seraglio. Any capacity for rational judgement which the Emperor may have had is rendered impotent through the lure of superstition. Roe, for example, scorns the fact that the King should have taken advice from a beggar, 'a pooer silly olde man all asht, ragd, and patcht', or that once he entertained, in all seriousness, a Bengali juggler who had brought to the court an ape who, it was claimed, held the power to prophesy and conjure tricks.[26] A further incident which features in the account of Roe as well as those of William Hawkins and William Finch is more symbolic. Jahangir had publicly converted his nephews to Christianity. Roe, who describes the grand baptismal parade of the three boys through the streets of Agra, also records the general suspicion levelled at the Emperor; 'Others supposed he suffered this policie to reduce these Children into hate among the Moores for their conversion',[27] thereby prohibiting their claim to the Sultanate. William Finch, described the incident as one of pure 'dissimulation', 'so to make the Christian Name not as an Ointment powred out, that the Virgin Soules may be converted, and love Christ, but as filthy matter running out of rotten hearts and poisoned lips'.[28]

Behind the obvious implications of this episode, however, it is possible to detect a further shock to the Western scheme of things. The abuse of all potential male heirs to the throne was a common effect of the absence of any laws designed to secure heredity. The entire kingdom of the 'Great Moghul' was built by side-stepping genealogy. The Orient destroys the concept of filiation and nullifies the principle of paternity (indeed, for the early merchants, the only discernible filial principle seemed to be the one which connected the despot to a barbaric deity). As Niccolao Manucci put it in the final paragraph of his *Memoirs of the Mogul Court*; '[t]hus do matters go in the Mogul kingdom; sons, grandsons, and great-grandsons are making preparations for the terrible wars which must ensue upon the death of the old king. For, there are many aspirants to dominion, it being one of them a saying that in such a case a father should not trust a son, nor a son his father'.[29] The French physician Bernier illustrates this Occidental anxiety in his *History of the States of the Great Moghul* with the following anecdote;

> Shariyar was the most beautiful of all the princes. Once when he was troubled with a severe pain in his eyes, he was cured by the Mukawab Khan. The Emperor (Jahangir) heard of this cure and cynically remarked that no doubt his eyes would remain entirely well until they were put out by his brothers—as indeed came to pass.[30]

These observations of 'evil deeds' noted by the travellers emphasize the gravity attached to the principle of heredity. From a Western perspective, the sacred principle of heredity informs both religious and political thought. The importance of the laws of inheritance to Western statecraft is well stated by Burke for without these laws the Crown could not be settled and the fabric of the ancient constitution dissolves, staining 'the throne of England with the blot of a continual userpation, and calling into question the whole line of our kings whose laws determine liberties'.[31] But the principle of heredity is rooted even more deeply. For, if genealogy may be regarded as the law of Law in the Christian West, it is because it establishes the relationship between 'the Law of the Father' and those who must obey. It is the principle through which the totemic father organizes desire, regulates pleasure and manages enjoyment. Ignorance of genealogy only constitutes the loss of continuity and the anarchic evil of uncontrollable urges, dark pleasures and illicit enjoyment.

Femininity/Effeminacy

In one of the earliest accounts of commercial travel, written in 1470, the Russian merchant Athanasius Nikitin describes the women of India as 'harlots, or witches, or thieves, or cheats; and they destroy their masters with poison'.[32] The corrupt form of enjoyment as embodied in the figure of femininity is a classic feature of Western symbolic orders and the spirit of these invectives was resuscitated in the travellers' literary treatment of the women found in the Imperial seraglios. Oriental women were depicted as the quintessence of intellectual vacuity and spiritual emptiness, devoting their lives only to pleasure and luxury. Plato, for example, blamed the despotism of the Persian monarchy on the fact that the young princes had to suffer a 'womanish education conducted by the royal harem'.[33] This education being one of extreme luxury ignored the acquisition of traditional Persian skills of shepherding and soldiering. The same criticism is levelled at the women of the Moghul court whose life of luxury sets the backdrop to the court and bypasses the intellectual tools required for good government. According to Forbes: '[w]hether confined within the secluded harem, or of more easy access in a voluptuous city, the Oriental females, far from cultivating intellectual entertainment, pass their time either in listless apathy, or personal decoration'.[34]

This indulgence in 'personal decoration' is a feature of harem life that absorbs the attention of many authors. Manucci, who lists the 'extraordinary' daily expenses of the court, comments on the clothes and jewellery provided for the women whose every inch of flesh was decorated with silk saris laced with gold, pearls and other precious stones that were often brought in on great golden trays 'solely as an opening for a conversation'.[35] While, 'their amusement at night is generally to have large torches lighted on which they will spend more than one hundred and fifty thousand rupees'.[36]

The economy of these descriptions is that they signify simultaneously a number of different forms of corruption that are traditionally associated with femininity. First, the definition of surplus enjoyment as unproductive expenditure is given full expression. This self consuming and expensive form of enjoyment eclipses the meaning of value particularly for the merchant travellers. Second, these expenses expose, for the reader, the vanity of Oriental women: 'on their fingers are rich rings, and on the right thumb there is always a ring, where in place of a stone, there is mounted a little round mirror, having pearles around it. This mirror they use to look at themselves, an act of which they are very fond, at any and every moment'.[37] Third, the care which they lavished on themselves is considered part of the process of ensnaring men. Here, feminine narcissism threatens the more egocentric fantasy that man himself might be the object of feminine desire. And finally, the jewels received from the Sultan, debases, what might otherwise have been regarded as respectable positions in the hierarchically organized seraglio, with the stigma of prostitution.

Everything in this fantasy about the Imperial harem consequently seemed to be directed toward pure enjoyment and unadulterated gratification. Women were thought to be regarded by the courtesans as part of a collection of rarities from around the world akin to trophies of war. The fantasy bestowed upon the Great Moghul the power to exploit resources and a boundless appetite for sexual satisfaction. This superabundant vitality is all the more transgressive for being debauched. The reverend Terry writes that 'there lodge none in the Kings house but his women and eunuchs, and some little boyes which hee keepes about him for a wicked use'.[38] And Bernier describes the behaviour of Shah Jahan during the visits of common dancing girls (*kenchens*) to organized festivals as 'transgressing the bounds of decency . . . it was not enough for chah-jehan that the kenchens visited the fairs; when they came to him on the Wednesdays to pay their reverence at the Am-Kas he often detained them the whole night and amused himself with their antics and follies'.[39]

While life in the seraglio was fantasized as being aimed towards the surplus accumulation of pleasure, the fate of the harem women was one which led only to *purdah*. This seeming paradox was partially resolved by a prevalent belief that, in spite of their confinement within the walls of the inner court, Indian women enjoyed life only in acquiescence. Forbes explains this in picturesque terms after being granted rare permission to enter the women's chambers (vacated):

> I had the opportunity of seeing the haram: all the windows look into the enclosed gardens, and have no prospect of anything beyond them. It seems calculated to furnish every pleasure that can be expected by the unfortunate females immured under the Argus-eyes of the duennas and eunuchs. Baths, fountains, fruits and flowers, the European fair ones would think a poor compensation for liberty; the Asiatic ladies, accostemed to this confinement, are not discontented with their lot.[40]

Women, according to this view, took pleasure in being forced to withdraw into a life of meaningless luxury. A direct relationship is established between confinement and 'every pleasure' against which even the enjoyment of liberty seems insignificant. The pseudo-erotic image of an Oriental princess bathing in her private quarters surrounded by fountains, fruits and flowers, while guarded by eunuchs has, of course, been a central stereotype in establishing the lazy pleasures of the East (so famously depicted by Ingres). In fact, what is found to be troubling about these images is not simply the indolent atmosphere of the harem but the presence of the watchful slave-guard. The whole business of confinement itself seems crucial to the notion of corrupt enjoyment.

Guarded and secluded from visitors, the harem signified a further dimension to the issue of Oriental enjoyment. The physical location and dynamics of the women's quarters indicated that the Sultans enjoyment was exclusive to himself and inaccessible to others. Internal administration placed the women under a complicated system of guardianship which enlisted the services of eunuchs, *duennas* (governesses), and *daroghas* (matrons). The 'entry of men inside the mahal was meticulously checked . . . [the visitors] name, physiognomy and other details were carefully noted down and verified at many check points'.[41] Besides, it was not only men who were forbidden entry but 'whatever is brought in of virill shape, as instance in reddishes . . . so frequent the wickedness of this people, that they are cut and jagged for feare of converting the same to some unnaturall abuse'.[42] Such seclusion also stages a withdrawal from both the community and representation. It is a trope common to literary and philosophical treatments of despotism (as in Burke's famous depiction of the sublime despot in *A philosophical Inquiry into the Origins of Our Ideas of the Sublime and Beautiful* or, Beckford's similar portrait in *Vathek*) that the machinery of despotism, and the figure of the despot himself must be obscured from sight under cover of a dreadful night. That is to say, that the form of despotism in order to approach any sense of excess has to be given an obscure formlessness. Obscurity thus plots the despot as being apart and beyond the limit of representation. Any form, any character already reduces his power and captures it within the capacity of language while granting him a subjectivity.

But the secluded harem has another effect upon the traveller: the prohibition of men and phallic objects contributed to the process of jealousy felt for the Sultan's exclusive enjoyment as well as to an anxiety over this form of symbolic castration. Enjoyment was not so much excluded as cut off (*coupure*, to use the Lacanian terminology), and, the traveller was made to feel emasculated. In 'short', the traveller was made to feel like the figure of the eunuch. What 'arose' was a provocative overturning of the acceptable state of affairs where the male traveller in fact enjoyed less freedom than the women.

Herein lies the most crucial paradox about the fantasy of harem life. While indolent and acquiescent, these women were thought to have enjoyed a great deal of power over the male traveller. What came to be noticed as a symptom of this threat to the Western scheme of things was that some of the women in the harem were armed with 'bows and arrows, a poynard and cimiter', and that the King (who becomes both the Master and the guest of the women) was 'during his sleep, guarded by women slaves, very brave and highly skilled in the management of the bow and other arms'.[43] In inverting the hierarchy of masculine reason over feminine sensuality, life in the harem also undercut the supposedly proper location and identity of political power. Descriptions contained in all of these Oriental memoirs associate political power with plethoric enjoyment particularly since it was suspected that the women of the harem acted as the 'cabinet council of the Moghul'.

> For just as the King has his officers outside, he has the same among the fair sex within the palace. Among these ladies are some who occupy the same offices that are held by grandees outside; and it is by mouth of these illustrious persons, when the King does not come forth, that the officials outside receive the orders sent them from within.[44]

The idea of the wrongful accumulation of power appears in many, if not all, accounts of the eunuch. Like Oriental women, the eunuch is avaricious and accumulates wealth in excess of his needs. Manucci writes that 'among the other qualities of this sort of animal is their extreme covetousness in collecting gold, silver, diamonds, and pearles . . . the tongue and hands of these baboons act together, being most licentious in examining everything, both goods and women coming into the palace'. Their position of power derives from their guardianship of the women. As Manucci goes on to note: 'they hold themselves in estimation, for they are the favorites of princesses, who are very liberal to them, in order to win them, and from time to time get permission to enjoy that of which I cannot speak. They are useful for the introduction secretly of men into the harem'.[45] What was further cause for concern, was that eunuchs, while considered to be mere attendants, often rose in ranks to command armies or govern provinces. As Grosrichard points out: 'Like the Roman pontiff, the eunuch renounces his own desire in order to command that of others.'[46]

The relationship between the vice of feminine enjoyment and power is only one aspect of a more general order of effeminacy that ripples through the seraglio. The energy of Oriental power upsets because it emanates from women and eunuchs. It is also seen to be located within a physical architecture that is described as over-indulgent and effeminate in style. Take, for example, the description provided by Roe of the Sultan's throne room; in describing the kings throne room, Roe shows more than mischievous ridicule:

> [A wooden pavillion] inlayed with mother of pearle, borne up with the fore pillers, and covered with clothe of gold. Above the edge overhead like a valence, was a net fringe of goode pearle, upon which hung downe Pomgranats, Apples, Peares, and such fruits of Gold, *but hollow*: within that the King sate on cushions, very rich in Pearles, in jewels, round about the court; before the throne the principall men had erected Tents which encompassed the court and lined them with velvet, damask and taffatae.[47]

Roe, however, cannot concede that this luxury was appropriate to the Sultan's position: 'it was rather patched then glorious, as if it seemed to strive to shewe all, like a lady that with her plate, set out on a cupboard her imbroydered slippers'.[48] The imagery employed by Roe is, of course, curious. Its moral effect, however, comes not from deriding the random, promiscuous design of the throne room but from its association with femininity. Such are the qualities of femininity employed by Roe in order to turn simple description into political invective (as Roe elsewhere states this is the 'basest place I ever saw . . . and the Moguls are an effeminate people').[49] On one hand, these descriptions of ornament create of the court an impression of frivolity and immorality in comparison to the serious and sober business of treaty negotiation (the purpose of Roe's embassy). On the other hand, the idea that ornaments were considered feminine had been a feature of Protestant discourses against the image at the time of Roe's visit to India. Ornaments took on the feminized qualities of charm and seduction and came to be regarded as orgiastic sites of contemptible lust before which the rational capacity of the eyewitness turns fallow and helpless. The denigration of the cornucopia of Moghul forms, the baroque surfaces and gilded surfaces of imperial display, were thus complicated by the debates surrounding both religious and civil forms of ornament and image worship raging throughout Europe at the time. Unashamedly carnal and cosmic, the Oriental world of appearances came to be regarded as an effeminate space which privileged the sensual over the rational and the poet over the lawyer. Everything about it seemed antithetical to a Western political order attempting to rid itself of the papal psychology of the imagination. Thus, where the Oriental court was an extravagant riot of colour, reformation England emphasized the simplicity of religious forms; where the Hindu obeyed images, the Protestant followed 'the inner light'; and where Eastern crowds celebrated with deliberate cacophonies, the lonely Western individual placed himself in a world of euphonious reasoned order.

Effeminacy and Passivity

These descriptions of effeminacy also allow travellers to develop the Aristotelian idea that the Barbarian people were more inclined to slavery. This point distinguishes travel accounts from much of the political philosophy written about despotism. Montesquieu, for example, claims that it is fear instilled by the individual despotic prince that results in the subservience of his subjects: 'When a despotic prince ceases for one single moment to uplift his arm, when he cannot instantly demolish those whom he has entrusted with the first employments, all is over; for fear, the spring of this government, no longer subsists.'[50] Fear, for Montesquieu, is what produces passivity and 'extinguishes even the least sense of ambition'. Travel accounts, on the other hand, are much less professional, far more scurrilous, and stress the effeminate nature of despotism, harem life and everyday life. Such accounts are used to establish despotism as being more than the product of the Sultan's individual passions. The protestant argument that the subject turns passive in front of the image is translated into the Orientalist idea that despotic regimes remain in power largely due to the effeminate and sedentary nature of the people: 'the inhabitants of the torrid zone are generally indolent and effeminate; the climate is equally inimical to bodily and mental exertion: physical causes produce these effects. History shews the fatal effects of arbitrary power and effeminate indulgence'.[51] Time and again, the charge of effeminacy (coupled with a lack of air-conditioning) is used as the barrier which prevents the Asian subject from adopting, 'the noble sentiments which animate free-born souls',[52] and which would prevent the formation of despotic government. Oaten, in pointing out that fault of despotism did not lie exclusively at the feet of the Ruler but, rather with the subjects themselves cites the opinion of Sebastian Manrique, who in 1612 arrived in Bengal as a friar of the order of St. Augustine in order to propagate Christianity. Manrique found the people of Bengal to be spiritless and: 'who understood nothing better than rough treatment, kindness was wasted on them. He who gives blows is a master; he who gives none is a dog'.[53]

But this effeminate and slavish nature is once again connected to an absurd sense of enjoyment: 'the languor occasioned by the hot climate of India, inclines the native to indolence and ease; and he thinks the evils of despotism less severe than the labour of being free'.[54] What the subject enjoys, in other words, is the satisfaction derived from a belief that an all-powerful figure, an arbiter of destinies, is in command protecting against some abysmal uncertainty that might befall at any given moment. As Anton Schutz, in summarising Zizek, puts it: 'all you need is to assume that the master, the despot, the collective receptacle or master of power, is simultaneously also the master of possibilities and . . . in effective command of what happens, of history'.[55] Even when perceived to be in a state of servitude, the idea of Oriental enjoyment is inextricably connected with corruption and excess insofar as such enjoyment is useless and justifies the excesses of despotism.

But a further point has to be stressed since Oriental passivity is what distinguishes the subjects of a despot from the subject of Catholic emperors or Absolute monarchs. In the Occidental scheme of things the subject retains minimal rights. A certain freedom, however theoretical and minimal, prevails. The Occidental subject is a subject because he is subjected to one who is also a servant, a vicar, or a *subjectum*. The theoretical point that emerges from the non-theoretical literature of the East is (the false fantasy) that Oriental inhabitants have no freedoms whatsoever. There is no theory of subjectivity that can arise out of this unimaginable excess other than the fact of subjugation itself.

Luxury/Leisure

The reason why femininity and effeminacy were considered such a disturbing locus for political power was that, far from softening the effects of Oriental leadership, they rendered it more extreme than any other form of government. The effeminate luxury of the court was inextricably linked to the barbarity of despotism. Describing his first interview with Jahangir, Roe states that he:

> was brought in by the cutwall: at the outward court were about one hundred horsemen armed, being gentlemen that attend the Princes setting out to salute him: In the inner court hee sate high in a gallery that went round with a canopy over him, and a great carpet before him, in great *but barbarous state*. Coming toward him thorow a lane of people, an officer came and brought me word I must touch the ground with my head, and my hat off.[56]

The carpeted and canopied pavilion, as already noted, belongs to that stock set of Orientalist images from these travel accounts. Yet, in this context, the carpet and canopy are not mere signs of indulgent splendour. Roe loads their significance in order to exaggerate the imperious figure of the King to the point of barbarity. At one level, the enjoyment of excessive luxury and effeminate diversions emphasizes the split between rich and poor: 'the one pampered by voluptuous indulgence, the other degraded below the monkeys which surround them'.[57] This theme is recorded in some of the earliest European narratives. Athanasius Nikitin (1486) for instance notes the discrepancy between the wealth of the Great Moghul's palace (where very stone is carved or gilded) and the poverty of the people:

> The land is overstocked with people, but those in the country are very miserable, whilst the nobles are very opulent and delight in luxury. They are wont to be carried on their silver beds, preceded by some twenty chargers caparisoned in gold, and followed by three hundred men on horseback, and five hundred on foot, and by horn-men, ten torch bearers and ten musicians.[58]

Terry makes a similar point in more comical fashion when describing the image of princes travelling through the streets:

> [they] ride on Elephants, or else are carried upon men's shoulders alone, in a slight thing they call a palankee, which is like a couch or standing pallat, but covered with a cannopie. This should seeme an effeminacie sometimes used in Rome, Juvenal thus describing a fat lawyer that fil'd one of them: *Causidici nova cum veniat lectica Mathonis plena ipso* [Matho the pleader comes in his new chaire, Fil'd with himself when he takes the air].[59]

The luxury of the Sultan's harem not only indicates a sedate form of sovereignty. It was seen to derive from greed, where every resource is devoted to the exclusive enjoyment of the Emperor and his court: 'If a land holder cannot pay his proper rent, the governor seizes not only his property, but even his wife and children.'[60] Luxury constitutes despotism, by taking everything in excess of requirement and giving nothing back: 'its principle is *coupure*, the cutting off all that circulates'.[61] Every European account of travels to the Moghul court in the seventeenth century devotes at least a chapter to the absurd accumulation of wealth. Hawkins's account, for example, revels in the Sultan's treasure-house. The following is one paragraph in a whole chapter devoted to an inventory of the Sultan's jewels, his clothes, armies, bestiary etc:

> swords of Almaine Blades, with the Hilts and Scabbards set with divers sorts of rich stones, of the richest sort, there are two thousand and two hundred. Of two sorts of Poniards there bee two thousand of Saddle Drummes, which they use in their Hawking, of these there are very rich ones of Gold, set with stones, five hundred. Of broaches for their heads, whereunto there Feathers be put, these be very rich, and of them there are two thousand. Of Saddles of Gold and Silver set with stones, there are one thousand. Of Teukes there be five hundred and twentie, this is a great Launce covered with gold and the Fluke set with stones, and these instead of their colours are carried when the King goeth to the warres, of these there are five hundred and twentie. Of Kittasoles of state, for to shaddow him, there bee twentie. None in his Empire dareth in any sort have any of these carried for his shadow but himselfe, of these I say there are twentie. Of Chaires of Estate, there be five, to say, three of Silver and two of Gold; and of other sorts of Chaires, there bee an hundred of Silver and Gold, in

> all a hundred and five. Of rich Glasses there bee two hundred. Of Vases for Wine very faire and rich set with Jewels there are an hundred. Of Drinking Cuppes, five hundred, but fiftie very rich, that is to say, made of one piece of Ballace Ruby, and also of Emerods of Eshmin, of Turkish stone, and of other sorts of stones. Of Chaines of Pearle, and Chaines of all sorts of precious stones and Ringes with Jewels of rich Diamants, Ballace Rubies, Rubies and old Emerods, there is an infinite number which only the Keeper therof knoweth. Of all sorts of plate, as Dishes, Cups, Basons, Pots, Beakers of Silver wrought there are two thousand Battmans. Of Gold wrought, there are one thousand Battmans.[62]

It should be added, however, that the despot is not simply one who can exploit resources greedily 'extracting oil out of sand', or 'sunlight from cucumbers'.[63] In theory, the despot already owns everything. For the rest of the population, in the Moghul empire, there existed no such notion as private property. It is this absurd enjoyment of all property that properly connects Oriental leadership to despotism: 'take away the right of private property in land, and you introduce, as a sure and necessary consequence, tyranny, slavery, injustice, beggary and barbarism'.[64] It is here that despotism supposedly defeats any principle of subjectivity. Everything, including inhabitants, is property belonging to the Emporer. His subjects are deemed to be nothing other than objects; things, *res*, sport. They are certainly animals in general, perhaps mankind in particular, but never subjects in law.[65] And, how can one imagine the principle of humanity without subjectivity. The greed of any Western monarch, potentate, or Company man is nothing compared to that of a despot.

Justice

The exclusive enjoyment over land rights is only one aspect of an overall luxury that interferes in the exercise of justice. Access to justice itself required permission to tread on land owned by the Sultan. It is important to note the significance of palace architecture and its exclusivity as a significant element in the overall derision of Oriental justice. It was already observed (mistakenly) from the use of over elaborate Imperial titles such as the 'Asylum of Pardon', the 'Shadow of God', or 'the Fountain of all Honours' that the Sultan placed himself well above the supervision of the courts. This was all the more disturbing since they indicated the exclusive power of the Sultan to dispense justice according to his will.

> The Emperour stiles himself: *the King of Justice, the Light of the Law of Mahomet, the Conquerer of the World.* Himselfe moderates in all matters of consequence which happen neere his court, for the most part judging *secundum allegata et probata.* Tryals are quick, and so are executions: hangings, beheading, impaling, killing with dogges, by elephants, serpents, and other like, according to the nature of the market place. The governours in cities and provinces proceed in like forme of justice. I could never heare of law written amongst them: the King and his substitutes will is law.[66]

Not only is authority exclusive to the Sultan but it is inaccessible to others. It is exercised in a private domain where he keeps matters for, and to, himself: 'In the silence which attends despotism everything is dark and solemn. Justice itself is executed with privacy, and sometimes a solitary gun fired at midnight from the palace of the despot, proclaims the work of death.'[67] The idea of the Sultan's private domain is one which is used as emblem of all that is contrary to the juridical values of the Western. The private domain becomes signifier of a private mysterious will and the aesthetic structure of the Imperial palace is used to signify the difficulty of gaining access to the Emperor as dispenser of justice. While the over-elaborate architecture of this structure is described in most journals, Tavernier's is the most detailed:

> When the King administers justice he comes, as I stated, into the balcony which overlooks the square, and all those who desire to be present stand below, opposite to where he is seated. Between the people and the wall of the palace three rows of sticks the length of a short-pike are planted in the ground, at the ends of which are attached cords which cross one another, and no one, whosoever he may be, is allowed to pass these limits without being summoned. This barrier, which is not put up except when the King administers justice, extends the whole length of the square, and opposite the balcony there is an opening to allow those who are summoned to pass. Then two men, who hold by the ends a cord stretched across this opening, have only to lower it to admit the person who is summoned. A Secretary of State remains in the square below the balcony to receive petitions, and when he has five or six in hand he places them in a bag, which a eunuch, who is on the balcony by the side of the King, lowers with a cord, draws up and presents them to his majesty.[68]

Much more keenly aware of Western jurisprudence than other travellers, Bernier notes the effect of this inaccessibility on those who actually seek justice: 'how is a poor peasant or a ruined artisan to defray the expenses of a journey to the capital, and to seek justice at one hundred and fifty or two hundred leagues from home? He would be waylaid or murdered'.[69] Bernier subsequently notices that the intervention of the secretary of state, the eunuch or any other friend of the King would increase the chances of 'distorting the truth, and misrepresenting the whole affair'. The more complicated these rituals were, the more the palace was walled in or cordoned off through an elaborate architecture, the more despotic the system came to be regarded.

In all of these journal entries, it is the combination of luxury and the dispensation of justice which causes most concern. Luxury may imply the Sultan's inordinate wealth, exclusive ownership of property, or the closed walls of the royal palace. It also implies the indolent enjoyment of leisurely diversions. Not a day passes but there is not a curiosity to be noted, an event to be remembered, or an observance to be laughed at in the exercise of justice. These events, which usually take place during the daily durbars, are described as being more than examples of cruelty.[70] They become examples of cruelty staged as spectacular events for the exclusive enjoyment of the Sultan. Roe, for example, describes the attendance of Jahangir at ritual executions: 'once weekly where sometimes he sees the execution done by his elephants with too much delight in blood'.[71] Quite how much delight in blood is permissible Roe does not calculate. Perhaps the most celebrated emblem of the spectacle of Eastern cruelty comes in the form of the Tippoo Sultan's mechanical toy tiger which shows a royal tiger (representing the triumph of the *khood a dand Sircar*, or God given) devouring a prostrate Englishman. For Forbes, this automaton, while not a spectacular piece of cruelty in itself, 'affords us great reason to suppose he would have enjoyed direful spectacle'.[72] In continuing his description, Forbes strengthens the charge of tyranny levelled against Tippoo by drawing parallels with Nero, yet even Nero 'had the grace to turn away his eyes from the horrors of his reign'. Tippoo, on the other hand, becomes the more tyrannical of the two because, as spectator, he keeps a 'register of our sighs and groans'. It is the participation in the rituals of torture and execution, in the aesthetics of display, which maintains the level of tyrannical power. That this level of enjoyment far exceeds that which is permissible is made all the more poignant on those occasions where the Sultan would, in a fit of excessive passion, execute men with his own hand, instead of leaving the work to the official executioners, where he takes over and presents himself as part of the spectacle:

> He put to death in my time his Secretary, onley upon suspicion; whereupon the King not having patience, arose from his seate, and with his sword gave him his deadly wound, and afterwards delivered him to be torne by Elephants.[73]

More disturbing is that to the spectator ignorant of the full meaning and symbolism of Mughal court ritual, which must surely be the position occupied by the authors of these travel journals, these incidents appear to be leisurely diversions with no discernible political ends. They are presented to the reader as occasions where the Sultan indulges in sport in order to satiate his whimsical desire to see cruelty done:

> The King not yet contented but desirous to see more sport, sent for ten men that were of his horsemen . . . these men one after another were to buffet with the Lyon, who were all grevously wounded, and it cost three of them their lives. The King continued three months in this vaine, when he was in his humors, for whose pleasure sake, many men lost their lives untill some fifteen young Lyons were made tame, and played one with another before the King, frisking betweene mens legs, and no man hurt in a long time.[74]

Accounts of these indulgent events allow authors to establish, explore and exploit, one of the most persistent stereotypes of the Eastern potentate as an arch-schemer. First and foremost, the despotic character suggests cunning and an endless appetite for double-dealing. The following account, although having less of a game-like quality, demands a belief in the treachery and deceit of the jealous Sultan as if he were playing a game:

> It is said that Begum-Saheb (one of the Princesses in the harem of Shah Jahan) although confined in a Seraglio, and guarded like other women, received the visits of a young man . . . Chah-Jehan was apprised of her guilt, and resolved to enter her apartments at an unusual and unexpected hour. The intimation of his approach was too sudden to allow her the choice of more than one place of concealment. The affrighted gallant sought refuge in the capacious cauldron used for the bath. The King's countenance denoted neither surprise nor displeasure; he discoursed with his daughter on ordinary topics, but finished the conversation by observing that the state of her skin indicated a neglect of her customary ablutions, and that it was proper she should bathe. He

> then commanded the Eunuchs to light a fire under the cauldron, and did not retire until they gave him to understand that his wretched victim was no more.[75]

Sly and witting, the Oriental despot is characterized by his unwillingness to put, what in the West would be regarded as his imperial wisdom to any other use than the illicit enjoyment of cruelty. It is through the descriptions of the Sultans leisurely activities and the enjoyment of excess wealth, that these narratives manage to convey a sense of the injustices that attach to despotic rule.

Illusion

It has already been mentioned that, for these travellers, the Moghul court contradicts efficient order since power is held by women, by eunuchs, by the people who command his presence every day. And it has been noted, that examples of the Emperors appetite are provided against the lavish backdrop of the court and emerge from a world apparently mad on ostentation. There is, nevertheless, more to this process of distinguishing Eastern from Western forms of government than simply by focusing on courtly pretension. The key to despotism is not simply in the display and enjoyment of wealth and power. It is in the idea that the entire display is no more than a deception of power designed to manipulate those who are subjected to it. The duplicity of the Sultan, which reflects the duplicity found in nature, and among the Eunuchs of the harem, has already been noted. On one level, the deception of power, which is probably no more than tactical warfare, had brutal consequences for the British. Forbes, for example, describes the fate of two British residents who were summoned to Tipoo's durbar, and 'received with respectful politeness, which he knew how to assume. After being seated on the carpet they were each presented with a cup of coffee . . . In a few minutes [they were] either carried out in the struggles of death, or expired at the tyrants feet'.[76]

On another level, the deception of Sultanate power indicated a more profound emptiness at the heart of Oriental government. This illusory insubstantiality of the court is hinted at by Roe having described the Sultan's daily routine of showing himself to the crowds:

> Hee comes every morning to a window called the jarrneo, looking into a plaine before his gate and shewes himself to the common people . . . from whence hee retires to sleep among his women . . . this course is unchangeable, except sicknesse or drink prevent it, which must be known: for as all his subjects are slaves, so is hee in

> a kind of reciprocall bondage, for hee is tyed to observe these houres and customs so precisely, that if hee were unseen one day, and no sufficient reason rendred, the people would mutinie; two days no reason can excuse, but that he must be seen by some to satisfie others.[77]

The public display of the Sultan's body, which is as regular, solemn and as spectacular as an astral phenomenon, introduces the whole suspicion of fakery and impotency. The daily spectacle disguises the dangers and intrigues of the court. Away from the window, Jahangir suffers the 'vice' of drink. A gloriously opiate-addled lethargy which infuses the sultanate court is hidden well away from public sight; a concern shared by Roe's predecessor William Hawkins. Each night Jehangir indulges by drinking and smoking opium:

> And then he ariseth, and being in the height of his drinks, he layeth him down to sleep, every man departing to his own home. And, after he hath slept two hours they awake him, and bring his supper to him, at which time he is not able to feed himself; but it is thrust into his mouth by others, and this is about one of the clock; and then he sleepeth the rest of the night.[78]

Elsewhere in his narrative, Roe becomes suspicious of the value of all this wealth. During Jahangir's birthday celebrations, the Emperor sits cross-legged on a pair of scales and his weight is measured against gold and jewels which Roe believes to be make believe: he describes sacks full of that which:

> they say was silver, gold and jewels and precious stones, but I saw none, it being in bagges might bee pibles. Then [he is weighed] against cloth of Gold, Silke, Stuffes, Linnen, Spices and all sorts of goods, but I must believe, for they were in fardles. Lastly, against Meale, Butter, Corne, which is said to be given to the Beniani, and all the rerst of the Stuffe: but I saw it carefully carried in, and none disturbed.[79]

If Roe's descriptions of sultanate rituals and ornament are so detailed and so vivid, they are so in order to validate the claim that there is but no substance to despotism beyond the frippery. It is all show: 'To describe it rightly, it was like a great stage, and the Prince sate above as the Mock Kings doe there',[80] or '[t]his sitting out had so much affinity with a theatre, the manner of the king in his gallery: the great men lifted on stage, as actors, the vulgar below gazing on'.[81]

For Roe, Oriental luxury exceeds the order of resemblance by masking the empty relations of power. Throughout Roe's account the world of luxury is a world of dissimulation; fruits of gold are in fact hollow, sacks of jewels may be full of pebbles, and the whole scene is staged to glorify a 'mock King'. Objects and persons are never what they seem. Borrowing directly from a favourite maxim of Protestant iconoclasm, Roe concludes his description of Jahangir's Imperial pavilion, by making scathing reference to the transitory nature of the Oriental vanities: *sic transit gloria mundi.*[82] All of this theatrical display of Imperial power, for Roe, was based upon deceit rather than fact. Its extravagance hid an emptiness within the structure of power itself. Oriental government was more deceitful a form of power in that it managed to captivate, seduce and, ultimately, dupe those attendant subjects. The formal arrangement of Moghul rule, as stated much later by a company director although 'beautiful in its simplicity upon paper, is apt to charm the imagination and mislead the judgment of men'.[83] The theory that the King is King only through appearances was well noted by travellers such as Roe, and with it the power of images to manipulate the affections of the 'vulgar' spectators. This deceitful manipulation through the arts of representation is what made the idea of despotism so abhorrent.

Yet, a paradox emerges. In terms of the fantasy, the more that emptiness is envisaged at the heart of despotic power, the more tyrannical it becomes. The more sedentary, drunk, effeminate the despot gets, the more despotic he becomes. Despotic power finds its paradigm in the image of the drunk, lazy, and inefficient Sultan. The force of despotism lies in the dazzling display that is nothing more than dissimulation. If there were an equivalent it might be Descartes's philosophical fiction of the 'evil genius' as the one who creates the illusion of truth. Dissimulation, consequently, comes to be regarded as the origin of illegitimate force, it is what institutes despotic power. And in manipulating and manoeuvring the desires and behaviour of those who are subject to its display, this dissimulation is not without real effect. The fantasy of excess rests on nothing.

Conclusion

Excess is constituted as a deficiency. It is constituted as such on three levels. First, the fantasy of the non-Western 'subject' prone and subject to despotic excess is perceived to be uncivilized; wanting in control, laws, and the requisite code of pleasures that authenticate his subjectivity as legal.

Second, there is the suspicion that excess is based on deception and nothingness. The third point is one which will be pursued in the next chapter and that is that excess is something that is missing from the controlled make-up of Western legal subjectivity. It is something (or, profound nothingness) that has been lost to the East. Indeed, given the impossibility to think of the excess except through fantasy, then this excess is radically lacking.

But these fantasies of Oriental excess are not just a repository of the disqualified and deactivated desires. They become part of institutional life, and of the Occidental and juridical colonization of subjectivity. That is to say, in denigrating what is excessive, a more mundane theory of pleasure emerges that instructs and legislates Western and global subjectivity. The fantasy of excess becomes tutelary; a necessary part of the management of pleasure and subjective behaviour. In an historical sense, these early Orientalist tracts are to be read as attempts to exempt the Western from the corrupt excesses that may have characterized the medieval political world and to externalize and transfer such unwanted excess to the Orient. The idealization of the legal subject thus takes place as a specifically non-Eastern figure.

CHAPTER 4

Envy and Subjectivity in Orientalism

> We imagine primitives to possess some of the qualities of ideal poetry—full of zest, clairvoyantly sensitive, realistic, whole, natural, and passionate; and so we might well look at their songs hopefully.

> England was from the Anglo Saxon period an intensely governed country; if it has also been at various times an over-administered one, the desire of many travellers may have consisted in a flight from the conditions of English civilisation itself. The English penchant for the dream and the vision may in turn be part of a general escape from the conventions of practicality and common sense which make up so much of the native psyche. The Tradition of empiricism or pragmatism is not in contradiction to the equally large inheritance of ghosts, dreams and visions; they are the opposite sides of the same coin of the realm.[1]

Introduction

What was uncovered in the last chapter was a jurisprudential attitude towards excessive enjoyment that condemns 'the Oriental' to a fantastical space in which everything is deemed to be a corrupt surplus. It is the claim of this chapter that travel narratives as well as Orientalizing excess, pitching it over the Western horizon, also reveal desire and envy for the same object of horror. It was not the case, as Montesquieu implies, that the East was different things at different times: 'sometimes detestable, other times admirable'.[2] Horror and desire occur simultaneously. It is obvious that Western visitors were also beguiled by the excesses of the East at the exact moment of distancing themselves from it and travel narratives bear within their grammar this constant struggle between horror and desire, distance and engagement. This chapter examines this desire for excess in terms of the more specific trope of envy (*invidia*).

The matter and mechanics of envy[3] have been the subject of jurisprudential debate since John Rawls's attempt to exclude the syndrome from his concept of justice under a veil of ignorance. Justice, even social justice (equal rights and equal opportunity), can only arise if society is in a position 'where, by hypothesis, no one is moved by rancor and spite'.[4] Other than in Rawls's hypothetical original position, the suspicion raised by all claims to equality is that such claims are based on an individual's envy of what another has (rights, goods etc), and what might be denied to him. 'Envy', as Aristotle points out, 'is pain at the good fortune of others.'[5] In the context of early encounters in the East, it might be thought that envy would be a useful way of describing Western attitudes towards differences in Oriental resources and manners. Envy at least provides a standard which measures self worth against the other.

However, the argument pursued in this chapter will be based on something less than a comparative approach to the differences between East and West. Instead, envy will be treated as a by-product of the specific relationship between desire and pleasure (or rather, the impossibility of desire fulfilment) and as betraying something about what the legal subject really wants. That is, he no longer wishes to simply be what he is meant to be; he no longer wishes to be simply the end-product, the passive subject of civilization; he no longer wishes to behave according to the proscribed set of pleasures. Rather, we have to take into account that the legal subject often wants to be carnal, liberated, or to be another in order to have access to what he believes the other has. Such a romantic desire to possess the earth, to be in touch with our outlawed emotions, has to be factored into the institution of subjectivity.

In slightly more synoptic terms, the argument made will be that the codes of pleasure that colonize the legal subject (of which the Western traveller is a specific example) erects an obstacle that prevents him from achieving what he desires (namely the excess enjoyment he fantasizes as belonging to the Oriental subject he so despises). This 'obstacle of pleasures' produces in the legal subject a much more heightened state of desire that expresses itself as envy. Such envy is for the very excess that constitutes the Oriental subject as an object of denigration. The fantasy of Oriental excess renders a Western subject envious of all the things, energies and power, that he suspects the Eastern non-subject might enjoy. Envy, in other words, emerges for that which exceeds civilized norms.

But all that which exceeds civilized norms, it will be argued, awakens in the Western subject a suppressed memory of pre-civilized man. Envy for the Oriental subject's enjoyment, is for a fantasized mode of existence that pre-existed the early modern civilized state of being. Such a state of being, such a fantasm, now comes to be represented through early Orientalism, in the figures of the despot and his subjects, as well as in the fancy that the East was the birthplace of all civilization. The Western subject desires to be the other that is created in fantasy because the other, particularly the Oriental other, comes to represent something that he himself once was (or might have been). The East thus stirs up such ancient primeval memories from the depths of the West; it reminds and realizes the vitality and potential lost from sophisticated society and institutionalized life. Such a hankering after the non-sophisticated domain of pre-historical life, so well expressed in these early modern travel narratives, constitutes a strand of modern Western thought that links Rousseau, the Libertarians, the Romantics, psychoanalysts etc; in short, it distinguishes all those 'discontented' with civilization. But this 'discontent' cannot be thought of as an aberration in the make up of legal subjectivity. The desire to be (or the envy for) someone different (caveman, superhero, bird, pop-star, white, black, or to have different parents, or a different nationality) seems to be too common, too normal, an occurrence for it not to be a significant factor in the preparation of subjectivity. Thus, in the context of this project, the trope and targets of Orientalist envy will be treated as vital yet paradoxical in forming Western subjectivity. They will also be treated as a juridical feature of the colonialist impulse to understand, chart and possess the transition from the raw to the cooked, from feral child to cultivated man.

Before proceeding a number of preliminary points might be made about the relationship of narrative to pleasure and excess, and the passion of envy that is revealed. We will focus on the travel reports in order to demonstrate how pleasure thwarts desire and then institutes envy. Thus, an examination of travel narratives as a specific genre indicates the manner in which they institute pleasure over what they describe. At the same time they betray a desire for what they describe and the impossibility of reaching this pleasure. Travel narratives are haunted not by the strangeness of the other *per se*, but by our (civilized man's) relationship to the pre-civilized image of ourselves. This then leads to an envy for the place of the other as symptomatic of what the civilized subject has lost.

Narrative

That this form of jurisprudence is conducted through a narrative genre that is unrecognizable as formal legal writing cannot go unremarked. Travel narratives already betray, and codify, differing levels of pleasure in a way that the non-ordinary form of legal texts cannot, and perhaps should not! As Louis Marin puts it 'the right to write, the right to listen to tales: these are synonymous with the right to pleasure'.[6] The elements of narrow colonial jurisprudence are concerned with the authority of rules and a mode of didactics that attempt to regulate the colonized subject. A broader jurisprudence is invoked in these travellers' accounts that attempts to instruct and persuade its readership through pleasure. Marin's articulation of the pleasure of narratives progresses in a manner that provokes a number of jurisprudential questions. He suggests pleasure is not opposed to reason but is 'an envelope for the seriousness of instruction and morality'.[7] Indeed, what makes these tales so intriguing (over and above contemporaneous and similarly toned philosophers intrigued by the Orient) is that they interrupt the whole discourse of renunciation and denigration that was examined in the last chapter, while nevertheless holding onto an agenda of rationalizing and ordering the world. Whether or not we care to believe these authors, they place themselves in the position of being both witnesses and raconteurs. So that at the first (authorial) level of analysis, the traveller gives himself the pleasure of telling a tale borne of the assumption that he himself has witnessed the Moghul world. He is party to something so extraordinary that his readers cannot have experienced anything like it. Thus, the pleasure of narration is also the pleasure of seemingly mastering or accessing the unknowable excesses of the Orient (or, in more Hegelian terms, it is the pleasure in being recognized, by a suspected readership, as master of an esoteric and rare knowledge). At this basic level, narratology provides a model for jurisdiction insofar as it contracts the world into one appreciable entity that can be surveyed. It sets up the Orient as a district of the world. The pleasure of power, and the assertion of the subject's place in the world, emanates from this contraction.

The most obvious manifestation of this pleasure of contraction lies in the treatment of Oriental nature. It was noted, in the last chapter, that the denigration of the natural life of the Orient was based around its profusion and perceived aberrancies, and nature was deemed to infuse the figure of the despot with animal qualities. Yet, beneath even the bitter prose these authors indicate an admiration for the existence and variety of Eastern life. This admiration goes beyond the exploitation of natural resources that India had to offer. For, even in its abundance, nature also provided security from excess. In this context, it is notable, and hardly surprising for an Englishman, that Thomas Roe expresses his love for the Emperor's gardens:

> A delicate grove of two miles large, a quarter broad, planted by industry with Manges, Tamerins and other fruits, divided with walks and full of little Temples and Altars of Pagods, and Gentilitial idolatory, many fountains, wels, tankes and summer houses of carved stone curiously arched, so that I must confesse, a banished Englishman might have been content to dwell there.[8]

Or, in the following passage from Reverend Terry, the sense of escape from the excesses of the Orient is described in terms that seems to presage the later Romantic treatment of nature as a beautiful, and sometimes sublime, respite from mundane existence.

> For places of pleasure they have curious gardens, planted with fruitfull Trees and delightfull Flowers, to which Nature daily lends a supply as that they never seeme to fade. In these they have pleasant Fountaynes to bathe in, and other delights by sundrie conveyances of water, whose silent murmure helps to lay their senses with the bonds of sleepe in the hot seasons of the day.[9]

The tone of these passages are themselves relaxed and tranquil. So that even the idols that decorate the gardens, those symbols of evil, seem more acceptable. What these passages indicate is the ambivalence in the attitude toward excessive enjoyment. Gardens do not simply tame nature, they provide a sanctuary where the despot may relax. They have within themselves a regulatory function that keeps a check on the voluptuous figure of the despot.

> the high walls . . . are the necessary guradians of a Muhomedan's honour, and the safeguard of his pleasures. Within this protection, secluded from the world, the voluptuous Mussulman, laying aside the grandeurs of the day, with the irritation of the mind which accompanies ambition, abandons himself to soft repose; and, in the stillness of a starry night, acquires that serenity of mind which

> lulls the soul into pleasing complacency; forming a delightful contrast to the stormy passions of the agitated day. Negligently stretched upon his couch, he listens to the melodious song; and contemplates the graceful forms of the surrounding dancers; amid the odiferous smoke of incense.[10]

A number of interrelated points might be made. The contraction of excess enjoyment into a more understandable lexical framework indicates a taming of excess into pleasure. In terms of the overall project of colonizing India, this marks a typical moment in the history of Western civilization. Pleasure performs the task of differentiating Western subjectivity from the domain of carnality. These gardens were not innocent pastimes, but part and parcel of the manner in which animal instincts are to be subject to interdiction. The garden cultivates man, so to speak, colonizing him as a subject of pleasure. This basic level of pleasure mixes with others. The traveller takes pleasure in asserting his unique position within the world, describing and transmitting information about a rarefied world.

But the colonization of subjectivity is achieved through the dissemination of these texts among a broader range of readers. So that central to the pleasures of narratology is the idea that reading produces its own delights. It might be thought that these records of the strange fearful and fabulous might disturb the subject. But the subject who reads is cast adrift only in order to anchor himself again. Reading reminds and reassures the reader of the security of his a vantage point. Everything, or at least the world, seems to revolve around his perspective.

In general terms, the solitary act of reading such travel narratives, produces a satisfaction that mirrors Western codes of civility whereby the individual conducts his private passions in some quiet recess of the world. A pleasant distance is maintained from the whirl of social activity. More specifically, however, the reader is given the pleasure of being held in thrall and seduced by what he takes to be the truth of India, or Turkey, or the South Seas. The more scandalous this truth is taken to be the better. The reader, like the traveller in whose name these texts are written, becomes a witness, albeit a second, or third hand witness. His pleasure comes from being a vicarious party to proceedings, indeed from being a vicarious traveller who sets about discovering and opening up new spaces (the discursive Orient, the discursive New World). And so, to borrow from Benedict Anderson's famous argument, these readers become bonded to an 'imagined community of readers', enmeshed in a whole network of fellow witnesses and travellers. Thus emerges a sense of proximity to a strange and distant land and to a community of readers. And just as the author imagines himself to be some sort of master, so too are his readers able to grant themselves a moral superiority over the characters and society about which they read. Enchanted, and spellbound they might be, but a specific subjectivity nevertheless emerges from, and is colonized by, this pleasure in which the juridical or disciplinary elements of Occidental narratology are hidden. An elevated confidence seems to be self-bestowed. It is in instilling this sense of sovereign mastery over the topics of description that the pleasures of reading travel narratives coheres and renders superior a sense of English civility over all other civilizations. Moreover, in granting the reader at least a sense of critical discernment between what is proper and what is licit, the reading subject emerges as a good citizen; a legal subject.

Desire

Pleasure might render a domain of subjectivity far removed from the carnality of nature and the excessive despotic enjoyments found in the East. And, such descriptions contained in early travel accounts might seem like an attempt to reduce the power of excess, to civilize and contain it within representation. However, what is also revealed in these travellers's tales is an underlying desire for the very thing that is meant to be prohibited. Pleasure, therefore, must be distinguished from the desire that these authors and readers, these travellers, also betrayed. Indeed, pleasure must be read as the clue to what exceeds the normative boundaries of subjectivity; the Western state of pleasure institutes a subject who consistently reaches out for something more, something beyond his own colonized existence. Civilization, as Freud argued, produces its fair share of (neurotic) subjects discontented with its repressive force. But in pointing this out Freud coheres a whole tribe of eighteenth century romantics, ideologues and libertines all of whom wish for a different order of subjective experiences and freedoms, and all of them critical of the cosmetic (bourgeois) structure of civilization. Elements of this desire for what was deemed to be excessive, what exceeded the colonized subject of pleasure, breathe through the pages of early travel accounts of the Orient. Take, for example, an account of a garden constructed and tended by Sir James Forbes at his residence in Baroche. There is here an obvious tension between a Western scheme of pleasure represented by the garden and desire for something beyond the Western fence. In approving of the garden as a idyllic repose he cites Jeremiah: 'their soul shall be a watered garden: they shall sorrow no more'.[11] The Biblical reference clearly locks into the idea of a life of pleasure (or a life lacking in sorrow). And it does so by emphasizing how pleasure inhabits the interior domain of subjectivity (the Christian soul). But Forbes is not content with the Christian sanction of pleasure. His description takes on a more devotional tone and he seeks ratification from the same heathen religion decried for its polytheistic excess. Thus, on a pedestal near his favourite seat beneath a Tamarind tree, Forbes inscribes a dedication to the Water nymph of Hindu Mythology:

> To Medhummad'ha, lovely nymph
> Let Spicy groves luxuriant rise
> Around this blest retreat,
> And Indra balmy zephyrs breath
> On every peaceful seat.[12]

The devotional tone of the inscription may be an idiom of nothing more than an early example of scholarly Indophilia, or it may be simply a multi-religious version of Pascal's Wager, that it is safer to bet on as many Gods as possible in order to ensure salvation. Even if we accept these basic reasons for the inscription, it provides evidence of a significant process through which Western subjects were to be seduced by what was considered dangerous to the well founded estate of subjectivity. It must be argued that this seemingly innocent description is symptomatic of a deeper desire for another state of life, of having been seduced by what the other has or of wanting to be like the other.

Such a process of seduction operates at exactly the same level as denigration. It was noted in the last chapter that early travellers were appalled by the corrupt excessive behaviour of the Sultan's court. It cannot be said, however, that the effect that the illusion of despotic enjoyment was meant to have on the Sultan's own subjects did not have a similar (or, indeed exactly the same) effect on the Western traveller. The opposite is the case, and as soon as the Sultan becomes an object of derision for the English visitors, his escapades begin to fascinate. Norbert Elias stresses the importance in examining ceremony and etiquette as means of describing the manner in which behaviour is moulded. So much depends upon the central ruler and his close entourage: 'each of his steps, each of his gestures may be of such momentous and far reaching importance'.[13] But the same fetishing of charisma applies to a foreign order of rule. This is made clear in a number of instances and certainly so in the case of Hawkins. In dancing attendance on the Moghul Emperor, Hawkins's primary objective was to secure a treaty. In so doing, he cups his ears and listens attentively to the Sultan's every word. He watches out for his every signal. Each gesture, each whimsy, becomes a clue to the Imperial decision. Just as every lover becomes a detective in the early stages of courtship and tries to decipher the desires of another, so Hawkins seems desperate to place the chaos of these signs within an understandable lexical framework. Such is the inflaming power of all things enigmatic, it is inevitable that the Englishman will be seduced into the ways of the Moghul court. The result of this is that Hawkins eventually began to dress as a Muslim of the court. He won the confidence of, and drank with, the Emperor Jahangir, and was 'given' an Armenian wife, the King's daughter Mubarique Shah. Upon arriving at Agra, Hawkins had initially asked Jahangir's permission to establish a factory at Surat. Jahangir refused, and offered Hawkins a place at the court, an appointment of 400 horses, an annual income, and the honourable title of 'Khan'. The 'Inglis Khan', decided to remain in India for some time on the Sultan's promise that:

> If I would remayne with him, he would grant me Articles for our factorie to my hearts desire . . . and he would allow me by the yeare, three thousand and two hundred pounds sterling for my first, and so yearley, hee promised to augment my Living, till I came to a thousand Horse. For the Nobilitie of India have their Titles by the number of their Horse.[14]

The controversy caused by such figures being seduced by and adopting Eastern styles of dress and behaviour has been the subject of numerous studies. Inevitably, Hawkins was mocked by his contemporaries, described as 'a typsy-swiller of the most pronounced type'.[15] But the point to be stressed here is that the capture of the Western subject by another non-Western modality of behaviour illuminates a desire to belong to this non-order of excess and to possess the surplus enjoyment of the Orient. Thus, to provide an obvious illustration, the surplus wealth of the Oriental monarch simultaneously measures extreme corruption (where, in Thomas Roe's observation 'the propertie of all is come to the King, no man takes care for particulars; so that in every place appeares the vastations and spoiles of warres without reparation')[16] *and* exposes all that the Western observer wants for himself. The earliest of these travellers to the Moghul court, Thomas Coryate, describes a gift to the King as 'one of the richest Presents that I have heard to be sent to any Prince. Elephants so gloriously adorned as I never saw the like, nor shall see the like againe while I live'.[17] In itself, the gift giving ceremony testifies to an Oriental jurisprudence of property in which all things are in fact owned by the Sultan. Nevertheless, the wonder of the gift-object, the singular status of the giving of the gift as a particular event in Coryate's life, is exactly what escapes the pleasure that travellers took in criticizing despotic greed.

The process of seduction was not confined to the obvious promises of wealth and luxury. We noted in the last chapter that the elaborate rituals of Oriental court life were the subject of deep revulsion, regarded, as they were, as key to the charge that despotism was the exercise of empty ill-gotten power. Different and select aspects of courtly rituals formed part of the perception of the East as a veiled and dangerously carnal world. They were as much part of its exotica as were 'spices and drugges, silke, sandales and Elephants teeth'.[18] They were as much part of its fearful collection of fabula as were the legends of colossal beasts and deities. Nevertheless, all this seduced and captured the Western imagination and it is clear from many accounts that the Western traveller sought to share in the excessive enjoyment held by the Eastern courts. Eighteenth century Orientalism maniacally dances to the discordant yet amorous strains of courtly music. Portraits of Westerners dressed in muslin and silk twisted into scarlet and gold turbans, belong to a cult of exoticism in which the West is held in thrall by the dress and rituals of Eastern nobility.[19] But the process of seduction by the aesthetic order begins much sooner, in fact it begins the moment the Western traveller uses the luxurious ephemera of the Oriental court in order to denigrate the political theory of despotism and its jurisprudence of excessive enjoyment.

The very phrase 'eighteenth century Orientalism' brings to mind the idea of gentlemen connoisseurs finding decorative objects in the East, sometimes of academic interest. And, for Said, such an image supports a regime of knowledge whereby the East is tamed. However, the argument made here is that from the seventeenth century, Western travellers captured by the aesthetic order of Eastern courts actually bought into a different way of conducting themselves. This process of seduction, in other words, testifies to a desire to escape the normative rules of Western civilized subjectivity.

Such desire must be distinguished from the noetic order of the subject's intentions and will. The desire to be other than civilized occurs in spite of what the subject consciously wants or expresses. The following anecdote is interesting in so far as it is taken from the journals of Sir Thomas Roe who must be described as the most moral of observers, keen to protect his status as a civilized Englishman and ambassador for James I. Like his predecessor, Hawkins, Roe's purpose in India was to secure a treaty of trade with the Moghul Emperor Jahangir. One night, during celebrations for the Sultan's birthday, Roe was woken from his private quarters and summoned to the Emperor Jahangir's rooms. Once there, Roe was ordered to produce a portrait which he had shipped from England. The portrait was of a woman to whom Roe had been engaged, who had died before his appointment as ambassador and who remains nameless. The Emperor, so enamoured by the woman's beauty, demanded the painting as a gift. After much hesitation Roe parted with the painting. This he confesses was done only after being promised its return and in the vain hope that pleasing the Emperor would buy the much sought-after treaty. The incident is used to illustrate the aesthetic tastes of the Sultan, but it illustrates the manner in which even the notoriously upright Roe came to engage with what he also regarded as corrupt behaviour. Roe, perhaps the most vehement critic of the aesthetic frippery of the Moghul Sultanate and of its use of empty ornament, ends up mimicking its very process using images in order to gain affection and favour. It is important to note, here, that this process of being seduced into a different manner of behaviour renders the subject passive. Roe succumbs in spite of his better conscience. It seems more in the nature of a ritual itself than a moment in life, that one is tempted by the object of denigration or fear. But the word 'temptation' does not adequately describe this (non-Christian) process. There seems to be no choice in the matter. In fact, on a historical level of analysis, so deeply did the British come to be seduced by the lavish trappings of Indian imperialism that all the irrational mechanics of superficial display and pageant were to become the indispensable condition of the juridical and political structure of colonial administration during the days of the British Raj. This political use of Oriental display occurs at precisely the same time that the British sought to introduce the resolutely anti-imagistic utilitarian reforms into India during the nineteenth century. This aspect of Orientalism, and its effect upon subjectivity, will be examined in a later chapter. Suffice it to say, Roe's use of the painting as an attempt to secure a treaty with Jahangir, might be described as an early example of the way in which the British themselves were to use and control images in order to manipulate the affection of those they were to govern. In short the British had to adopt what they had sought to repress and the use of imagistic display was to become essential to the formation of colonial legitimacy.

The Problem with Desire

The above related incident displays an unconscious desire to be like the other. But more than this it also illustrates a more Lacanian point that desire is directed toward the objects to which the other has access and that seem to provide the other with the frenzy of excessive enjoyment. Thus, the British were enthralled, captured and enticed by what was paraded before their eyes and the English nabobs and factors began to behave in similar fashion in order to possess the same level of enjoyment. The public displays of torture that amused the despot and sickened the travellers were copied by the English and punishments (public whippings, etc) handed down by the English courts provided 'free entertainment'. Again, in order to partake in the perceived excesses of the Emperor, early English settlers attempted for themselves the very same living conditions found in the Sultan's court; the lavish trappings of the Emperor's court soon provided a model for the type of unimaginable lifestyle that could never be permitted back in (protestant) England.

> The head of the factory lived in almost as great a state as the Mogul Governor. Outside the door of his bedchamber stood servants with silver staves and when he appeared they followed him from room to room. If he went downstairs a picket of liveried guardsmen sprang to attention in the hall, and if he left the factory Bandarines and Moors under two standards marched before him. He was provided with well filled stables for pleasure or services and he had his own chaplain, physician, surgeon, linguist and mint-master. At his entry into the dining room trumpets blew and while he sat at table violins played softly.[20]

What is interesting about the above passage is that the President does not quite obtain the levels of excessive luxury of the Moghul Emperor. In spite of the clear desire to have and to hold whatever it is that the Oriental monarch had access to, there is a difference. Presidential life is only '*almost* as great a state' as the despot. Public whippings are not described in the same wild terms used to rebuke the reign of terror and torture supposedly managed by the Emperor. While numerous reports, particularly around the time of the impeachment and trial of the Governor-General Warren Hastings (for corruption), criticized the opulent living conditions of the English in India, a degree of difference was always maintained between the English nabob and the Oriental despot. For those such as Burke, the threat of nabob corruption was that it approached but never quite reached the 'dread majesty' of Oriental despotism. There were political issues at stake during the trial of Warren Hastings, not least of which was the desire to uphold English values of civilization, which might explain why the corrupt Englishman could not be equally compared to the despotic character of the Oriental subject. However, this form of distancing English corruption from Oriental excess may be explained otherwise. It was impossible for corruption to ever reach the same *fantasized* state of excess. The desire to have what the other has (excessive enjoyment) is a desire for an object that is impossible to have. In mimicking the imaginary structures, processes and trappings of Indian government and, yet, in marking out their difference, colonial authority could not therefore indulge in the copious excesses, the superabundant vitality, or the fun which they perceived had been enjoyed by the Nawabs, Sultans and Maharajahs. These poor melancholic, upright, yet impotent, Englishmen, seduced by what they believed to be the passion of Oriental government were unable properly to participate in the enjoyment they simultaneously denigrated and desired.

What exactly explains this impossibility? In strictly positivist terms, recent revisionist scholarship attempts to highlight the inauthenticity of what was described in these reports. In other words, what was described and denigrated as forms of excessive enjoyment never actually existed and might have other explanations. From Turkey to India, the harem, for example, symbolized, the centrality of sex to Oriental politics. Recent scholars dispute the idea that the harem was an inner cabal or hidden cabinet responsible for running the evils of despotic politics.[21] The same mistake is pointed out in relation to ceremonies described by early travellers, whereby petitioners would give the Emperor lavish gifts (*nazar*), as symptomatic of a corrupt and greedy system. Such gift giving, in fact does not indicate corruption and excessive greed, but is based on a mystical theory of reciprocity that simply did not exist in the Western imagination. More crucially, it may be that despotism itself was not really despotic. Weber, in fact, describing the 'fire-side' equity of Oriental justice (a term left loosely defined) suggests that both patrimonial (law of master and serf, patron and client or lord and vassal) and Sultanate decisionism, far from being arbitrary, in fact dissolves into a sophisticated form of administration.[22]

All these examples, if *true*, point to the idea that there was *in fact* no excessive enjoyment in which Westerners might indulge. But whether or not these travel journals are inauthentic, false, or based on misrecognition (wilful or otherwise) is neither here nor there. What matters is that the descriptions of Oriental excess represent a fantasy of the Orient that nevertheless has an effect on subjectivity. That is, to repeat, these fantasies effect upon the subject a desire to travel beyond the legislated pleasures of English civility. It was precisely because excessive enjoyment does not exist other than as a set of fantasies that there was/is a radical failure to steal the enjoyment of the other. Regardless of the veracity or falsity of these reports, what is significant is the sheer repetition of commonplaces, themes, motifs and even events narrated by Haklyut, Roe, Terry, Bernier, Forbes and company. The recurrence of already overwrought detail, far from adding credibility and cogency, interrupts the discourse of knowledge and produces a fantastic hallucinatory effect. The reader cannot, with any degree of moral certainty, know if this is the True Orient. Distance from the object of description remains locked within every detail and the object that the subject desires to know and possess is shrunken in understanding. Moreover, diminished and isolated from the object of his desires, the subject is thwarted by the same scripted source of pleasure that defines him. Pleasure is the *sine qua non* of Western civilization in so far as it controls and represses the *fulfilment* of any desire (and not just the desire itself) to be pre-civilized, or carnal. It has already done its work and has constituted the subject as a defined being. The argument that Englishness (and the corrupt figure of the English nabob) has to be differentiated from Oriental despotic excess, is therefore partially correct. Indeed, it is the civilized pleasures that constitute the English/Western subjectivity that acts as a barrier of repression. If we remind ourselves of the types of pleasures that attach to the writing and reading of these travel reports, it becomes easier to appreciate the mechanics of pleasure as a constraint upon satiating desire. The narrator/reader/traveller gives himself the pleasure of mastering an unknown section of the universe. He has already contracted the Orient into an appreciable unity that is removed from the disorder of excess. He secures himself from the imagined dangers of this excess in pleasurable fashion (he fences himself in his garden). Above all, he gives himself the pleasure of witnessing the oddities of the Orient. That is to say, as an observer, he already places himself at a distance and removes himself from the object of description that he wants to be/possess. He is thus captured, spellbound and incapacitated by his own fantasy. It is here that pleasure most viciously accomplishes its function as a *regula* and constraint upon subjectivity. The point to be stressed is a fairly standard application of the Lacanian theorem that the object of desire remains radically unattainable (rather than untrue, or non-existent).

It is the most recurring commonplace of the harem that demonstrates, simultaneously the thrill of witnessing an aberrancy, the textual pleasures of opening up and contracting a new space and the impossibility of desire fulfilment. Consider, for example, Thomas Roe's description/confession of having furtively glimpsed the private quarters of the Emperor's wives.[23] In spite of what he tries to repress, in the name of propriety, Roe acknowledges the exoticism and sensuality of the seraglio. The 'glimpse' he says is brief, more a glance. Nevertheless, he manages to paint a vivid scene. He notes that the women are decorated in diamonds and pearls.[24] He dwells upon their fingers, their faces, their black hair and coy laughter, trying desperately, through tiny peep-holes, to objectify their 'full proportion' and to access the forbidden. Indeed, the surplus of feminine enjoyment that we saw denigrated in the last chapter is converted into a different, more manageable, superlative pleasure in the words of Robert Orme: 'nature seems to have showered beauty on the fairer sex throughout Industan with a more lavish hand than in most other countries'.[25]

Moreover, the sub-theme of secrecy that supports the fantasy of the harem as secluded and formless is turned into 'mystique'. Perhaps the most clichéd of all Orientalist tropes, the attribute of mystique, plays on the figure of the one who is uninitiated into a particular ministry or cabinet. But this mystical sense of being uninitiated, or being forbidden entry into a secret place, adds to its erotic charge.

> [The eunuchs] inform me that the seraglio contains beautiful apartments, separated, and more or less spacious and splendid, according to the rank and income of the females. Nearly every chamber has its reservoir of running water at the door; on every side are gardens, delightful alleys, shady retreats, streams, fountains, grottoes, deep excavations that afford shelter from the sun by day, lofty divans and terraces, on which to sleep coolly at night . . . [these] apartments are decorated with gold and azure, exquisite paintings and magnificent mirrors.[26]

Bernier's visit to attend to a sick patient in the seraglio, is even more extraordinary in betraying that sense of seduction: 'a Kachemire shawl covered my head, hanging like a scarf down to my feet, and an eunuch led me by the hand, as if I had been a blind man'.[27] What maintains the frisson of delight in these descriptions of the seraglio, are the veils, the clothes and the screen. The importance of cloth in the seduction of Westerners was not lost on these authors. Forbes, for example, deliberately quotes Ezekiel's portrait of an Oriental lady: 'I clothe thee with broidered work, I girded thee with fine linen and covered thee with silk: I decked thee with ornaments . . . Thus was thou decked with gold and silver; and thy raiment was of fine linen, and silk and thou wast exceedingly beautiful.'[28]

What these descriptions and the sub-theme of secrecy reveal is that seduction is prompted by surfaces rather than depth, images rather than 'reality', and veils rather than flesh. Seduction takes place before or beyond any understanding, it is stimulated not by inaccessible substance, but by what masks the inaccessible. What maintains the frisson of delight in Roes description of the seraglio, are the veils, the clothes, and the reed screen through which he peeps. It is appearance rather than substance which is found to be seductive. Throughout Roe's account no success is obtained in understanding the hidden meanings of the Sultanate rituals. That the layout and plants of the Imperial gardens were themselves burdened with significance, escapes Roe. Their substantive meaning remains inaccessible and hidden beneath what is displayed. One never knows what lies beyond these displays. Seduction merely plays upon their surfaces.

In other words, seduction, the very thing that holds the traveller spellbound and gives him pleasure and excites his desires to be other than he is, is exactly what prevents access to the object of desire. The act of concealment simultaneously gives pleasure and denies access. At every turn, barriers are erected and veils are drawn.

The process here seems to follow the dialectic of desire according to which any obstacles placed in the way of an object increase its desirability: we covet what is forbidden. For Zizek, 'the aim of the prohibition is not to "raise the price" of an object by rendering access to it more difficult, but to raise this object itself to the level of the thing around which desire is organized'.[29] At a basic palpable level, Roe admits that he is unable to describe what he calls 'the full proportion' of the women in the harem. The eroticism of the scene is channelled through the tangle of matter that obstructs access, and a fuller vision of the women's bodies.

The question remains therefore as to what happens to this excess desire once it is frustrated.

Frustrated Desire Leads to Envy

A profound envy (what Lacan termed the *lebensneid*) builds up for the happiness enjoyed to surplus excess by others yet which remained barred to everybody else. Envy should not be confused with jealousy. As Lacan puts it:

> *Lebensneid* is not ordinary jealousy, it is jealousy born in a subject in his relation to another, insofar as this other is held to enjoy a certain form of jouissance or superabundant vitality, that the subject perceives as something that he cannot apprehend by means of even the most elementary of affective movements.[30]

Lacan draws a lesson from St. Augustine's *Confessions,* (book 1, cap 7): 'I have myself seen jealousy in a baby and know what it means. He was not old enough to talk, but whenever he saw his foster-brother at the breast, he would grow pale with envy.' For Augustine, the anecdote indicates that no man is free from sin (*invidia*). For Lacan, on the other hand, the suggestion is of the structuring power of the evil (invidious) eye.[31] Indeed, Lacan puts it in far stronger terms by suggesting that envy structures our relationships between ourselves, others and the world of objects subjected to our gaze: 'What makes the human world a world covered with objects derives from the fact that the object of human interest is the object of the others desire.'[32] In this primitive and aggressive atmosphere, it would be easy to apply the allegory to the figure of the Oriental subject, the subject in infanthood, who is closer to the material source of desire and a rival with a head-start to all the resources of nature.

But Augustine suggests that *invidia* is more than jealousy for material wealth (or even surplus value). What the small child envies is not what he might need. It is not for want of nourishment that the child envies his foster-brother. What causes the child to 'grow pale with envy' is exactly what causes the Western traveller to grow pale. That is, the other person has a position or access to something that was once his but is no longer.

Travel journals thus expose the 'envy complex' which was to become a factor in colonial mastery; what the Western subject wants is access to the excessive, feral and carnal energy long removed from Western modes of subjective existence and now fantasized as being in the Orient. The pleasures derived from travel narratives speak of the pain of loss and such pleasures are the pleasures of return. In this sense desire is always a longing for a lost origin. In this sense it is vital to note that the envy felt by the older child, in Augustine's anecdote, was envy for a position of excessive enjoyment (where the milk from the mother's breast 'flows in such abundance from its source', more freely than was needed) that was once his. It is, therefore, as if it is the Oriental other and not the Western subject (as it is so often assumed) who is responsible for the theft of enjoyment.

And, as an accidental emissary of the unconscious, this is what the traveller reports back to his monarch and his fellow subjects. The language of denigration attempts to conceal desire. But it does so badly. Through the fissures and cracks of the traveller's report, waves of desire are expressed as envy (*lebensneid*). The fantasy of excess enjoyment, thus produces and fabulates something of an uncanny quality about its object. That is to say, according to the proper parameters of what constitutes 'the uncanny', there is even something 'hauntingly familiar' about the fantasy of the Oriental who is excessive and animal in desires. While strange, the despotic/indolent/uncivil character of the Oriental reminds the traveller of something long ago forgotten, a previous incarnation of himself.

It might be thought that the cognition/recognition of this violently instinctual domain, that is supposedly discharged from modern man, may well render infirm the rational individual. But that is not in itself a radical claim. Indeed the irrational, or in this case the excess, does not necessarily shatter subjectivity and Western civilization does not entail that its model of subjectivity eradicates its archaic origins. Excursions Eastwards are always some sort of archaeological expedition, undertaken in order to find oneself, or in order to contemplate humankind in all his aspects. Rather, these narratives that describe the strange uncanny realms of the universe betray a hidden underside to the civilizing program which is, in fact, to reconcile the primitive past to the sophisticated present. What they express is a desire for something that might make subjectivity more commensurate with the whole universe. These early modern examples of travel literature betray an attempt by the West at recreating itself, to tell the truth of subjectivity, by re-examining its bawling infancy.

We are used to thinking about the modern subject as one who presupposes an absolute sovereignty, but this state is built on a lack. What the modern subject lacks is the excess that would make him a total being. Or, to put it according to Bataille's formulation, the object of desire is the universe or the totality of being, warts and all. The lack suffered (what Lacan might term the *Manque a Etre*), in other words, manifests itself in envy, in the 'wanting to be like the other'. The other may be irrational and may not be an ideal, but she represents the missing link to the secret of subjectivity. What the subject lacks is completeness, a totality of being, the totality of world history, the totality of the universe, an Empire. The subject cannot be absolute until it comprehends and confronts what it suspects might be its own history of becoming. The computation of complete subjectivity cannot begin to add up until this suspected aspect of excision has been factored in. What is supposedly discarded from history is recognized as necessary in order to understand the subjects development from *homo natura* to *homo historia.*[33] Reason, therefore, has to be comprehended in relation to this primitive energy: 'reason recreates itself in its childhood, in its archaic beginnings'.[34] It needs to make sense of itself and to understand its history for 'what it really is'. And, in order to understand 'what it really is', it has recourse to a whole set of fantasmatic projections. Within this ambivalence lies the seeds of an Imperial complex that attempts to embody and encompass the whole of history as its own. The attempt to understand the excessive pre-subjective domain, however much such attempts are based on fantasmatic constructions of the Orient, underscores the colonial impulse inherent in, and juridical element of, Western subjectivity. The microscopic study into the particularity and depth of created beings is nothing other than the urge to possess (or to enjoy that possession as *jouissance*) the excess in order to become more absolute. Herein lies the beginnings of the modern desire for universality; legal rationality has to be united with all that seemingly opposes it so that the omni-jurisdictional can become even more omni-jurisdictional.

CHAPTER 5

Ex Oriente Lex: Orientalism and the Colonization of Sublime Enjoyment

> Lady J. is pretty well; a tiger about a month old, who is suckled by a goat, and has all the gentleness of his foster-mother, is now playing at her feet. I call him Jupiter.[1]

> The question of the sublime was doubtless first of all an attempt to measure the decline of the Orient.[2]

Introduction: From the *Campus Venereus* to the *Hortus Conclusus*

Although described as inhospitable, Oriental nature also offered a certain amount of pleasure. In his study of the everyday life of an English nabob during the eighteenth century, Percival Spear mentions that 'the evening diversion par excellence at the beginning of the century was the taking of one's ease in "gardens 'neath which rivers flow" with the help of arrack, punch and shiraz wine'. The description is innocent enough but what is significant is the way in which the garden became central to images of imperial and colonial luxury. Accounts written by company officers stationed in India during the eighteenth and nineteenth centuries emphasize the importance of maintaining English style lawns and gardens both as a source of national pride and as a place to relax.[3] There was, however, more to these gardens than the pursuit of an English pastime. In his *Oriental Memoirs*, James Forbes noted that:

> the high walls [of the garden] are the necessary guardians of a Muhomedan's honour, and the safeguard of his pleasures. Within this protection, secluded from the world, the voluptuous Mussulman, laying aside the grandeurs of the day, with the irritation of the mind which accompanies ambition, abandons himself to soft repose; and, in the stillness of a starry night, acquires that serenity of mind which lulls the soul into pleasing complacency; forming a delightful contrast to the stormy passions of the agitated day. Negligently stretched upon his couch, he listens to the melodious song; and contemplates the graceful forms of the surrounding dancers; amid the odiferous smoke of incense.[4]

For Forbes, it was as if gardens, in providing tranquillity, also upheld a regulatory purpose. They provided an odiferous, graceful and melodious sanctuary where the 'voluptuous Mussulman' would relax and shut out 'grandeur' and irritation. They controlled the excesses of nature and sedated those 'stormy passions' associated with despotic character. A similar sentiment is to be found in the journals of Thomas Roe for whom the Emperor's gardens provided an environment in which the excesses of nature not only seemed tame but where otherwise terrifying and ugly heathen idols seemed acceptable:

> A delicate grove of two miles large, a quarter broad, planted by industry with Manges, Tamerins and other fruits, divided with walks and full of little Temples and Altars of Pagods, and Gentilitial idolatry, many fountains, wels, tankes and summer houses of carved stone curiously arched, so that I must confesse, a banished Englishman might have been content to dwell there.[5]

In these accounts and others a sharp and obvious contrast is made between the descriptions of gardens and those of Oriental nature in general. Where nature had been described as wild, dangerous and uncontrollable, the garden provided safety and tranquillity. The overly fertile, serpentine and horrifying enjoyment inherent in Oriental nature (where animals kill for a pleasure that goes beyond utility) is distinguished from the sedate and useful, even necessary, pleasures of the garden. Cultivation re-configures nature converting the threat of excess into simple pleasure. The open unimaginable field of excess enjoyment looks set to be contained within enclosed spaces; or, in the flat humour of school latin, the *hortus conclusus* is reclaimed from the *campus venereus*.

This distinction is not entirely simplistic. The theme of nature as a shelter from turmoil and disorder was important in romantic literature. For Wordsworth, the garden constitutes a 'spot of time', a corner of the world, in which to escape the riot of modernization.[6] Forbes's description is predicated on such romantic sensibilities and it must be noted that his memoirs were written after the publication of Burke's *Inquiry into the Origins of Our Ideas of the Sublime and the Beautiful* which exerts a clear influence. He is influenced further, and more explicitly, by the romantic sensibilities of the Sanskrit scholar William Jones. Properly, the distinction between wild and cultivated nature is the distinction between the sublime and the beautiful. Burke, in particular, uses the unmanageable ferocity of wildlife as a central example of the sublime.

Everything that could be said of excess enjoyment corresponds to the romantic philosophy of the sublime. Both categories refer to an emotional horizon beyond the reach of theoretical reason and mere pleasure. The romantic distinction between the beautiful and the sublime attaches to a jurisprudential tradition of distinguishing between pleasure and enjoyment. Indeed, Burke himself distinguishes between pleasure (attributed to the will) and the pain associated with the sublime (and inflicted by a superior power). Or, as Zizek puts it: 'the sublime is beyond the pleasure principle . . . it is a paradoxical pleasure produced by displeasure itself (the exact definition of enjoyment [jouissance])'.[7] After all, the sublime in nature is that which, in its 'approach to infinity'[8] and in its uselessness, is always in excess of pleasure. However, a difference between excess enjoyment and the sublime exists if the shift from one to another is analysed as a form of sublimation. In psychoanalytic terms sublimation is the supression of excitation. Imposing the category of the sublime converts the primitive and uncivilized energy of excess into something (*das ding*) more socially acceptable: '[The collectivity] finds a space of relaxation where it may delude itself . . . That is how collective, socially accepted sublimations operate.'[9] It is according to this process of sublimation that romantic discourse on India was to confront and contain the 'stormy passions' of the East, and deal with its idolatry. Seen in these terms the romantic process of sublimation is, therefore, a form of prohibition.

For a number of eighteenth century scholars (William Jones, Herder, Schlegel, etc), the perfect expression of the sublime in nature was to be found in the East with its profusion of species, haunting landscapes, ancient forests or its gigantic aspects. Consider, for example, the following description of the Tartary which:

> is as a stupendous edifice . . . If the mansion be so amazingly sublime, the land around it is proportionably extended, but more wonderouslly diversified; for some parts of it are encrusted with ice, others parched with inflamed air, and covered with a kind of lava; here we meet with immense tracts of sandy deserts, and forests, almost impenetrable; there with gardens, groves, and meadows, perfumed with musk, watered by numberless rivulets, and abounding in fruits and flowers.[10]

Classically, however, the category of the sublime referred to man's relationship to the Gods. In this sense it is noteworthy that the language used by Forbes to describe his own garden in Baroche often tends towards a 'discourse of exaltation'. The garden becomes associated with a sublime joy and he cites Jeremiah ('their soul shall be a watered garden: they shall sorrow no more').[11] On a pedestal near his favourite seat situated beneath a tamarind tree, Forbes inscribes a dedication to the water spirit of ancient Hindu mythology:

> To Medhummad'ha, lovely nymph
> Let Spicy groves luxuriant rise
> Around this blest retreat,
> And Indra balmy zephyrs breath
> On every peaceful seat.

All that is missing from this discourse of exaltation, or for the garden to become a sublime object of apprehension, is the chaotic and boundless terror which properly accompanies sublime joy. Such terror—useless and beyond nature's normal parameters—was what earlier travel writers found to be a characteristic of Oriental enjoyment.

'[T]error is in all cases . . . the ruling principle of the sublime'[12] states Burke, who then goes on to substitute the word 'terror' for 'wonder', 'astonishment' (*stupeo*), 'being thunderstruck' (*attonitus*) and 'amazement'. Whatever the predominant passion caused by the sublime, all other emotions are 'suspended, with some degree of horror'.[13] It is the unmanageable ferocity of wildlife rather than the well cultivated beauty of the garden that elicits the kind of astonishment that exceeds pleasure. The inscription in Forbes' garden might hint at sublime joy, but it is both more and less than an index of horror. As a process of sublimation, it may also be seen as an attempt to domesticate the sublime and to eradicate its excess so that the plural ways of the Hindu Gods and laws become fathomable. Cultivation reconfigures both nature and the sublime.

Forbes's description of his garden, and any other form of sublimation, therefore expresses an ambivalent attitude toward the idea of the sublime. On the one hand, the sublime is recognized as a new aesthetic category for that which exists beyond the pleasures of beauty, a source of awesome inspiration before which the human subject 'shrinks into the minuteness of [his] own nature'.[14] While on the other hand, Forbes's account is symptomatic of a tendency to colonize, cultivate and civilize the Oriental sublime and to eradicate its excess so that enjoyment becomes something else—something more manageable and pleasurable. In supposedly surrendering himself before the sublime, the romantic simply disguises his desire for mastership: 'the sublime object may be used in this scenario to gratify a subject who, in spite of his masochistic protestations, has no intention of renouncing his position of mastery'.[15] The process of sublimation is essential in establishing the conditions of mastery.

The taming of nature is to be regarded as symptomatic of a general tendency to cultivate and colonize Oriental excess. The purpose of the rest of this chapter will be to examine this process of sublimation both as a key feature of Orientalism and as that which formed an essential part of the juridical project of colonizing subjectivity. For the same process is found to be expressed in a number of works on Oriental art and antiquities, on Hindu religion and, most significantly, in the project to translate the laws of Manu. As shall be argued, it is this last project which fully exposes law's 'symbolic significance for the history of Orientalism'[16] and the manner in which romantic Orientalism was shaped by jurisprudential concerns. A secondary observation will be made concerning the manner in which the exercise of common law jurisdiction depended upon the notion of the sublime and the way in which this source of authority exceeded the confines and specificity of nationhood. What emerges from the shadows of the sublime is a notion of subjectivity that is ensnared by common legality.

Asiatic Jones and the Sublimation of Oriental Scholarship

Under the administration of William Hastings in the eighteenth century, scholars such as Charles Wilkins and Nathaniel Halhed initiated studies into the Indian past. Having established the first printing press in India, Halhed published his *Grammar of the Bengali Language* and Wilkins published the first translation of the *Bagavad Gita*. Ostensibly, such works were issued both to inform Englishmen interested in India and to 'conciliate the affection of the natives'.[17] But there was more to these works, and the desire for exotic knowledge betrayed a deeper obsession with India that centred around the remoteness of its antiquity and the origins of its culture, religion and law. Orientalist scholars, spurred on by such discoveries as the ancient cave temples of Elephanta, turned to the East in an attempt to calculate the origins of *all* culture. The caves of Elephanta, for example, were not simply dark, mysterious and terrifyingly colossal. Their sublimity also resided in the suspicion that their antiquity was thought to pre-date any known culture. The implication was that somewhere in the East existed the cradle of civilizations and that the clues as to its precise location was to be found in ancient Sanskrit texts.[18] Contained in this literature was a history that went further back in time than Christianity or, even, the immemorial origins of English Common law!

> I, who cannot help believing the Divinity of the Messiah, from the undisputed antiquity and manifest completion of many prophesies, especially those of Isaiah, am obliged of course to believe the sanctity of the venerable books to which that sacred person refers as genuine (the books of Moses); but it is not the truth of our national religion, as such, that I have at heart—it is truth itself; and if any cool unbiased reasoner will clearly convince me that Moses drew his narrative, through Egyptian conduits, from primeval fountains of Indian literature, I shall esteem him as a friend for having weeded my mind from a capital error, and promise to stand among the foremost in assisting to circulate the truth which he has ascertained . . . I am persuaded that a connexion subsisted between the old idolatrous nations of Egypt, India, Greece and Italy.[19]

Nature and the antiquity of the Orient are simply two forms of excess that excited the Orientalist scholar. As Voltaire suggested the Brahmin had 'sublime ideas' about the supreme being and the peculiar theocracy of Hinduism which we saw denigrated in the last chapter, this prompted Orientalist speculation on the sublime location of divine power.

These appropriately disparate forms of the sublime stimulated the work of the Welshman Sir William Jones who was regarded as perhaps the most obsessed of all early scholars and about whom a few biographical points are apposite. Details about the life of William Jones (c. 1746–94) suggest that his was one almost completely devoted to Eastern scholarship. His biographers never fail to repeat that, even before travelling to the East, he had published his *Grammar of the Persian Language* (1771) and *Poems, consisting chiefly of Translations from the Arabic Languages* (1772). Any residual scholarly commitments outside this exotic field were dedicated only to the more mundane study and practice of law as a judge on the

Welsh circuits.[20] Even so, it was the recognition of Jones's talents as an Orientalist by Warren Hastings which earned him an appointment as a puisne judge in the presidency of Bengal.

In Calcutta the judge devoted much of his time to the study of various Oriental cultures: 'my daily studies are now, what they will be for six years to come, Persian and law, and whatever relates to India'.[21] While the enjoyment derived from his studies might not belong to the same register of excessive enjoyment attached to Oriental forms, it is nevertheless expressed in hymn-like prose: 'as the thirsty antelope runs to a pool of sweet water, so I thirsted for all kinds of knowledge, which was sweet as nectar'.[22] Again, it is sometimes expressed as 'infinite pleasure':

> If envy can exist with an anxious wish of all possible entertainment and reputation to the person envied, I am not free from that passion, when I think of the infinite pleasure which you must receive from a subject so new and interesting [as sanskrit]. Happy should I be to follow you in the same track.[23]

Even the justification for his studies was Orientalized, and his scholarly appetite was determined by, and surrendered to, a more despotic cause: 'the *Mahomedans* have not only the permission, but the positive command, of their law-giver, *to search for learning even in the remotest parts of the globe*'.[24] However, this compulsive obsession with studying as many things Oriental as he could commanded a certain price: 'I do not expect, as long as I stay in India, to be free from a bad digestion, the *morbus literatorum*, for which there is hardly any remedy, but abstinance from too much food, literary and culinary.'[25] Jones, incidentally, was to die in Calcutta from an inflammation of the liver.

In addition to his judicial tasks Jones founded the Asiatic Society of Bengal in 1784. Modelled on the Royal Society, its aims were to 'furnish proof to our posterity, that the acquisition of [Indian wealth] did not absorb [our] attention, and that the English laws and English government, in those distant regions, have sometimes been administered by men of extensive capacity, erudition and application'.[26] Jones himself, the gentleman scholar-administrator, undertook full scale studies in the history, religions, customs, manners, geography, chronology, zodiac, mystical poetry and pastoral drama of India, and is recognized as having founded modern philology. He assiduously gathered a portfolio of icons, drawing images of Hindu Gods and symbols that would later haunt the gothic imagination of those such as Thomas de Quincey. Broad and eclectic though his research was, its determining influence on imperial manners should not be underestimated. It shored up respect for a fundamentally inaccessible set of cultures, and informed policy on the treatment of Muslims and Hindus. Yet, such an obsessive and zodiacal inquiry, in order, at least, to be in touch with all forms of Oriental knowledge, betrayed a desire to accumulate a different type of wealth to that sustained by company officials. It may be that, as Edward Said has already argued, early Orientalism laid down a cultural foundation that enabled the establishment of colonial power. Information was to be managed so as to be understood and controlled. Yet, it ought to be remembered that the acquisition of knowledge was always already implicit in the idea of imperialism. In classical terms, the colonized world was to be understood as that which had 'fallen under inquiry' and the antecedents of Roman law implied the *imperium* to be a source of knowledge.[27]

It is obvious, then, that the study of the Orient was a source of pleasure. That is to say, in opposition to the category of excess enjoyment, this pleasure had a controlling function (see Chapter One). Yet, a distinction has to be drawn between the pleasure of study and the effective quality of the object studied. For Jones, like the other Orientalists, India was the source of the sublime. But this claim, repeated in the following passage which employs images and expressions of the sublime, follows the same trajectory as that shown in the attempts to cultivate Oriental nature:

> When I was at sea last August, on my voyage to this country, which I had long and ardently desired to visit, I found one evening, on inspecting the observations of the day, that India lay before us, and Persia on our left, while a breeze from Arabia blew nearly on our stern. A situation so pleasing in itself, and to me so new, could not fail to awaken a train of reflections in a mind, which had clearly been accustomed to contemplate with delight the eventful histories and agreeable fictions of this eastern world. It gives me inexpressible pleasure to find myself in the midst of so noble an amphitheatre, almost encircled by the vast regions of Asia, which has ever been esteemed the nurse of sciences, the inventress of delightful and useful arts, the scene of glorious actions, fertile in the productions of human genius, abounding in natural wonders and infinitely diversified in the forms of religion and government, in the laws, manners, customs, and languages, as well as the features and complexions of men. I could not help remarking, how important and extensive a field was yet unexplored, and how many solid advantages unimproved, and when I considered, with

> pain, that in this fluctuating imperfect, and limited conditions of life, such inquiries and improvements could only be made through the united efforts of many, who are not easily brought, without some pressing inducement or strong impulse, to converge in a common point, I consoled myself with a hope, founded on opinions, which it might have the appearance of flattery to mention, that if in any country or community, such a union could be effected, it was among my countrymen in Bengal, with some of whom I already had, and with most desirous of having, the pleasure of being intimately acquainted.[28]

The phrases and metaphors used by Jones consciously engage with the themes of romantic sublime. The 'inexpressible pleasure' in the face of unexplored territories directly transferred onto the Orient Burkean ideas of ignorance inciting the sublime passions. Typical of romantic sensibilities, the sublime Orient is expressed through the feminized descriptions of Asia ('nurse of the sciences, inventress of the delightful arts') and directs our attention to the formlessness and excesses of femininity described in the last chapter. Elsewhere, Jones is more explicit and suggests that 'The [mythology of] the Hindus and Arabs are perfectly original; and to my taste their compositions are sublime',[29] for the Indians are those 'who receive the first light of the rising sun'.[30] That the study of the Orient produced such an 'infinite pleasure' was due not to the nature of study *qua* study, but to the nature of the object of those studies. What is interesting about the above passage, however, is that there is a shift away from the feminine and unexplored sublime to the more mundane descriptions of a society of aquaintances. The thirst for knowledge, and the pleasures of Oriental scholarship, were rooted in the very idea of the sublime East. And, *vice-versa*, 'inexpressible pleasure' turns into expressible pleasure as Jones seeks artistic reward by means of sublimation. The hidden, undiscovered and excessive forms of the East provided the initial motor propelling 'the delightful and glorious arts' and became the condition of the tamer pleasures of societal research, and of mastery through knowledge.

This simultaneous attraction and utilization of the sublime can be traced over all the disciplines that form objects of Orientalist study. The architectural ruins of India, for example, was a key motif in the sublime imagination. One of the key company artists of the time, William Hodge, excelled in depicting the supernatural atmosphere of India so that both mundane and exotic aspects (e.g. the terror of suti) are set in front of gloomy architectural ruins.[31] In the words of Jones, relentlessly pursuing connections:

> the remains of architecture and sculpture in india, which I mention here as mere monuments in antiquity, not as specimens of ancient art, seem to prove an early connection between this country and Africa; the pyramids of Egypt, the colossal statues described by PAUSANIAS and others.[32]

Indeed, India itself was characterized as the ruins of ancient and sublime civilizations (a common argument in contemporary literature was that the Indian civilizations had been ruined by Moghul mismanagement). Yet the architectural remains, and the ruin of India, were an excuse to dominate and re-build the land. The suspicion that the Oriental ruler embodied a limitless capacity of enjoyment, coupled with the unpredictable nature of alien manners, provoked the need to reconstitute a sense of order fashioned according to prim European standards. It was by controlling the mysterious sublime of the Orient that colonialism was to pave the way for a strategy of rule based on the management of pleasures. In this sense, colonialism may be characterized as the attempt to dominate, control and assimilate the dangerous excesses of enjoyment illustrated in the last chapter.

The use of the Oriental sublime can even be traced in Jones's own compositions and receives striking exemplification in Jones's *Hymn to Ganges.*[33] Here, Jones locates the British within the sublime time of ancient Indian history. British imperialism is characterized as inevitable and as part of India's destiny. As prophesied by a mythological Brahmin, the British would arrive in India in order to rule by 'good laws well administered'. Again, in the *Ode to the Surya*, Jones composes a mythical scene that employs all the commonplaces of the romantic sublime (the obstructed caves, the pure fountains, the obscure paths). What is prophesied on this occasion is the arrival of Jones himself.

> From the bosom of your silver isle,
> Where skies more softly smile,
> He came; and, lisping our celestial tongue,
> Though not from *Brahma* sprung,
> Draws Orient knowledge from its fountains pure,
> Through caves obstructed long, and paths too long obscure.[34]

In this ode Jones submits himself to a sublime landscape that is larger than he, and he is a mere recipient of a language that pre-exists his own existence. Yet it is precisely his status as a foreigner that allows him to be the gift bearer, to return to the Indians what was theirs in any case.

Put simply, the sublime provided the pivot around which both romantic speculation and imperial mastery revolved. This irresolute attitude towards the sublime was expressed time and again over different fields. Jones's position was not unique, and artists and philosophers were drawn to the East in search of romantic inspiration and those elements that lent themselves to sublime feelings. Yet at the same time as submitting to it, this aspect of Orientalism, this process of sublimating the excess, yielded and mythologized British authority and was crucial to the control and management of the East and its potential subjects.

The Sublime Antiquity and Force of the Law

> Menu sat reclined, with his attention fixed on one object, the Supreme God; when the divine sages approached him.[35]

The colonization of the Oriental sublime must be understood, above all, as a symptom of jurisprudential thought. Sublimation is, after all, the transference, or re-assignment of excess enjoyment, into something more socially acceptible, and so operates as a form of prohibition. Given this it is not surprising to find the same jurisprudential concerns centred around William Jones's projects to translate Hindu laws. Just as he found 'infinite pleasure' in the study of Sanscrit and Hindu mythology, so the study of Indian laws became an equally romantic pastime. 'Do you not agree' he wrote to Schultens as early as in 1774, 'that nothing should be more pleasant or noble than the study of native and universal law?'[36] Yet again, it was the object of study itself that satisfied the romantic desire for, and submission to, the sublime. As Jones observed 'a spirit of sublime devotion ... pervades the whole work [of Hindu law]'. On a more mundane level, however, these translations differed significantly from others such as his translation of Kalidasa's plays. In being directly applicable, this was a form of Orientalism which constituted the text as an object of knowledge while also creating of the 'Indian', a subject of law. The totality of this exercise would have included:

> six or seven law books believed to be divine with a commentary on each of nearly equal authority; these are analagous to our Littleton and Coke, next Jimut Bahur, the best book on inheritances; and above all a digest of Hindu law in twenty-seven volumes precisely in the manner of the original digest.[37]

The project was never completed by Jones in its entirety, although, what survives of that project are the Laws of Manu, translated in 1794 as *The Institutes of Hindu Law: or, the Ordinances of Menu.*

What was so sublime, to Jones's mind, about the Hindu laws of Manu, in particular, was that they were revealed and written down rather than composed and invented: 'It was not MENU who composed the system of law, by the command of his father BRAHMA, but a holy personage or demi-god, named BHRIGU who revealed to men what MENU had delivered at the request of him and other saints or patriarchs.'[38] Menu, or Manu, was not simply the hand, or the amanuensis; he was, as it were, the first hand and the holiest of amanuenses! The law descends, having been promulgated 'in the beginning of time by MENU, son of BRAHMA, or, in plain language, the first of created beings, and not the oldest only, but the holiest of legislators'.[39] So old are these laws ('the laws [of menu] are considerably older than those of SOLON or even LYCURGUS')[40] that Jones declares himself to be 'lost in an inextricable labyrinth of imaginary astronomical cycles, *yugas, mahayugas, calpas, and menwantaras*, in attempting to calculate the time when the first MENU, governed this world, and became the progenitor of mankind'.[41]

While clearly interesting from an Orientalist point of view, it is unclear why, *as a lawyer*, Jones would wish to allocate any legal authority to a high Hindu text such as Manu? A number of reasons, simultaneously practical and ideological, are given by Jones, his contemporaries and modern commentators. It is important to analyse these given reasons in order to reveal the way in which they hang on the idea of the sublime and on the process of sublimation.

The 'Best Practicable System of Judicature'

At one level of analysis, the codification of the original texts of Indian laws arranged according to scientific method simply eased the process of decision-making by judges of the Calcutta Supreme Court. Apart from Jones, judges were unwilling to learn Sanskrit and were consequently ignorant of the laws they were applying to Indian subjects. Instead, they had to rely on the the 'written opinion of native lawyers' and translations of particular laws were provided only when required. The inefficiency of this process of discovering and applying Hindu, or Muslim, law was increased due to the lack of trust afforded to the relevant court officials: 'pure integrity is hardly to be found among the Pandits and Maulavis'.[42] Copies of the work enabled British judges to avoid relying on these intermediaries and to detect any misinformation that these pandits and maulavis may have provided in the courts. In this sense, Jones's attempt to translate the law was symptomatic of the training of all common lawyers.

The process of translating the Hindu and Muslim laws might be regarded as equivalent to that of legal education in the Inns of Court and simply provided direct access to what was hidden in the depths of an esoteric language. The secular lawyer assumed the mantle of the priest as guardian of a sacred text and of its meaning. Whether written in a 'strange tongue' or in English, a training into legal priesthood was, and remains, necessary in order to unlock the mysteries of legal knowledge (*arcana juris*).[43] The hieroglyphic nature of law was regarded as universal. Translation provided the opportunity for the lawyers of the supreme courts to have access to legal wisdom without the intermediation of the pandits and maulavis (translation, like despotism, is an attempt to control meaning. Jones identifies with a transcendental foundation of all signification. It is already a despotic act).

In strict doctrinal terms, however, the idea that a translation of indigenous laws would ease the judicial process of determining rules to be applied somewhat elides a more substantial point. It remains unclear as to why Hindu laws should be used in place of the common law given that in 1608 the English courts had stated firmly that 'if a Christian king should conquer the kingdom of an infidel . . . the laws of that kingdom are abrogated'.[44]

On this point, a number of reasons were given for keeping intact the laws of the 'native' subject. For Nathaniel Halhed, it was a matter of following the antecedents of Roman imperialism: '[The Romans] not only allowed their foreign subjects the free exercise of their own religion and the administration of their own civil jurisdiction, but sometimes, by a policy still more flattering, even naturalized parts of the mythology of the conquered, as were in any respect compatible with their own system.'[45] The following reason provided by Forbes, however, recognized the limits of Imperial authority.

> It is imposible to separate the political tendency of laws from the genius of government from which they emanate. The spirit of the Englsih constitution assigns to the mass of the people an extensive control over the exercise of public authority; and deems the executive government to be the representative of the public will. This spirit pervades the whole body of its laws; these laws necessarily reflect back and reproduce the principles from which they spring; and it is a matter of grave reflection, that if this species of reaction should ever be produced in India, from that moment it is lost to this country for ever. The efficient protection of our native subjects in all the rights which they themselves

> consider to be essential to their happiness is certainly the most sacred and Imperious of all our duties . . . It is not the question, whether the English or the Hindoo code of religion and jurisprudence be entitled to the preference; but whether the Hindu law and religion . . . are, or are not to be, maintained, or whether we are at liberty to invade both.[46]

According to Forbes, the 'invasion' of Indian law and its replacement with the common law did not form part of British Imperialism. As Jones continually emphasized, such an agenda would have compromised the spirit of liberty which was essential to the jurisprudence of the common law. In his recommendations to Edmund Burke for the 'Best Practicable System of Judicature', Jones observed that the replacement of Indian laws would have entailed a violent imposition of one institution upon another and would have implied that the English assume the despotic attributes of intolerance to which they were necessarily opposed: 'A system of *liberty*, forced upon a people invincibly attached to opposite *habits*, would in truth be a system of cruel *tyranny*'.[47] The *spirit* of liberty implied that the very system and set of institutions on which it depended could not be transferred to, and imposed upon, other cultures. However, the real paradox and irony of this sentiment was that for these Hindu and Muslim subjects, the enjoyment of their own laws had to be sanctioned and determined by a foreign system, a foreign institution, and foreign legislation:

> a legislative act [is needed] to assure the Hindu and Musselman subjects of Great Britain, that the private laws, which they severally hold secret and a violation of which they would have thought the most grevious oppression, should not be superceded by a new system, of which they could have no knowledge, and which they must have considered as imposed on them by a spirit of rigour and intolerance.[48]

This rhetoric of liberty, in other words, disguised the constitutional theory that there was *posited* a non-Indian geographical location of authority; the seemingly autonomous survival, existence and application of Indian laws hung upon a set of instructions relayed from London to Calcutta. And it should not be forgotten that behind this legislative authority lay an obvious ulterior Imperial motive that involved buying the respect and affection of the Bengalis. These additional and superficial reasons for the preferential use of Hindu and Muslim laws, given by Jones in his letter to Burke, point to mercantile interests and the importance of maintaining good relations between the English (or, in Jones's case, the Welsh) and the subjects of Bengal:

> Any system of *judicature* affecting the natives in *Bengal*, and not having for its basis the old *Mogul* constitution, would be dangerous and impracticable . . . The natives must have an *effective* tribunal for their protection against the *English*, or the country will soon be rendered *worse than useless* to Britian.

Holding back on the application of the common law was part of an established code of behaviour that sought to ensure the happiness and respect of 'the natives [who] are charmed with the idea of making their slavery lighter by giving them their own laws'.[49] Jones's reification of the spirit of liberty thus masks a motive for maintaining imperial authority through the judicial system: 'The Hindus are incapable of civil liberty; few of them have any idea of it; and those who have do not wish it. They must (I deplore the evil, but know the necessity of it) they must be ruled by an absolute power'.[50]

It might be argued further that the translation of a sacred Hindu text into English ensured the manipulation of that text. Sanskrit texts had their untranslatable words, and contained forms of signification and meaning unthinkable in an English idiom. Indeed, all projects of translation put signification and the status of the original into question. Translation necessitates mistranslation and glosses over the remnants of enigmas and puzzles, which are impossible to solve. Where, to subvert Spivak's original argument, did Sanskrit end and English begin?[51] Translating a legal text into English in order that its rules may be enforced in a court of law simply erases the ability of that text to speak in its own language, in a language other than that of the British court system. Hindu or Mohammedan laws were translated and tailored to fit British conceptions of justice. John Strawson makes the claim in relation to Jones's project of translating the *Al Sirajiyyah*. Islamic law, he suggests, was given legitimacy only 'by reference to European criteria which are taken almost as fact'.[52] Legal Orientalism thus denied and obscured the diverse literary traditions of both Hindu and Islamic jurisprudence.

What is at stake, at this (practical/ideological) level of analysis, is the use of the courts and the process of translation to manouevre and contain the law. It might be supposed, therefore, that Hindu law, for example, was to be kept as a mark of difference. Nations might be defined according to their laws, and their systems of interdiction, and so a Hindu was to be kept in his place and differentiated according to the law to which he appealed. The

Hindus are Hindus by virtue of their laws. Certainly the point is implied by Forbes in criticizing early attempts by the English to abolish the practice of suti: 'If we are to govern Hindoos by their own laws, why do we tear them up by their roots, they are no longer Hindoos if they are subject to innovation.'[53]

The sublime universality of laws

But there was more more to this process of translation than the control and manipulation of positive laws, and the 'staging of difference'. For Jones, and here his attititude was symptomatic of contemporary jurisprudential concerns, there was a genuine recognition of the spirit of Hindu law that actually refers him to similarities and connections between Eastern and Western notions of legality. Or, put slightly differently, the spirit of Hindu law refers to the other face of European legality that Jones and common lawyers such as Blackstone had been trying to recuperate throughout the eighteenth century. In what seems like a typical piece of apologia, linking a system of laws to the manners and civilization of its people, the following passage introduces Jones's recognition and obsession with the idea of legal sublimity:

> It is a maxim in the science of legislation and government that *laws are of no avail without manners*, or, to explain the sentence more fully, that the best intended legislative provisions would have no beneficial effect even at first unless they were congenial to the disposition and habits, to the religious prejudices, and approved immemorial usages, of the people, for whom they were enacted; especially if that people universally believed that all their ancient usages and established rules of conduct had the sanction of an actual revelation from heaven.[54]

While this idea of antiquity and sublime revelation is a feature of Hindu law, it also resonates with the reflections on the originary time and place of the common law that had been rattling around the minds of its own lawyers. It was common for eighteenth century doctrinalists to use the category of the sublime to describe the complexity, disorder and obscurity of the common law. For Blackstone, in particular, this irregular form of the law was founded in an idea of nature from which England was to derive the law of the land. Like the sublime ruins of gothic castles, churches and abbeys, the law was magnificent, venerable, winding, difficult, inspiring and at times neglected. Far from rendering common law defunct, the idea of neglect simply meant that it contained latent, undiscovered perfections.

It was because of its sublime nature, that the law was capable of evolving new and 'beautiful' solutions to problems: 'my system is formed; and I did not carry it *to* the law, but found it *in* the law'.[55] A second level of analysis, beyond the practical concerns of authority, has to be considered and, at this level, the focus is on similarity rather than difference. That both Hindu and common law shared ideas about their beginnings, and celebrated their obscurity in similar ways might seem like weak comparison, but to Jones, and other Orientalists of the Asiatic society, it implied that both systems may well have emerged from the mists of a common time immemorial, and a common place. It is at this mystical and sublime moment, whose precise time was lost in the labyrinthe of astronomical cycles, that Jones saw the familial connection between Eastern and Western sources of law: 'the Hindus believe [their law] to be almost as old as creation. It is ascribed to MENU, the MINOS of India, and like him, the son of JOVE'.[56]

In this respect, eighteenth century jurisprudential claims that English law was to boost its legitimacy if it 'conformed to the norms of a community of legal systems' have to be remembered.[57] Familial connections were essential to the iconic unity of the English law. As Jones puts it: 'The great system of jurisprudence like that of the Universe, consists of many subordinate systems, all of which are connected by nice links and beautiful dependencies.'[58] In this sense correspondences were even sought and found between the laws of Manu and Justinian's *pandectae*:

> If we had a complete digest of Hindu and Muhammedan laws, after the model of Justinian's inestimable Pandects, compiled by the most learned of native lawyers, with an accurate verbal translation of it into English; and if copies of the work were reposited in the proper offices . . . of the Supreme Court, that they might occasionally be consulted as a standard of justice, we should rarely be at a loss for principles at least and rules of law applicable to the cases before us . . . The great work, of which *Justinian* has the credit, consists of texts collected from law-books of approved authority, which in his time were extant at Rome; and those texts are digested according to a scientifical analysis; the names of the original authors, and the titles of their several books, being constantly cited with references even to parts of their works, from which the different passages were selected; but although it comprehends the whole system of jurisprudence . . . that vast compilation was published, we are told, in three years; with all its imperfections, it is a most valuable mine of juridical knowledge; it gives law at this hour to the greatest part of Europe; and though

> few English lawyers dare make such an acknowledgement, it is the true source of nearly all our English laws that are not feudal in origin. It would not be unworthy of a British government to give the natives of these Indian provinces a permanent security for the due administration of justice among them, similar to that which Justinian gave to his Greek and Roman subjects. The labour of the work would also be greatly diminished by two compilations already made in Sanscrit and Arabick, which approach nearly in merit and in method, to the Digest of Justinian . . . The *Vivadarnava* [*Bridge over the Sea of Litigation*] consists, like the Roman Digest, of authentick texts, with the names of their several authors regularly prefixed to them, and explained where an explanation is requisite, in short notes taken from commentaries of high authority.[59]

Even at the mundane level of individual rules of contract or inheritence, familial connections between the common law and other legal sytems had to be sought and found. As Boorstin, commenting on Blackstone, notes: 'the ancient or foreign rule is first used to explain, and then to justify the English institution'. An example of this is provided by Jones:

> That the Hindus were in early ages a *commercial* people, we have many reasons to believe; and in the first of their sacred law-tracts, which they suppose to have been revealed by MENU many *millions* of years ago, we find a curious passage on the legal *interest* of money, and the limited state of it in different cases, with an exception, which the sense of mankind approves, and which commerce absolutely requires, though it was not before the reign of CHARLES I that our own jurisprudence fully admitted it in respect of maritime contracts.[60]

There was, then, no clear discrimination against this foreign legal order. The word 'foreign' simply meant 'ancient', and 'ancient' meant the possibility that at some time—beyond the time of memory—Hindu, Roman and common law systems were conjoined, or even identical to one another.

Furthermore, what was to prove beneficial to the Imperial enterprise was that this universal law had universal jurisdiction and applied across the whole human race irrespective of differences. That the Hindu code of laws was comparable to the *corpus iuris civilis* points to the place of the legal text in classical ideas of Imperialism. These comparisons and connections appealed to the policy of the Roman *imperium* according to which the essence of legal authority devolved from the textual body of its laws. Similarly, Manu was to take the place of the Pandects as law's *ur*-text and thus transfer its authority right across the globe. After all: 'Legislative provisions have not the individual for their object, but the species; and are not made for the convenience of the day but for the regulation of ages.'[61] Even in this age of reason, Law was to be considered universal, beyond mere geography, and as deriving from, and revealed by, the Gods. For Jones: '[Hooker's] idea of heavenly law is just and noble; and human law as derived from it, must partake of the phrase as far as it is perfectly administered.'[62]

The universality of law, so crucial to the idea of Empire, did not derive from differentiating Western from Eastern jurisprudence. It was, rather, based on their similarities, or at least a similarity in so far as both posited a mysterious and sublime cause at the centre of their institutional organization.

The 'dread force of law'

In the context of Imperialism, the sublimity of Hindu laws offered the English further advantages. The sublime was connected with power, and control over the sublime would be control over power: 'I know of nothing sublime' states Burke 'which is not some modification of power.'[63] Or, as Jean-Luc Nancy puts it: 'In the sublime, enjoyment touches, moves, that is also commands.'[64] For Burke, and for later romantics such as Jones and Forbes, the sublime was rooted in objects which are obscured from sight; darkness, confusion, ignorance and terror are what excited romantic passions. Just as the dread of night and the fear of ghosts lay in their obscure forms, similarly, the despot was one who exercised his form of justice in private: 'Those despotic governments, which are founded on the passions of men, and principally upon the passion of fear, keep their chief as much as may be from the public eye.'[65] It was this inaccessible private domain, a commonplace of much gothic fiction, which characterized despotic enjoyment as exclusive, absolute and terrifying.

In dressing up its own pre-history with a mantle of sublimity, in emphasizing its obscure origins, it was to be the law that occupied the place of the despotic potentates; it was to be the law that inherited the exercise of power by replacing the 'dread majesty' of the Sultans. As Nietzsche later put it, legal authority rests on 'the assumption that the rationale of every law is not human in origin, that it was not sought and found after ages of error, but that it is divine in its origin, completely and utterly without a history, a gift, a miracle, a mere communication'.[66] To reveal the origins of law as something positive, as opposed to divine, would be to obviate its imperative tone. Thus: 'To draw up a law-book like Manu's, is tantamount to granting to a people mastership for the future, perfection for the future,—the right to aspire to the highest Art of Life. To that end, the law must be made unconscious: this is the object of every holy lie.'[67]

This shift from the denigration of despotic enjoyment to the use of its energies (*pouissance*) in the more socially acceptable form of law can be traced through Jones's own work. On the question of despotic power he expressed two differing opinions. On the one hand, of course, he stood opposed: 'My temperament cannot stomach the arrogance of princes and nobles.'[68] He reiterated the point again when comparing press gangs to Oriental tyranny: 'Be assured, my dear lord, that while the *illegal* pwer of pressing subsists, the peasantry are no more free than the people of Constantinople or Morocco. It is only a base mode of excercising cruel tyranny.'[69]

Yet, on the other hand, Jones saw in the process of sublimation the chance to convert the excess energy of Oriental forms into something useful. In this light, Jones's comments on the use of the Hindu oath in the English courts, which required witnesses to be sworn by a Brahmin in front of consecrated fire, are important. In his address to the grand jury, Jones emphasized at length why the phrasing of the Hindu oath is so necessarily awful:

> because, though in form it invokes the Supreme Being as a defender, yet by implication it addresses Him as an avenger; and though it openly expresses a benediction, yet it virtually implies imprecation: the expression could not be full, without raising too violent and too painful an image . . . a sublimer idea could not enter the mind of man; since it is a clear deduction of reason, that the bare suspension of the Divine energy but for a moment, would cause the instantaneous dissolution of all worlds, and the tumultuous extinction of all who inhabit them.[70]

It is noteworthy that the figure of punishment invoked by Jones bears the same features of the terrifying Gods—the black complexion and the red eyes—that previous travellers had denigrated as idolatrous symbols of polytheistic excess. It is an exemplary feature of common law jurisprudence that any such fantasies of excess come to be assimilated and monopolized rather than rejected. Jones was as easily drawn to the idea of an alien deity such as *Kali* as he was to the sublime powers of despotic excess:

> In general I observe, that the *Hindu* writers have exalted ideas of criminal justice, and in their figurative style, introduce the *person* of *punishment* with great sublimity: "Punishment" they say "with a black complexion and a red eye, inspires terror, but alarms the guilty only"; Punishment guards those who sleep, nourishes the people, secures the state from calamity, and produces the happiest consequences in a country where it is justly inflicted; where unjustly, the magistrate cannot escape censure, nor nation, adversity.[71]

It was, in other words, these once terrifying figures of Oriental excess that were to inform eighteenth century jurisprudence and provide the law with a theoretical dais from which to instruct.

The Law-Givers: Manu, Solon, Tribonian, Jones

The effect of sublimation thus converted the exclusive enjoyment of the Sultans, and the obscene excesses of religious idolatry, into more accepted and useful forms of control. The sublime allows power to emerge and to be 'posited' as legitimate force. However, just as superabundant enjoyment is what distinguished the despot from his subjects, so too sublime power conferred a similar, but more accepted, status on the judge/legislator. As Deleuze and Guattari observe, the machinery of despotism is driven by the one who establishes a filial link between his subjects and a superior deity. The Oriental despot held a particular place as a mediator and messenger of the Gods. According to Grosrichard the despot had to submit to the law because to do so was to endow the law with universal characteristics.[72] And, simultaneously, because the law was regarded as universal it empowered him to act and speak imperatively. The Law created the despot and the despot created the law. That the despot was simultaneously subject to the law, and in a unique position to create the law might be characterized in terms of a split. This being so, it may be argued that this split is what allows the charisma of authority to emerge.

This same split economy of power, and of jurisdiction, is discernable if we analyse Jones's own position in relation to the law. In typical fashion, and throughout his writings, Jones maintained his submission before the law. In a letter to Earl Spencer, he declares his refusal to take sides in the battle between Burke and Hastings in the run-up to the latter's impeachment. His allegiances are only to aspects of the law. Thus he has 'an equity-*side*, a common-law-*side*, an ecclesiastical *side*, and an admiralty-*side*, but I am quadrilateral by act of parliament'. Jones's quadrilateral nature (Janus squared) involves his submission to a higher cause: 'it is my sole duty to convey law as though a channel'.[73]

Jones's subservient relationship to the law conformed to the correct manners demanded of its institution. Yet this passive position within the dogmatic structure of the law assigned Jones to a particular place that distinguished him from those other (pre-) colonial subjects of law over whom he held authority. He was no mere passive recipient of the law, but a messenger and conduit of an already established truth. Jones, himself, recognized the power conferred upon him over his subjects. It is a power, he freely admitted, that made him tremble: 'All the police and judicial power, therefore, of this settlement, where at least half a million of natives reside, are in my hands: I tremble at the power, which I possess.'[74]

The simultaneity of passivity and authority is more pertinently discernable in relation to the translations of the legal codes. For here Jones was more than a judge: 'I speak the *language of the Gods* as the Brahmens call it, and am engaged in superintending a *Digest* of Indian law for the benefit of *twenty four millions* of black subjects in these provinces.'[75] Jones bestowed upon himself the status of a law-giver and, continually, referred to himself as occupying the same position as that of Solon. Indeed in the following passage Jones admits to a position that Solon would have envied:

> I have the delight of knowing that my studies go hand in hand with my duty, since I now read both sanscrit and Arabik with so much ease, that the native lawyers can never impose upon the courts, in which I sit. I converse fluently in arabick with the Maulavi's, in sanscrit with the Pandit's, and in Persian with the nobles of the country; thus possessing an advantage which neither Pythagoras nor Solon possessed, though they must ardently have wished it.[76]

Given that the sublimity of law renders it universal, the law-giver need not be Greek. And so, on occasions, Jones described himself as a reincarnation of Manu himself, who 'having written the laws of BRAHMA in a hundred thousand couplets, arranged under *twenty-four* heads in a *thousand* chapters presented them to the primitive world'.[77] What Manu presented to the primitive world, the modern day amanuensis, Jones, was to present to the civilized world of European judges, and governor-generals. Again, in a private letter sent from Calcutta to London in 1786 in which Jones expressed his plans for the systematic translation and compilation of

Hindu and Mohameddan laws, Jones likenes himself to Tribonian, the compiler of the Justinian code and declares that the mantle of Justinian himself was to fall upon his patron, Lord Cornwallis, the Governor-General of Bengal. Jones's personal pandit or Maulavy, Mujdudden, is given the title *omni exceptione major* taken from Justinian's institutes.[78]

The category of the sublime thus clears a space to be occupied by a mediating figure. As Pierre Legendre puts it: 'In theology, the power of God or absolute place of the mythical Third must always pass through a mediating figure—that of the pope, the emperor or the priest—before it becomes an object of subjective attachment.'[79] Similarly, in Jones' imperial jurisprudence, it is the law-giver—Manu, Solon, Justinian or Jones himself—who was to occupy that charismatic position as mediator between the Gods and his subjects.

The Affect of Subjectivity

In sublimating excess enjoyment, and in rendering a mythological status for himself and for the British, Jones constructed out of the law a domain of affection. Face to face with the terrifying powers of the sublime, the subject has no option but to be dominated and thereby defined. For Jones the power of the legal sublime found in the Hindu scriptures provides for a replication of Burke's theory at the level of legal subjectivity. The legal sublime renders urgent the question of devotion and belief. Consider his description of Manu. Even though it is 'a system of despotism and priestcraft', or perhaps because of this, the Hindu laws of Manu, are imbued with:

> a spirit of sublime devotion, of benevolence to mankind, and of amiable tenderness to all sentient creatures, pervades the whole work; the style of it has a certain austere majesty, that sounds like the language of legislation and exhorts a respectful awe; the sentiments of independence on all beings but God, and the harsh admonitions, even to Kings, are truly noble, and the many panegyrics on the Gayatri, the mother, as it is called, of the vedas, prove the author to have adored . . . that divine and incomparably greater light, to use the words of the most venerable text in the Indian scripture, which illumines all, delights all, from which all proceed, to which all must return, and which alone can irradiate (not our visual organs merely, but or souls, and) or intellects.[80]

In establishing this affective domain, the sublime is used for the psychoanalytical control and institution of the subject. The terror of the sublime, and the suggestion that laws derive from origins which exceeded perishable man, established the proper emotional attachment to the law. Sublime enjoyment operates around the idea that man is small when he confronts the vastness of nature. It is from this standpoint that the subject is confronted with his own limits. The numerous drawings and paintings made by romantic artists in India, recording the microscopic detail of everyday life, reflected the concern with the interiority and contours of subjective life. They were also concerned with the way in which subjective life was instituted. As James Beattie observed:

> Grammarians are not agreed about the etymology of the word sublime. The most probable is that it may be derived from supra and limus; and so denotes literally the circumstance of being raised above the slime, the mud, or the mould of this world.[81]

Such a concern for circumscribing subjective life was consciously transferred into the jurisprudential sphere by Jones. The legal subject *per* Jones is not a self defined entity. Rather subjectivity is to be defined only in relation to the vast sublimity of law. In the context of colonial legality, the translation of the Hindu law codes and the subsequent theorization of the sublimity of law was a key moment in the colonization and cultivation of subjectivity. Faced with the sublimity of Law, the legal subject has no option but to give himself up to it. What we have seen from the numerous (excessive) quotes from Jones's work is a confidence to now talk about the Hindus and Muslims as subjects. The process of sublimating excess enjoyment similarly converts the Oriental individual into a subject of law. Such confidence was decidedly borne of the the translation of the Hindu law as a sublime source of authority.

Conclusion

The sublime provides a terrifying yet empty space from which to instruct and colonize the subject. The category of the sublime allows 'man' to move away from the feminine, the gayatri, or the formlessness and towards rationality.[82] But that the sublime was to be found through Orientalism and also found to be of relevance to Western (common law) juridical thought is noteworthy and essentially unmasks the other face of Europeanism. In this sense, the application of Jones's project was not limited to the commercial interests of the East India Company. The translation of Manu was not an attempt to recreate an alternative history of the law, but to ascertain the origins of the essence of law and the secrets of its subjectivity.

What was needed was an idea of universal subjection and submission not to the state, or a monarch but to the law as an universal phenomenon mediated by the judge as *sublimis.* What the romantic fantasy of Oriental excess did was to uncover the theoretical arsenal needed to establish this omni-jurisdictionality. It exposed a desire to institute a terryfying excess as the presupposition of legal universalism. In drawing out the perceived similarities between Hindu and common law, Jones provided a plan for a universal law in which *all* are to be subjects of the law. By the eighteenth century, Oriental excess was to provide the co-ordinates by which the legal subject was to be dominated by the law.

CHAPTER 6

Anglican Pleasures in the Orient: Staging the Rule of Law

Thrice happy, blest Brittania's bounded Kings!
To clothe the naked, feed the hungry, wipe
The guiltless tear from lone Affliction's eye;
To raise hid Merit, set the alluring light
Of Virtue high to view; to nourish Arts,
Direct the thunder of an injur'd state,
Make a whole glorious people sing for Joy.
Bless humankind, and through the downward depth
Of future times to spread that better Sun
Which lights up British soul; for deeds like these,
The dazzling fair career unbounded lies;
While (still superior bliss) the dark abrupt
Is kindly barr'd, the precipice of ill.
O luxury divine! O poor to this
Ye giddy glories of *despotic thrones*!
By this, by this indeed is imag'd heaven,
The boundless good, without the pow'r of Ill.[1]

Ius ac fas omne delere (cic.att 1, 16, 6)

Introduction

In a pamphlet entitled *Inquiry into the Science of Food Preservation*, Jeremy Bentham sets out his plans for a system of storing food through the exclusion of heat. The world, then obviously more than now, would have found indispensable a contraption that could preserve the usual daily comestibles; vegetables, fruit, milk, meat and fish. Bentham found other uses; it could also be built, for example, on a larger scale in order to store dead bodies in a national bank for anatomical study. But such a unit, Bentham stresses, should not freeze its contents since freezing would cause the texture of food to break up. Even from such a slight description of the purposes of a sideline project one could quite easily distinguish the basic philosophical themes that concerned the radical utilitarians. Everything must be saved, nothing is to be wasted, for all of it is useful and intrinsic to a plan; 'every thing uses or serves another thing'.[2] Indeed the principle of exclusion characterizes the very fault in whatever system the utilitarians sought to reform. Utilitarianism ought not to have limits: 'Limits it has no other than those of the earth.'[3] Thus, for example, the procedure of common law trials suffers from the fact that jurors were unable to consider evidence rendered inadmissible by the judge: 'Exclude evidence, exclude justice', was the slogan Bentham scribbled across the range of his evidence scholarship. The second noteworthy point, is symptomatic of a standard fear, shared by most anti-deconstructionists, from which Bentham was not immune. Everything should be done to minimize the destruction of the texture of materials. The purity of forms, fabric, teachings and understanding must be maintained if they are to be at all useful. Indeed Bentham's fear of being misunderstood is what informs his notoriously detailed and eccentric writing style. From his scrupulous and overly careful writings to the bequeathment of both his works and his body to University College, a whole range of prophylactic measures were taken by Bentham in order to overcome the natural, accidental or wilful contamination of both texture and text.

Yet, as inevitable as the process of contamination, the principle of exclusion ineluctably infects the whole of utilitarian thought. Indeed, 'everything' is arranged around exclusion. Even if it is at the tired old meta-level of pointing out the paradox of 'excluding exclusions' from our thought, utilitarianism can never be all-inclusive. Something must go to waste. The question is *what* (apart from exclusion) is being excluded? If even the most useless object can be turned to profit then what could possibly fall beyond salvage?

It is neither mere coincidence, nor an arbitrary feature of his wonderfully all-encompassing dilettantism, that Bentham should turn to the idea of a refrigeration system. What bugs Bentham, and what eventually gets to him is heat and all of its torrid effects; infection, impurity and, as we shall argue, despotism and excess. The maximum amount of happiness for the maximum amount of people entailed the minimum amount of heat. If everything about utilitarianism is arranged around this exclusion of heat, then this exclusion seems to mark the limits, the boiling point, of utilitarianism. This is the point at which its philosophical texts have to be examined for contamination, and, indeed, the point at which all the variations of post-utilitarian modern rational thought become infected.

As for Bentham himself, the posthumous fate of his body seems to reflect the failure of utilitarian thought to seal itself hermetically from extreme and adverse atmospheric conditions. It is somewhat sad yet poignant to note that the body bequeathed to University College in the form of an auto-icon has been removed from display on advice of experts from the Textile Corporation Centre. As a result of humidity, an infestation of beetles known as the 'wooly bear' had been eating away at the textiles clothing his waxed body, undoing its very texture. The auto-icon has now been freeze-dried.

Utilitarianism is the most temperate of all philosophies which makes its study within the context of British India, well before the invention of efficient air conditioning systems, all the more fascinating. This chapter will examine, first of all, the efforts made by utilitarians to exclude Orientalism as a useful pedagogic tool of colonial government and to replace it with the more tempered 'principle of pleasure'. In broad terms, by the time the British gained the upper hand and started to rule India, the missionary and utilitarian agendas were committed to the renunciation of decadent pleasures and the eradication of as many forms of bad behaviour as possible. The frenetic activity of colonialism throughout the nineteenth century may be regarded as 'designed to protect the other from his jouissance', even at the point of destroying the other.[4] According to such an account, Indian culture ceased to be a major source of inspiration to the English. With some exceptions, the country became a dull and arid land where the supposed glamour of life in the colony was confined to the specifically English rituals of afternoon tea on the verandah, bridge at the club or drinks in the barrack rooms. The fan-palms had found their way into the Victorian drawing-rooms back in England. The art of the subcontinent was made available to all, images of deities were displayed in museums in London and wild animals, not as colossal as they were at the time of early travel narratives, had shrunk in size in order to fit Regency zoos. The fantasy figures of wealthy, despotic Sultans (such as Tipu Sultan and Haider Ali) were eventually killed in battle. Once the country came to be held by the British crown, the exotica which had already been exposed to the frigid gaze of European Orientalism became banal and their descriptions well rehearsed. Like the khaki-toned photographs of the late nineteenth century, the Orient had been drained of its colour.

Nevertheless, the utilitarian theory of pleasure, it will be argued, inevitably commits itself to a structural relationship to the fantasy of excess and useless enjoyment. It creates a space for it as a sovereign necessity; that is to say, excess remains more than nothing, and more than an archaic vestige of Orientalism. It is, in fact, revealed to be quintessentially necessary to the idea of rule and legality. What will be proposed here is that the relationship between Western notions of pleasure and Oriental excess was to be reconfigured during the nineteenth century. Oriental excess, and all of its symptoms, are not as so often claimed, completely eradicated by utilitarian reforms and the move towards a bureaucratically administered state. Rather, excess becomes less a fantasy and more a useful notion in establishing bonds of fealty between the state defined according to the vagaries of the rule of law and the subject. The idea of excess becomes assimilated, incorporated into the very structure of rule that seeks to undermine its non-civilized status. As we shall see, it becomes useful.

Utilitarianism

For Bentham, who rivalled Jones's ambition to become the Solon of India, the 'principle of utility' belongs to an affective order. The point is emphasized by Mill that utilitarianism 'holds feeling at least as valuable as thought, and poetry not only on a par with, but the necessary condition of, any true philosophy'.[5] What is posited within this order of sovereign affects is, of course, the principle of pleasure. It is interesting to note in passing that the language used by Bentham to describe pleasure is at times religious in nuance. Pleasures have, Bentham says, the force of 'sanctions'. That is to say that they bind individuals in the same manner as sacred blood ties.[6] Utilitarianism 'assumes [pleasure] for the foundation of that system, the object of which is to tear the fabric of felicity by the hands of reason and law'.[7] Pleasure is the prerequisite foundation for positive laws, it is what 'gives binding force to any rule'.[8] But it is so in order to promote pleasure itself. The principle of utility devotes its energies towards the promotion and maximization of pleasure and happiness both among individuals and the community. And, as a necessary concomitant, utilitarianism must also negate that which is broadly categorized as pain.

> every writer, from Epicurus to Bentham, who maintain the theory of utility, meant by it, not something contradistinguished

> from pleasure, but pleasure itself, together with exemption from pain.[9]

It is from the perspective of a society free from pain that Mill is able to illuminate his social agenda and the manner in which utilitarian values may be smuggled into a broader liberal political and legal philosophy: 'the present wretched education, and wretched social arrangements, are the only real hindrance to [pleasure] being attainable by almost all'.[10] Furthermore, what promotes pain and hinders the attaining of pleasure is law, or, rather 'bad' law. Whether at the level of substantive decision-making, or at the level of expediting procedures for its correct administration, the utilitarian critique emphasized the way in which 'bad' law (or a bad legal system) blocks the pleasures that liberty affords:

> in a world in which there is so much to interest, so much to enjoy, and so much also to correct and improve, every one who has this moderate amount of moral and intellectual requisites is capable of an existence which may be called enviable; and unless such a person, through bad laws, or subjection to the will of others, is denied the liberty to use the sources of liberty within his reach, he will not fail to find this enviable existence.[11]

The wider importance of utilitarianism to colonialism, and subsequently the importance of colonialism in legitimizing this philosophical system is given fuller treatment in Mill's essay, *Considerations on Representative Government.* It is here, in Chapter Eighteen, 'on the government of dependencies by a free state', that the quantification of happiness is addressed in relation to the 'Hindoo' subjects of the British Empire. In so doing Mill provides utilitarian justification for colonial government:

> there are strong reasons for maintaining the present slight bond of connection . . . It is a step, as far as it goes, towards universal peace, and general friendly co-operation among nations. It renders war impossible among a large number of otherwise independent communities; and moreover hinders any of them from being absorbed into a foreign state, and becoming a rival power, either more despotic or closer at hand, which might not always be so unambitious or so pacific as Great Britain. It at least keeps the markets of the different countries open to one another . . . And in the case of the British possessions it has the advantage, especially valuable at the present time, of adding to the moral

> influence, and weight in the councils of the world, of Power which of all in existence, best understands liberty.[12]

Everything good about colonial government is calibrated in terms of greater accrual of benefits; it promotes universal peace, comity between nations, moral influence, and liberty. It also prevents despotism. It should be noted, that at this stage of the argument Mill is not opposed to despotism per se. Were it not for the fact that a good despot is a 'rare and transitory accident',[13] he would agree to native rule in India if it were to lead to a higher state of improvement among the 'semi-barbarous'. Nevertheless, colonial administration is justified if it does not sink into the criminality of 'bad' despotism, and so long as it does not assume that 'one people may keep another as a warren or preserve for its own use, a place to make money in, a human cattlefarm to be worked for the profit of its own inhabitants'.[14]

Having declared their philosophic radicalism while illustrating the benefits of colonial administration, the utilitarians provided the intellectual basis for a movement of reform that was to be applied in India. As Eric Stokes has argued, Bentham's influence in Indian affairs, particularly in the field of law reform was striking. Utilitarianism ushered in an era of paper-planning and mundane law codes: 'the sword was to be exchanged for the pen, and the soldier-diplomat to give way before the administrator-judge'.[15] Those such as Macauley and Trevelyan encouraged the teaching of English to Indians as a means of conducting business and facilitating the progress of free trade. Macaulay, in fact, attempted to define for India a manifesto, and for the British in India, what he termed, 'a reason for living': 'It is scarcely possible to calculate the benefits which we might derive from the diffusion of European civilisation among the vast population of the East . . . To trade with civilised men is infinitely more profitable than to govern savages.' And again, a couple of pages later in the same speech: 'Are we to keep the people of India ignorant in order that we may keep them submissive.'[16] Progress, in other words was to be measured according to the yardstick of Europeanism: 'What the Greek and Latin were to More and Ascham our tongue is to the people of India.'[17]

The specific achievements by the utilitarians in the field of Indian law reform have already been covered substantially and in detail by others. It will suffice to list but a few of the more important and salient of these reforms in order to illustrate some of the philosophical underpinnings. By and large, such reforms concentrated on promoting happiness under a rule of law whereby individual rights, security, and liberty are legitimated and guaranteed by subjecting sovereign powers to the same laws as the citizen.

What would differentiate British rule in India from that of its Moghul predecessors was the idea of a pre-existing legal foundation free from the inventions and caprice of individual officers. This meant obliterating those evil hindrances to justice that had hitherto defined the legal system. The Indian legislative council was inspired by Benthamism to a series of acts in the mid-nineteenth century designed to facilitate the efficient administration of justice. The *Civil Procedure Act* of 1859 'promised to secure so far as judicial institutions can secure that blessing, as good and accessible an administration of civil justice as the lights of the age are capable of conferring on it'.[18] The *Penal Code* 1860, and the *Code of Criminal Procedure* 1861 brought changes to criminal jurisdiction. The priority was to rid legal procedure and the rules of evidence from prolixity and technicality. These features, characteristic of the common law in general, had already been regarded by Bentham as part of the 'sinister interests of judge and co.'. Prone to delays, common law procedure and the complicated rules over the admissibility and weight of evidence encouraged a system that effectively barred proper access to justice and played into the hands of fee-gathering lawyers. Thus the Civil Procedure Act and the Code of Criminal Procedure were noteworthy for abandoning the technicality of written pleadings and enforcing *viva voce* proceedings. It should be noted, however, that orality, in and of itself, does not lend itself to a less technical system of procedure and that an ulterior motive other than that of mere technicality may be given for these changes: 'The magistrate is compelled to learn the facts of the case from the witnesses themselves, instead of trusting to a deposition of a corrupt omlah in a corner.'[19] In this light it is interesting to note that more recent reforms to the English civil justice system express a preference for written depositions over oral testimony, precisely in order to combat time wasting.[20]

In a slightly different vein, Fitzjames Stephen's *Indian Evidence Act* 1872, sought to rationalize the common law rules regarding the admissibility and weight of evidence during common law trials. Crucially, the adversarial rules regarding admissibility turn on the question as to what constitutes relevant evidence to be put before a tribunal of fact. By searching through the pertinent case law, and by employing J.S. Mill's inductive system of logic, Stephens (who styled himself the 'Benthamee Lycurgus' of India) was able to whittle down and codify rules for testing relevancy of evidence.

In keeping with more modern ideas about the relationship between the rule of law and state power, Fitzjames Stephen further recommended splitting the functions of judicial and executive power which had hitherto been combined and which he had identified as the cause of much of the procedural inefficiency and maladministration. Stephens emptied the executive office of any dealings with civil justice. Although, interestingly and controversially, this splitting of functions was not to be applied in the sphere of criminal procedure. The spirit of legislative authority that informed Stephens's own peculiar brand of utilitarianism is fully exemplified here: sanctions and punishment under criminal jurisdiction was a mark of sovereign state power and was to remain in the hands of an executive collector-magistrate. Moreover, such power was deemed necessary in order to prevent an increase in the use or threat of military force.[21]

The latter caveat is instructive and indicative of general utilitarian principles. As well as promoting the principles of pleasure, access to justice and liberty under the law, an efficient legal system was key to the idea of strong government. In turn, both efficient law and strong government were the seed-beds for this much sought after growth-spurt in maximum happiness: 'All that the law can do or ought to try to do is to provide a rational and convenient framework in which the new state of things may grow up.' And, again: 'it only remained to work the system with energy and perseverence, so that the rule of law might complete its civilising mission'.[22] It is in this sense that British Imperial rule was to be compared, by Stephens, to the *pax romana*:

> This peace actually was, and the more highly educated Romans must have seen that it was about to become, the mother of laws, arts, institutions of all kinds, under which our own characters have been moulded. The Roman law, at that period as clumsy as English law is at present, but nearly as rich, sagacious and vigorous, was taking root in all parts of the world . . . and all the arts of life, literature, philosophy and art were growing by its side.[23]

But what unites all the different strands of utilitarianism is both the promotion of maximum pleasure and the minimization of procedural obstacles. The principle of pleasure is thus defined in the negative, by what it excludes. And, the way in which the success of an administrative, executive or judicial system is measured is according to whether or not it mitigates against evil hindrances, rather than in terms of a happiness-effect. This is certainly true of the reforms implemented in British India. As Eric Stokes points out:

> It would be foolish to pretend that Bentham's ideal was in any sense attained, and that justice in India remained far from cheap,

> simple and expeditious. But this has been equally true of most countries where the rule of law has been established, and Bentham's influence requires to be tested by the extent it has mitigated the evils afflicting the administration of justice rather than the extent to which it instituted a positive system of its own . . . the [Indian] system as a whole was better organised and more logical than its English counterpart.[24]

The Utilitarian Expulsion of Enjoyment

What is excluded from the utilitarian system in the name of pain, however, is not simply bad law, bad procedure, or obstacles to justice. These features are in fact symptoms of a much deeper structural displacement. As we have already noted, the rule of law and its administration through an efficient court system displaced the idea of personal discretion and exercise of despotic power which the West had long suspected was characteristic of Eastern government. Key figures in reforming Indian administration, such as Thomas Macauley, James Mill, Henry Maine, and Fitzjames Stephens, dismissed the readiness of Clive and Hastings to admire and conserve Indian institutions, and opposed the priestly superstitions and political despotism of Indian society. Instead the utilitarians attempted to apply standards of civilization based on the mature sciences, classical ideas of liberty and, above all, legal rationality. Modern and radical utilitarianism replaced the fluctuating customs and unwritten law in which, according to Western jurisprudence, the secular mixed with a sublime theocratic order of things. Asian legality, or what Weber calls 'sultanism', was confounded by what was perceived to be magically conditioned norms with no clear rules of action and a high degree of flexibility. Here, was arranged the 'whole range of life rituallistically . . . in which special laws prevail over general law'.[25]

The spirit of sublime devotion that had obsessed William Jones and informed the policies of Cornwallis was now described as priestly superstition. Emphatically, Jones's attempts to codify and apply Hindu law was dismissed by Mill as:

> a disorderly compilation of looses, stupid or unintelligible quotations and maxims; selected arbitrarily from books of law, books of devotion, and books of poetry; attended with a commentary which only adds to the mass of absurdity and darkness; a farrago by which nothing is defined, nothing is established.[26]

There emerges with utilitarianism a much stauncher dismissal of Orientalism than hitherto expressed; an unwanted (or, at least, a previously wanted) and useless Orient. This is the Orient characterized by Fitzjames Stephens as stagnant and completely at odds with the social growth advocated by utilitarian reform:

> the fact that the institutions of a village community throw light on the institutions of modern Europe, and the fact that village communities have altered but little for many centuries, prove only that society in India has remained in a stagnant condition. It is a crude form of socialism, paralysing the growth of individual energy and all its consequences.[27]

Pleasure, so essential to utilitarian thought, is thus defined in the negative. And it is here in this process of negation that pain, as well as bad law and procedure is all subsumed into an Oriental frame of reference. Indeed, all that is seen to be the enemy of the system is found in Oriental despotism. Any other philosophical, religious or political system of thought, Bentham argues, which attempts to question the sovereignty of pleasure 'deal in sounds instead of senses, in caprice instead of reason, in darkness instead of light'.[28] It is the 'principle of caprice' or what Bentham qualifies as the twin principles of sympathy and antipathy which constitute the predominant principles adverse to that of utility. For, Bentham despotism was to be opposed, not simply as a corruption of government, but because it belongs to an affective *and* phantasmatic order of thought. It is, in other words, insufficient to characterize the capricious despot as relying simply on affects. Indeed, caprice shares with utility a place within an affective scheme. Utility is simply an 'affection of the sensible variety'.[29] Rather, the tendency of the despot is further characterized by what Bentham calls the 'phantastic principle' and it is this which takes over the affections. That is to say, the way in which rights are conferred under a capricious or despotic system 'has been the work, not of the affections but of the imagination'.

However, if this is the case, then there is nothing much to separate Orientalism from the mere defects of the common law. Consequently, as Bentham admits, even the colonial government of Bengal comes in for criticism in applying common law maxims, the music of which 'absorbs the whole imagination [drowning] the cries of humanity along with the dictates of common sense'.[30]

If the common law itself is capable of falling out of the sensible sphere and in danger of hurtling into a phantastic void, then there must be a further distinction which separates Eastern despotism from the common law. Utility, here, begins to revolve around the temper and disposition of the despot. The despot, unlike the greedy and sinister common lawyer, is one to whom a certain disposition attaches. Moral frameworks which determine right from wrong, natural from unnatural, serve 'as a cloke, and pretence, and aliment to despotism; if not a despotism in practice, a despotism in disposition'. And so, Bentham has to elucidate the word 'disposition':

> 'I feel in myself,' (say you) 'a disposition to approve of such or such an action in a moral view: but this is not owing to any notions I have of its being a useful one to the community. I do not pretend to know whether it be an useful one or not: it may be, for aught I know, a mischievous one.' 'But is it then,' (say I) 'a mischievous one? examine; and if you can make yourself sensible that it is so, then, if duty means anything, that is, moral duty, it is your *duty* at least to abstain from it . . . it is not your cherishing the notion of it in your bosom, and giving it the name of virtue, that will excuse you.'[31]

A despotic disposition, in other words, involves a failure to consider the usefulness of an action, or thought: 'Thus it shows a more depraved and dangerous disposition, if a man kill another out of mere sport, as the Emperor of Morocco, Muley Mahommet, is said to have done great numbers, than out of revenge.'[32]

It is not yet clear that such a disposition is directly connected to the idea of excess enjoyment. It is, in fact, left to Bentham's disciples to properly theorize that relationship and to make the connection between despotism and animal appetites. Such an opposition between utility and that which is beyond utility is put in more direct terms by J.S. Mill. There is, he claims, simply a difference between types of pleasure: 'It is quite compatible with the principle of utility to recognise the fact, that some kinds of pleasure are more desirable and more valuable than others.'[33] Within a utilitarian society, life has no higher pursuit than the pursuit of pleasure, but these pleasures are human and civilized and 'cannot be equated with those of a swine (an attack often levelled at the Epicurean) or those sensual indulgences injurious to health'.[34]

> Human beings have faculties more elevated than animal appetites, and when once made conscious of them, do not regard anything as happiness which does not include their gratification . . . no

> intelligent human being would consent to being a fool, no instructed person would be an ignoramus, no person of feeling and conscience would be selfish and base, even though they should be persuaded that the fool, the dunce, or the rascal is better satisfied with his lot than they are with theirs.[35]

The modern avatar of the Epicurean swine whose sensuous indulgences paralyzes all growth appears incarnated both as the Oriental despot and his subjects. If, in other words, the history of Oriental forms of government was to have one use for the utilitarians it was only to provide what is taken to be *proof* of Oriental excess. The fantasy of savage excess and animal instinct must therefore be acknowledged as a historical fact of life in the East.

Oriental history ensures that the Benthamite law-giver is to be 'possesed fully of the facts, to be informed of the local situation, the climate, the bodily constitution, the manners, the legal customs, the religion of those with whom they have to deal'.[36] Only when such history (notably, James Mill's *History of India*) has established the fantasy of the 'savage mind' as if it were a fact to be put before a jury then all other features of Orientalism must be deemed insignificant. The Benthamite legislator would thus have a clearer idea of his aims insofar as he has now a better measure of the principle of pleasure. Modern legality under these circumstances was to be defined only in opposition to its other; its conception of authority is therefore anti-feudal, anti-despotic, and anti-excess. To define what is useful it was necessary to return to pathological principles beyond utility and pleasure, and necessary to return to the symptoms of violent and savage instincts and dispositions. Moreover, it is this philosophical opposition between pleasure and excess enjoyment that consequently informed the reforms to the system of judicial administration in British India.

All this is not to say that the fantasy of enjoyment was, or remains, obliterated. It is simply replaced, re-housed, repatriated. Utilitarianism, in other words, without admitting to it, depends on what Bataille described as the 'negative character of the pleasure principle' in order to acquire, produce and conserve human life. The extent to which utilitarianism relies on Orientalism and is affected by its heat has now to be considered.

Utility's Excess

At a mundane level, it may be sufficient to point out that colonial rule occasionally inclines towards an archaic form of authority associated with Oriental (Moghul) rule. At this level, it is sufficient simply to measure the angle of this inclination without heeding the structural relationship. In the context of colonial rule, utilitarianism was caught in a paradoxical relationship between the principles of liberty and authority, between J.S. Mill's political theory and Fitzjames Stevens's jurisprudence of legislative authority as the maintenance of Empire. Indeed, as Stokes notes, the spirit of Anglican reforms in India was met by a rival conservative philosophy that shared 'an emotional kinship' with Hindu feudalism and its immemorial past. Moreover, a number of viceroys, he suggests, 'distrusted the chilly dogmatics of the reforming spirit, which was to eradicate in the name of utility all the historical associations connected with British power'.[37]

According to such studies of 'utilitarianism-in-context', the benevolent despotism of colonial government is seen as an aberrancy determined by historical and geographical circumstances rather than logic. Yet, as Daniel Bivona has already shown, the utilitarian rationality of bureaucratic imperialism implied an ideology of bureaucratic self sacrifice and imperial manners.[38] The bureaucrat is both perpetrator and victim, both master and slave. The bureaucrat subjects others to rule by virtue of being a subject himself. In Kipling's words:

> The Deputy is above the Assistant, the Commissioner above the Deputy, the Lieutenant-Governer above the Commissioner, and the Vice-Roy above all four, under the orders of the Secretary of State, who is responsible to the Empress. If the Empress be not responsible to her Maker—if there is no maker for her to be responsible to, the entire system of Our administration must be wrong.[39]

This understanding of bureaucracy already sits uncomfortably with Weber's analysis of modernity where the bureaucrat is made to work as unobtrusively as possible. Ideas of loyalty and self sacrifice became entwined with the new medievalism of conservatism and with a sultanic surrender to a belief in the extraordinary.

What is being asserted here is the failure of utilitarian reforms to exist without a structural bond to the fantasy of enjoyment. At another level, therefore, historical and geographical circumstances simply point to the limits and failures of utilitarianism.

It is vital to understand that the Anglican spirit of nineteenth century colonial India was largely self justification and as such had little purchase in achieving the consent of those governed. An inscription on the walls of St John's church, Middleton Row, Calcutta states: 'and they that Instruct

Many to Justice, shall shine as the Stars for all Eternity. Daniel XII 3'. The gift of law, in other words, rewards the giver. Sentimental socialism legitimated crown possession at a time when such legitimation was required in Britain. The years of company misrule had exposed the capricious tendency of company officials such as Warren Hastings at the expense of the 'great and permanent revenue of the sovereign'.[40] The legislative steps taken to rectify such corruption of the British might well have appeased the British, but utilitarian reforms were limited in their appeal to Indians themselves.

The problem was not specific to utilitarianism in India. The idea that the British exercise of power, which was put to full effect over the full course of the nineteenth century, was essentially empty is easily demonstrated by the fact that statute failed to establish any sense of sovereignty over British India. Extinguishing the Moghul government could not be won by force of positive law, and could not derive from juridical, or political, structures alone. Various treaties had already existed between the East India company and Indian rulers. In Surat, an agreement between Roe and Jahangir, in 1618, permitted the English to administer justice within their own factory. Madras, for example, was held under a grant (1661) which allowed the company to build a fort and mint money, to administer justice within the company's factories and to allow British judges to sit in the local *choultry* (shed) courts. Similarly, Calcutta was under control of the British after they had purchased the *zamindari* (a feudal system of collecting revenue from land tenures according to which peasants were dependant upon the unchecked whim of the landholders) of villages on the banks of the Hughly from the Nawabs (1698).[41] The *zamindari* thus granted juridical powers over native inhabitants from the Indian surzerain. As long as these treaties remained a source of authority, the British could not exercise unlimited juridical or governmental power. Judicial and Legislative measures had therefore sought, and effectively failed, to establish the English as *imperium in imperio* on numerous occasions since 1756. Formally, supreme executive and legislative power was vested in the office of the Governor-General in Council subject to the secretary of state responsible to the Crown (which eventually took the title of *Emperess of India* in 1876). However, without the use of excessive military force, these powers meant little and did little to prevent uprising and 'mutiny'.

Such difficulties in establishing sovereignty and persuading Indians to 'have faith' were to become more problematic for utilitarian reformers driven to maximise benefits for the greater number of people. An anonymous article published in the Calcutta Review of 1846 reviewing the administration of criminal justice in Bengal makes the point:

> Unrestrained by their actions—with large sums at their command–contaminated by daily intercourse with depraved natives, and forgetful of their god, they have been known to equal the worst zemindars in cruelty and oppression . . . The same sense of justice which compels us to admit, unhesitatingly, the superiority of the English government neccesitates us to point out defects . . . to abolish one inhuman practice . . . to disseminate the seeds of enlightenment among a few, is, as the Hindu poets say, to cast a drop of milk on the mighty ocean in order to turn it sweet. The mass of people must be educated.[42]

Nevertheless, these justifications and calls for education, when placed before many of the non-Christian Indians, simply dissolved into flat excuse. Where the Company had to justify itself to shareholders and the House of Commons, the Crown had to justify itself to Indian society. Bernard Cohn points out that the transition from company rule to Crown involved a shift from without to within.[43] The new Empire required that the British be accepted as insiders, part of the already diverse population. Seen from this perspective, utilitarian reform had little purchase. It recommended a rule which 'stood for cold, aloof impartiality, rejected all idea of winning over particular classes to its support, and almost prided itself on its estrangement from its subjects'.[44] The task facing the Crown was to construct a mode of authority acceptable to a potentially mutinous Indian populous, one based on consent rather than force. This was admitted by utilitarians such as Fitzjames Stephen:

> The Penal Code, the Code of Criminal Procedure, and the institutions which they regulate are somewhat grim presents for one people to make to another, and are little calculated to excite affection; but they are eminently well-calculated to protect peacable men and to beat down wrongdoers, to extort respect, and to enforce obedience.[45]

Fitzjames Stephens answer was to eventually agree to the conservatives, particularly Lord Lytton, in trying to attach a bond of loyalty between the Indian aristocracy and the British Crown. The moral basis of utilitarianism was to realize an ideal of happiness, and pleasure, but maximum pleasure could not be achieved without engendering bonds of loyalty and affection. In order to do this Anglicism had to rely upon Orientalism. Part of the argument made in previous chapters was that the luxurious arrangements and formal rituals of the Moghul courts were regarded as signs of a greedy despotic government. This indulgent world of appearances, in which an excess of pleasure was displayed, was used by travellers and philosophers as a means of characterising illicit authority. Victorian reform, however, seemed to find useful the very thing that was considered to be unproductive expenditure and as a solution, a necessary solution, utilized Oriental ritual in 'exciting the affections of the natives'. The 'civilising mission' rested upon the very image and symptoms of despotic excess which it sought to eradicate. Indeed in courting the other's desire for authority, the function of these rituals remained the same for both Moghul and British regimes.

Utilizing the Moghul Idiom

The importance to the British of employing all the signs of Moghul imperialism may be illustrated by comparing the following two incidents. Shortly after he was appointed Governor-General of India in 1813 Lord Moira had been invited to a formal audience with Sultan Akbar II. In accordance with then existing tradition and diplomatic custom between the British East India Company and the Moghul court, these practices were highly ornate ceremonies which sought to establish and maintain the veneer of a peaceful relationship. On this occasion Moira, significantly, decided to accept the invitation only on the condition that the Sultan waived all traditional ceremonial custom. This condition, intended to insult in the way only the British could, amounted to a refusal in all but name. Moira's furious insistence was a significant gesture in denying the symbolic value of an audience that would have reminded the British theirs was not the only authority in India. The existence of these Moghul imperial ceremonies implied that a dual source of authority and sovereignty—one British, the other Muslim—existed in certain Indian provinces. At a period when the East India Company had been trying to assert their paramountcy, waging wars of expansion and when Company officials thought it desirable to subject themselves and their possessions to the direct government of the British Crown, the notion of a dual source of authority would obviously have been controversial. At worst, the ceremonial interview would have implied Moghul supremacy over the dominions of the East India Company. 'Nothing', Moira generously admitted, 'has kept the floating notion of a duty owed to the Imperial family but our gratuitous and preserving exhibition of their pretensions.'

The agitation over these ceremonies continued and throughout the early nineteenth century, the British persisted in changing and slowly eroding as many of these symbolic peculiarities as possible. Lord Ellingborough went so far as to request that all titles held by Indian rulers of Salute states (Nawabs, Maharajas, Rajas Jam-Sahebs, Nizams, etc), even though unrecognized by the British, ought to be renounced and offered to the British Crown. Even empty titles were considered a threat to British supremacy; a supremacy all the more dangerous because it was borne of an inferiority complex. This anxiety extended to all the trappings of Indian rule: to rituals, titles and the luxurious ornaments of office.

The second incident involves a similar interview between Lord Amherst and Akbar II, in 1827. The two men apparently entered the function room at the same moment and at the same level. After the exchange of embraces in front of the central dais, the Emperor sat on his throne while the Governor-General occupied the state chair. Unlike previous occasions, no *nazar*, or tribute, was offered to the Emperor. The *nazar*, it ought to be noted, had been offered by the British to the Indian rulers throughout the seventeenth and eighteenth century, and had been a significant and symbolic gesture in recognizing the sovereignty of Moghul rule and the limitations of the formal administrative power held by the British. The tribute, or the price of protection, symbolically acknowledged submission to the recipient. On this occasion it was Amherst instead who received a string of pearls and emeralds.[46]

Returning to Moira's remarks about the Moghul ceremonials, it is obvious that even in the early nineteenth century their value did not go unnoticed. Lord Amherst, in his state interview with Akbar II, not only uses ritual to his benefit, but copies the very structure of Moghul ritual itself. In receiving rather than giving tribute (the *nazar*), Amherst merely reverses the roles and displays of power structures. It was recognized that where the company exercised material power, the emperor possessed mystic superiority, where the company was simply obeyed, the emperor was revered.

The ceremony (or 'ceremonials' as they became known) was recognized as a form of fealty. Forbes, describing the military durbars of the East India Company, notes: 'I often accompanied the English commander: politics, war, and public business, were then discussed, and orders issued for the ensuing day; complaints were heard, grievances redressed and the usual justice of Oriental governments administered.'[47] These rituals, he later claims were 'absolutely necessary among people so much attracted by outward appearance; and is equally unavoidable in some degree, wherever an Englishman resides in public character, vested with a delegated authority, whether he is entitled a governor, a chief, a judge or a collector'.[48] Consequently, Forbes was himself admonished by the local zemindary for taking even an evening walk without an 'ostentatious cavalcade'. By the late nineteenth century, there began a conscious attempt by the British to utilise these elements of ritual as a means of establishing social control without resorting to war. These were attempts to captivate the colonised subject in much the same way that earlier travellers had been captivated by the sensual wealth of Jahangir's court. They became essential in asserting the myth of British authority in a position whereby the pretensions of colonial power and authority did not, and could not, have their basis in fact. In order to rule effectively, to assert the idea of empire, to structure everyday life in the messes and cantonments, the British first had to tailor their imaginary to the requirements of India. They adopted Indian forms of splendour and extravagance, and mimicked for themselves the aesthetic of the conquered Moghul.

In contemporary accounts, Lord Wellesley, for example, is described as a Governer-General who modelled himself on the image of Roman proconsuls, waging wars of expansion and conducting himself with imperial splendour but who *also* sought actively to emulate Moghul imperialism. On his decision to build Government-House in Calcutta, it was stated by Lord Valentia that:

> The sums expended upon it have been considered extravagant by those who carry European ideas and European economy into Asia, but they ought to remember that India is a country of splendour, of extravagance *and of outward appearances*; that the head of a mighty Empire ought to conform himself to the prejudices of the country he rules over; and that the British in particular, ought to emulate the works of the Princes of the House of Timour.[49]

As far as the viceroys were concerned 'Illusion [was] necessary to life, that the pomp and circumstance with which men clothe political power [was] a vital succedaneum necessary to cover the defects of our naked shivering nature'.[50] And, as Malcolm put it in a letter to Gerald Wellesley:

> Bacon has told us what shrunken things the minds of most men would be if stripped of their vanities and pretensions; but where would you leave states if you were to knock away the thousand props, seen and unseen, by which they were supported?—many and some of the strongest of which have their foundations in what one of your mere general politicians or authors would pronounce, justly enough, folly, prejudice, ignorance or absurdity.[51]

The British attitude toward the enjoyment of the Indian courts cannot, therefore, be analyzed simply at the level of superficial indulgence. What had seeped into the unconscious of those such as Thomas Roe, and other seventeenth century travellers, eventually came to be absorbed into the colonial psyche as a new way of thinking about law and government.

The Grand Durbar and the Rule of Law

This hybrid idiom through which authority presented itself was given its most symbolic platform during various durbars which took place in British India from the late nineteenth century onwards. The word *durbar* refers to a court, or assembly hall, in which the Moghul Emperor received guests. However, the word also refers to the formulaic ritual of kingship and took as their primary function the administration of justice to those guests. As one of the earliest historians of the English version of the ceremony notes:

> Every morning the sovereign, or padshah appeared at a window of his palace: it overlooked a plain below. Here he performed his devotions in public; received the salams of nobles and people; read petitions and administered justice.[52]

Rewards, the presents, the nazars, as well as punishments were administered as matters of law and justice. Indeed, the durbar was essentially a court of law in which rewards were simply the adverse of punishments.

These functions were adopted by the first viceroy of India, Lord Canning, who undertook a series of tours setting up local durbars as an occasion to meet the large numbers of Indian Princes and issuing those who were loyal during the sepoy mutiny with honours such as the *Star of India.* Even at these local levels, a connection was made by the British Raj between the Oriental durbar and the introduction of civilization and technical rationality. As one modern commentator notes:

> Public gardens provided one venue, railway stations another, themselves a celebration of the same introduction of technology to India by the British. In the same way, the clock towers which the British erected in the centre of even the smallest stations celebrated the bringing of order and discipline through time keeping, to India.[53]

In addition to these itinerant durbars were grander ceremonies organized to celebrate the coronation of the English monarch as Emperor or Empress of India. The first of these, the Grand durbar, or, the Imperial Assemblage as it is sometimes called, held on 1 January 1877, celebrated the coronation of Victoria as Empress of India, but also that India from here on would be governed according to the rule of law. The scope and application of the rule of law, it should be noted, fits firmly into ideas of utilitarian pleasure. In the context of British India, the rule promises the pleasures of recognizing different religions 'without molestation', and, the ability of Indians to participate in public duty was to be encouraged: 'You the natives of India, whatever your creed, have a recognised claim to share largely with your fellow subjects, according to your capacity for the task, in the administration of the country you inhabit. This claim is founded in the highest justice.'[54] This 'site of ennunciation' thus provides fertile ground for further exploring the relationship between the utilitarian principle of pleasure and the fantasy of Oriental enjoyment. The coronation durbar of 1877, organized by Lord Lytton was shaped by a desire to stabilize relations with the Indian aristocracy, to create for the British Raj a Moghul past. As Thomas Metcalf has suggested, the Imperial Assemblage defined a strategy of rule which combined Orientalism with displays of the Union Jack in an attempt to convert the 'inert mass' of the Indian peasantry as well as the chiefs and princes through symbol and sentiment.[55] In Lytton's words, expressed in a letter addressed to Victoria, the assemblage would 'place the Queen's authority on the ancient throne of the Moghuls with which the imagination and tradition of our Indian subjects associate the splendour of Imperial power'.[56] Moreover, in proclaiming the rule of law, through the formulary of the durbar, the British invoked the Oriental idiom in order to transform this otherwise mundane doctrine of Anglican jurisprudence into an image of what India and Indians could become; civilized, uncapricious, non-despotic, participants in a destiny driven by universal values. If the rule of law is a phrase in search of a coherent set of ideas which corresponds to it, then the ritual of its proclamation dignifies that rule with a credible substitute for these ideas.[57]

It is worth dissecting the Imperial durbars in more detail for they were a peculiar hybrid of English medievalism and Moghul Orientalism. These occasions established for the Princes and their retainers a feudal order of precedence according to which each was ranked in order of importance depending upon family history, wealth, and other indicators of loyalty. What these Princes and Rajputs wore to the Imperial durbar—the colour of their turbans, cummerbunds and the tunics—was strictly regulated according to a complex code based on a desire to co-ordinate this feudal system.[58] Crests based on crude images of wild animals or Hindu deities, were drawn up for the Indian royal families by a newly established College of Arms based in Calcutta, and, were given to the families during the durbar as a substitute for the Moghul gift giving ceremony which would originally have taken place. The number of retainers and gun salutes given to each salute state varied according to heredity, rank and titles were also issued at the Assemblage. Whether or not feudalism was the correct characterization for a society based upon the plurality of religion and complexities of caste, blood and kinship was, in a strong sense, irrelevant. This sense of feudalism was projected onto India and reinforced at a time when medievalism appealed to British political Toryism and to the neo-gothic ideals of Victorian aesthetics. By invoking Anglo-Saxon imagery, Lytton's Imperial Assemblage attempted to create an Indian past that was linked to the past in England.[59] Not only did this suggest that the British were destined a place in India's history, but such medievalism ushered in ideals of chivalry, heroism, adventure, and *noblesse oblige*, thereby strengthening claims to legitimate Crown rule.

However, other aspects of the Imperial Assemblage were much more obviously Oriental in design. Recalling the travelling camps of the Moghul Emperors:

> Three large pavilions had been specifically erected for the large occasion at some distance outside, and overlooking an extensive plain to the north of the city of Dehli. The largest of these pavilions, which was semi-circular in form, about 800 feet long, facing the viceregal throne, was occupied by the governors of Madras and Bombay . . . the two other pavilions erected to the rear, right and left, of the vice-roy's throne were occupied by a large concourse of spectators including the governor-general of the Portugese settlements in India, the Khan of Khelat, the foreign envoys and consuls and European and native noblemen and gentlemen from all parts of India.[60]

In spite of its medieval flavour the size of the assemblage was regarded by many as a folly (*tamash*) and as very un-English.[61] The Viceroy's tent, described as large as a palace and which contained a large painting of Queen Victoria lit by gas lamps, was modelled upon the Sultan's pavilions described and derided by Roe. As was the case during the daily durbars conducted by Jahangir, the new subjects of the Crown were permitted inside the tent in order to pay homage to the Queen and present to her their *nazars*; heirlooms such as ruby necklaces, or, in one case, an umbrella carved out of a single piece of emerald. And, it was in this tent where the viceroy would present the armourial bearings. In shameless mimicry of past Moghul protocol, the ceremony began with Lord and Lady Lytton riding into the camp on a silver houdah mounted upon the back of, what was apparently, the largest elephant in India. Mounting the throne to the national anthem, Victoria was then proclaimed Empress of India (*Indiae Imperatrix*), although even here, an Indian title, *Kaiser i Hind*, had to be thought of. The term 'Kaiser' had been used by Muhamedan writers in describing the Roman Caesar. It implied the combined roles of Caesar, Czar, and, of course, the German Kaiser as symbol of Imperial power. The Kaiser's personal message to her Indian subjects was read out, both in English and in other translations, by the chief herald (reportedly the tallest man in the Indian army) followed by a hundred and one canon salvos and rifle shots (which apparently stampeded the elephants and killed bystanders).

In terms of its objectives, the Assemblage seems to have been declared a success: 'There can be no doubt of the fact, now universally acknowledged in India, that the proclamation of the paramount superiority of the British Crown was an act of political wisdom and foresight.'[62]

The coronation durbars of Edward VII (1903) and George V (1911) were no less Oriental in their design. Indeed, the Indo-Sarcenic influence on Lord Curzon's designs for the 1903 durbar was far more pronounced, and the Victorian medievalism played down. A Sarcenic dome had been constructed above the amphitheatre, surrounded by small kiosques and other Oriental ornaments. For Curzon, the role envisaged for British government in India was simply a continuation of that begun by the Moghuls. In order to naturalize this link between British and Moghul government, Oriental forms of ritual expression had to be adopted. This view is reflected in the following contemporary account of the 1911 durbar:

> We [the British] innovated nothing. The institutions, titles, customs, ceremonials were all part and parcel of what the British had inherited from the former masters of India, the Emporers of Dehli. The ceremonies by which a Maharaja or Nawab was installed, the meticulous exchange of official presents as between the subordinate ruler and the representative of the paramount government, the seating at these ceremonies and the order of precedence—all this was not something invented by the British or even by the ruler, but a survival of a state of affairs that had existed long before the British ever came to rule these parts.[63]

The objectives of the ceremony have already been made clear. As one description of the 1877 durbar states, it was to mark the relationship between 'ancient foes [who] have become staunch friends', and further 'to convince the people of India that there was nothing to fear, and something to hope, under the suzerainty of the Empress of India'.[64] In this sense the ritual ranks among the history of ceremonials and their political uses in buying the affections of subjects. The point was noted by Lord Curzon in his speech prior to the Grand durbar of 1903 held to celebrate the coronation of Edward VII: 'there is nothing strange, but something even familiar and even sacred, in the practice that brings Sovereigns into communion with their people in a ceremony of public solemnity and rejoicing after they have succeeded to their high estate'.[65] Nevertheless, the hybrid nature of this particular range of ceremonies reveals a stronger relationship between Anglican values and Oriental idioms of excess.

It may be that this relationship only applies within the context of colonialism. By invoking Anglo-Saxon imagery and mixing it with Moghulism, these durbars attempted to create an Indian past that was linked to an English past in order to stabilize relations to an Indian aristocracy.[66] In the words of Lord Lytton, in a letter addressed to Queen Victoria, the assemblage would place 'the Queen's authority on the ancient throne of the Moghuls with which the imagination and tradition of our Indian subjects associate the splendour of Imperial power'.[67] According to Wheeler, the use of the ceremony as a means of proclaiming the rule of law as 'an impartial and inflexible rule' resolves administrative problems about authority over any empire or state composed of plural customs, races and creeds. Such problems 'unsolved by Caesar, unsolved by Charlemagne, unsolved by Akbar', was solved, according to James Talboys and the unofficial historiographer of the event, Wheeler, by Lytton.[68]

However, the argument made here has broader reach. What emerges is an idea of courtship in which legal administration itself exposes its own desire for the other's desire. The Indian (subject) becomes the other that needs to be courted so that they too desire the rule of law, so that they too become members of the universal community of legal.

Conclusions

Colonialism simply offers us a way of observing the mechanics of how subjectivity and desire is colonised. In this case, the fantasy of Oriental excess is put to use in disguising the process of submission and buying the affect of the legal subject. Conversely, the legal order built on the no-nonsense, noh-mask, of utilitarianism could not survive without some structural link to the fantasy of glorious excess. Orientalism becomes assimilated into the structure of Western state polity. That of course, accounts for the slow demise of excess as a fantasmatic spirit floating around other histories. Assimilation becomes the most efficient way of defeating that which provokes and threatens. But the relationship between pleasure and excess can be seen the other way around. Excess as an idea, locked into a structure of rule, operates as a necessary element in the capture of subjectivity. Banal domains of administration have always had an intimate link to a surfeit of grandeur. Indeed, there is an argument to suppose that all forms of superordinate celebrity are in fact Oriental. Administrative reforms put in place by Diocletian during the Roman Tetrarchy made similar use of Oriental formulary; the institution of *amici augusti*, the honorific title of *dominus et deus*, the use of the Imperial throne, were all borrowed from Eastern forms of government in order to bolster the most mundane of reforms.[69] Orientalism so overwhelms the life and forms of Occidental regality that it can no longer be thought of in connection to its provenance. The mysterious theocratic nature of the office is thus an Orientalism within; it is the condition of fealty. There is, in spite of the greyness of the common law scheme of things, an 'Orient within', that remains necessary in the colonization of a subject who desires the law.

CHAPTER 7

Conclusion: Dust is Miscarried

> Meanwhile dismal sheets of dust constantly invade earthly habitations and uniformly defile them; as if it were a matter of making ready attics and old rooms for the imminent occupation of obsessions, phantoms, spectres that the decayed odour of old dust nourishes and intoxicates.[1]

So far we have traced a number of key avatars of excess enjoyment. In the first, the category of enjoyment assigns to foreign systems of interdiction a state of corruption supposedly unknown in the West. Permissive, illicit and, above all, excessive, it was used by Western travellers and philosophers to indicate difference, and demarcated the imaginary outline and structure of a foreign culture. Here, the ideal subject is contrasted and distinguished from the figure of the Oriental. The Occidental subject, in other words, is a subject of temperate pleasures; his Oriental counterpart is fantasised as over indulgent. In its second avatar, enjoyment, having been recognized for its fantasmatic energies, is converted, cultivated and appears as the romantic and Oriental sublime. Here, enjoyment, in its guise as the sublime, operates in order to connect domestic and foreign systems of (legal) thought. As we have seen, this second avatar provided further advantages to the Imperial cause. Moreover, the idea of the sublime lent to legality an extra-terrestrial, extra-secular, source of authority from which to regulate the universal subject of law. The idea of excess consequently becomes useful.

But to suggest that excess has a use is paradoxical to the point of being meaningless. By incorporating the symptoms and signs of Oriental despotism within the very principle of utilitarian pleasure, excess ceases to exist *qua* excess or, indeed, *qua* fantasy. Incorporation essentially kills off the threat of the Orient. There seems to be, in the historical trajectory of what has been described in this book, a desacralization of the East that seems wholly concomitant with the notion of an autonomous, muscular and secular subject. That the fantasy of excess might have lost its purchase in the relationship between East and West is a point reinforced by the following common law judgment. But, as shall be argued, its place in the construction and cultivation of legal subjectivity is still of relevance.

Consider the factual details of the following case picked out from the musty law reports of 1991 concerning an excavation and the accidental discovery of a bronze Hindu idol from the thirteenth century in the Indian state of Tamil Nadu.[2] Notwithstanding the provenance of the statue, the immediate story begins in 1976 when a local labourer, or 'coolie', called Ramamoorthi happened upon a solid metal object while shovelling around fallow dirt. The object turned out to be a major Hindu idol known as the *Pathur Siva-Natarja*, part of a family of bronze idols known by collectors as the Pathur bronzes. These bronze statues are familiar objects of worship and tourist souvenirs. They are of Siva standing on one foot. The whole divinity is surrounded by a circular halo of flames spewing out from the mouths of crocodiles who lie at either side of Siva. The land on which these particular bronzes were found by Ramamoorthi turned out to be the site of a temple endowed in the thirteenth century that had laid beneath in ruins for a number of centuries. As a result of this chance finding, further excavations unravelled more objects of worship including a stone object representing the phallus of Siva known as the Pathur Siva-lingam. This Siva-lingam was reinstated as an object of worship in the central sanctum of the excavated temple.

Save for an appearance as a witness in criminal investigations in India, the fate of Ramamoorthi is unrecorded by the Court of Appeal. It is one of the 'pricks' in the story, the *punctum*, or a loose end. Is he deemed complicit in the theft of the statue? Does he return to his hut? Is he rewarded for his labour? Unlike the status of Western travellers who discovered new territory, Ramamoorthi's discovery is simply incidental to the proceedings. He names and claims nothing and the story moves on, leaving him behind for dust. The Pathur Siva-Natarja, now removed from the grounds of the temple, was put on the black-market and exchanged hands among knowing recipients until the Bumper Development Corporation bought it in good faith from a London dealer. It was after the statue had been sent by

Bumper to the British Museum for appraisal that it was seized by the Metropolitan Police. The initial action brought by the Bumper Corporation against the Commissioner of Police of the Metropolis claimed the return of the Natarja and damages. The trial judge felt bound to consider whether any other claimants had a title to the statue superior to that of Bumper. As a result of the trial judges verdict Bumper's appeal sought to contradict claims from five other parties: first, the Union of India; second, the state of Tamil Nadu; third, the custodian of the Temple on his own behalf; fourth, the custodian of the temple on behalf of the temple; and fifth, *the Siva-lingam*, the stone phallus. It is the latter two potential claimants, the temple and the *Siva-lingam*, that interests us and the court. It is, according to jurisprudence of *locus standii*, the 'novel question'. Everything hinges on the question of legal personality and the comity of nations. According to Purchas LJ, legal personality being the creation of the law, might well be bestowed upon such inanimate entities as the University of London. An institution is an incorporated aggregate of human beings; but the existence of a human being is not the condition of granting legal personality. As such a temple, and arguably by extension the *Siva-lingam* could well be accorded *locus standii* in order to sue in an English court for recovery. The notion that a temple or *lingam* is a foreign entity, or an entity entitled to rights only under foreign laws is no bar to bringing a claim. The principle of the comity of nations, as long as it doesn't interfere with public policy, enables the court to recognize such entitlements that exist in India, or in the state of Tamil Nadu.

The decision seems to smack of rank spiritualism. However, what is being granted involves a reduction of excess according to two levels of analysis. First, the recognition that a temple or a divinity is a legal personality essentially diminishes the power of the divine. That is not surprising under a secular order. The same reasoning applies in India. Second, the question of Hindu law that recognizes these entities as having legal entitlements must be treated as a question of fact rather than a question of law. That is to say that inquiry into the jurisprudence of the Indian courts is a matter to be presented by expert witnesses and does not form part of the job description of English judges.

The fear and consequent denigration of Oriental religions described by early travellers to India such as Sir Thomas Roe and Reverend Edward Terry have now been exorcised. Neither do such fantasms hold any power of seduction. What was once considered to exceed the normative values of Occidental civilization have now become 'incorporated' (according to the proper judicial sense of the term), and its laws turned into questions of fact. Indeed, such signs of excess are not merely commodified. They have become part of corporate culture; the necessary accoutrements required to display taste in order to counter attacks that the 'city' is a culturally impoverished, money obsessed, de-humanized factory.

From images of the landless coolie who labours in intimacy with dusty fields, to the hyper-clean offices of global corporations, the excavation of the *Siva-lingam* seems to correspond to the death of the Orient as unimaginable threat and envy, as a source of the sublime or as providing a lending library of ritualistic forms. Nevertheless, it seems to me that two movements peculiar to twentieth century Occidentalism have managed to retain the juridical value of the fantasy of excess.

The first revolves around the late twentieth century phenomenon of Imperial nostalgia. Englishness is only ever Englishness by virtue of the melancholia of nostalgia. As Peter Ackroyd puts it: 'There is a word in Old English which belongs wholly to that civilization—"dustsceawung," meaning contemplation of dust. It is a true image of the Anglo-Saxon mind, or at least an echo of that consciousness which considered transience and loss to be part of the human estate.'[3] The political importance of the nostalgia industry has already formed the subject matter of post colonial theory cultural studies and sociology concerned with Thatcherism.[4] However, the claim here is that the longing implicit in Imperial nostalgia performs a vital function necessary to the colonization of subjectivity. It is through such nostalgia that the fantasy of excess lives on. The examples are too numerous; Paul Scott's *Raj Quartet* centres on the scene in which an English woman is gang raped by a group of Indian radicals. More interestingly, the film version of E.M Forster's *A Passage to India* revolves around a similar rape scene and the subsequent trial of Aziz the suspect. And it is against the false memory of this excess that the modern subject attempts to behave in a manner congruent with all the repressive values of civilization. The pleasures of nostalgia reinforce those pleasures necessary to the colonization of legal subjectivity. What emerges is a sense that the ideal subject is the subject who lives according to the principle of the rule of law. This is particularly so in the film version of *A Passage to India* where the audience are asked to sympathize with Fielding whose sense of *noblesse oblige*, his friendship with Aziz, derives from his legally defined sense of fairness. This nostalgia is not the nostalgia described by Mircea Eliade.[5] It is not the nostalgia for a primordial epoch in which man can appreciate himself as a totality of rational equipment and primitive desires. Rather this is a nostalgia for that period in which the fantasies of Eastern excess provided a set of co-ordinates against which legal subjectivity could be measured, fealty strengthened. It can be no mere coincidence that the rise in Imperial or colonial nostalgia—the films, the exhibitions, the furniture—runs contemporaneously with the crisis of Western legality and legitimacy.

The second phenomenon that I suspect has overtaken the function of Eastern excess is Freud's discovery of the unconscious. All the features of formlessness, the nightmares, the hallucinations, the call to explore and analyze the hidden depths of subjective life correspond to the features and fantasies of Oriental excess. The idea of the unconscious formulation of subjectivity in which excess fights against conscious pleasure perfectly encapsulates the concluding theme of this book; that Oriental excess is firmly incorporated into the domain of legal subjectivity.

Dust, signifier of death, the fulfillment of fate, seems to be an appropriate metaphor for the destiny of the fantasy of excess. It signifies death, the state of all returns in the Christian scheme of things. But it also signifies also a kind of vaporous and melancholic persistence.

Notes

Preface

1 During the final stages of preparing the manuscript for the book, my attention was drawn to an already existing and beautifully written argument uncovering the topographies of excess in seventeenth century travels to India: Pramod K. Nayar, 'Marvellous Excesses: English Travel Writing and India, 1608–1727' in *The Journal of British Studies* 44 pp213–38. Having read the article I am convinced that substantial and fundamental theoretical differences distinguish my work from his. For instance, Nayar institutes an actual and historically contingent split between the admiration and denigration of Oriental excess. While denigration and envy are treated in my book under two separate chapters, my argument holds that these two twin emotional strategies are coincidental. Furthermore, Nayar's argument, as I understand it, is something of an illustration of the orientalist discursive practices that attempt to deal with and understand India. While sympathetic to this, I would stress that the purpose of my argument is to uncover an unwritten period in the history of desire and legal subjectivity.

1 Introduction: the Colonization of the Legal Subject

1 Slavoj Zizek, *The Metastases of Enjoyment* (London: Verso, 1994) p54.
2 See Russell Smandych, 'History, Theory and the Cultural Imperialism'of Law' *Working Paper Series* (Griffith University, Socio-legal Research Centre, 2000). On the distortions of Western statecraft through colonial expansion see M.A. Mahmoud, *The Manipulation of Statehood, the Highest Stage of Imperialism*

(The Hague, 1969). See also Ranajit Guha, *Dominance Without Hegemony; History and Power in Colonial India* (Cambridge, Mass: Harvard, 1997). On the transfer of institutions across jurisdictions, see Alan Watson, *Legal Transplants; an Approach to Comparative Law* (Edinburgh: Scottish Academic Press, 1974).

3 The literature on colonial discursive strategies and subjectivity is vast. For an excellent introduction see Robert J.C. Young, *Postcolonialism: An Historical Introduction* (Oxford: Blackwell, 2001). See also Ann Laura Stoler, *Race and the Education of Desire: Foucault's History of Sexuality and the Colonial Order of Things* (Durham, NC: Duke University Press, 1996).

4 Edward Said, for example, admits that law was 'an occupation with symbolic significance for the history of Orientalism': Edward Said, *Orientalism* (Harmondsworth: Penguin, 1995) p78.

5 On the effects of the English Education Act see Gauri Viswanathan, *Masks of Conquest: Literary Studies and British Rule in India* (New York: Columbia University Press, 1989).

6 Pierre Legendre, *Jouir du Pouvoir: Traite de la Bureaucratie* (Paris: Edition de Minuit, 1974).

7 Gayatri Chakravorty Spivak, 'Can the Subaltern Speak?' in Carry Nelson and Larry Grossburg (eds), *Marxism and the Interpretation of Culture* (Chicago: University of Chicago Press, 1988).

8 Marcel Mauss, in M. Carruthers, S. Collins, S. Lukes (eds), *The Category of the Person, Anthropology, Philosophy, History* (Cambridge: Cambridge University Press, 1985).

9 On the use of the *ius gentium* in this context see Richard Waswo 'The Formation of Natural Law to Justify Colonialism' *New Literary History* 24.4 (1996) 743–59.

10 On the heretical position of Christianity within modernity see Slavoj Zizek, *The Puppet and the Dwarf* (London: MIT Press, 2003).

11 Legal anthropologists, for example, have tended towards an analysis of legal pluralism as a form of governmentality. Sally Engle Merry, 'Law, Jurisprudence and Social Thought: Colonialism, Postcolonialism and Legal Theory' in *Political and Legal Anthropology Review*, May 1994, Vol 17, No 1, pp95–100.

12 Max Weber, in H.H. Gerth and C. Wright Mills (eds and trans), *From Max Weber; Essays in Sociology* (London: Routledge & Kegan Paul, 1974) p185.

13 Ibid at pp76–77.

14 Sigmund Freud, in James Strachey (ed) *Civilization and its Discontents* (London: Hogarth Press, 1973) at p11.

15 Raymond Williams, 'Civilization' in *Keywords: A Vocabulary of Culture and Society* (London: Fontana Press, 1976) pp57–60.

16 Weber, op. cit., n12 at p185.

17 Rudyard Kipling, 'The Conversion of Aurelian McGoggin' in *Plain Tales from the Hills* (London: Penguin, 1990) at p118.

18 Ibid at p121.

19 *Calvin's case* 1608 7 *Coke Report* 1A.

20 Peter Fitzpatrick, *The Mythology of Modern Law* (London: Routledge, 1992) p110.
21 On the current common law jurisprudence regarding the status and comity of foreign law see the judgment of Purchas LJ in *Bumper Development Corporation Ltd v Commisioner of Police* [1991] 4 All ER 638.
22 Norbert Elias, *The Civilizing Process* (Oxford: Blackwell, 1994) at p319.
23 Ibid at p385.
24 Ferdinand Braudel, *Civilization and Capitalism 15th–18th Centuries: The Perspective of the World,* vol 3 (London: Fontana Press, 1984) p65.
25 Manners as a measure of civilization is a meaning acquired in the seventeenth century. See Jean Starobinski, *La Remedie dans le Mal: Critique et Legitimation de l'Artifice a l'Age des Lumieres* (Paris: Gallimard, 1989).
26 Weber, op. cit., n12 at p216.
27 For commentary on this aspect of Roman Law see Richard Waswo, 'The Formation of Natural Law to Justify Colonialism, 1539–1689', *New Literary History* 27.4 (1996) 743–59.
28 Jacques Derrida, 'The Animal that therefore I am', *Critical Inquiry* 28 2002 at 374.
29 Georges Bataille, *The Accursed Share,* vols ii and iii (New York: Zone Books, 1991) at p52.
30 Martha Nussbaum, *Hiding from Humanity: Disgust, Shame and the Law* (Princeton, NJ: Princeton University Press, 2004).
31 Sigmund Freud, *The Future of an Illusion* (London: Hogarth Press, 1970) at p12.
32 The Englishman as one embodying the rule of law is a theme often treated by E.M. Forster. See 'Reflections in India' in *The Prince's Tale and Other Collected Writings* (London: Penguin, 1998) pp242–51. More literary representations are to be found in E.M. Forster, *The Hill of Devi* (London: Penguin, 1998), and E.M. Forster, *A Passage to India* (Penguin Books, 1981). See also J.R. Ackerley, *Hindoo Holiday* (London: Penguin, 1983).
33 Condorcet, in Elias, op. cit., n22 at p42.
34 Elias, op. cit., n22 at p441.
35 'The law and repressed desire are one and the same thing'. Jacques Lacan, 'Kant with Sade' in 51 *October,* 1989, James Swenson (trans) pp55–75 at 68.
36 Anton Schutz, 'Legal Critique: Elements for a Genealogy', *Law and Critique* 2005 16: 71–93 at 78.
37 Ibid at 79.
38 Slavoj Zizek, *The Metastases of Enjoyment* (London: Verso, 1994) pp54–55.
39 Ibid at p64.
40 Slavoj Zizek, 'Against Human Rights', 2 *New Left Review* 34, 2005, p123.
41 Nasser Hussein, *The Jurisprudence of Emergency: Colonialism and the Rule of Law* (Ann Arbor: University of Michigan Press, 2003).
42 Freud op. cit., n31 at p11. Or as one recent novelist puts it in suitably melodramatic terms: 'Nothing is more frightening than no rules; people will

cherish the worst rules as long as they can avoid the prospect of a sky that spits in their face for no reason'. Tibor Fischer, *The Collector Collector* (London: Vintage Press, 1998) p39.

2 Plato and Orientalism

1 Voltaire, 'Zadig' in *Candide and Zadig* (Konemann: Kolne, 1998) p34.
2 'The transgression does not deny the taboo but transcends it and completes it', George Bataille, *Eroticism* (London: Marion Boyars, 1987) p63.
3 The principle of *agathon* as 'the good beyond essence' is discussed by Jean-Luc Nancy, 'Gift, Desire, *Agathon*' in J. Librett (trans), *Sense of the World* (Minneapolis: University of Minnesota Press, 1988) p50.
4 Michel Foucault, *The Use of Pleasure: The History of Sexuality*, vol 2, Robert Hurly (trans) (London: Viking, 1985) p70.
5 Plato, *The Laws* (London: Penguin, 1986) 2:672.
6 Euripides, *The Bacchae* (London: Penguin, 1986) 797–99.
7 Ibid at 745–48.
8 While this proposition constitutes an ethical theory of conduct it should not be confused with hedonism. Although, it should be noted that for Epicurus, pleasure must be guided by reason and prudence.
9 Cicero, *De Finibus* (Harvard: Loeb, 1999) 5:23.
10 Stephen Orgel, *The Illusion of Power: Political Theatre in the English Renaissance* (Los Angeles: University of California, 1991).
11 There are of course a number of accounts. Among the more frequently referenced are Captain Thomas Williamson, *Oriental Field Sports being a Complete, Detailed and Accurate description of Wild Sports of the East* (London: W. Bulmer, 1805); Charles Doyley, *The European in India* (London: J.F. Dove, 1813); R.V. Vernede (ed), *British Life in India* (Calcutta: Oxford University Press, 1997). Charles Allen, *Plain Tales from the Raj* (London: Futura 1975). For more analytical accounts see, Denis Kincaid, *British Social Life in India 1608–1937* (London: Routledge Kegan & Paul, 1973); Dale Kennedy, *The Magic Mountains: Hill Stations and the British Raj* (Berkeley: University of California Press, 1996).
12 Mikael Bakhtin, *Rabelais and His World*, Helene Iswolsky (trans) (Bloomington: Indiana University Press, 1993).
13 Stallybrass and White, *The Politics and Poetics of Transgression* (Ithica: New York University Press, 1986) p292.
14 Edward Muir, *Ritual in Early Modern Europe* (Cambridge: Cambridge University Press, 1997).
15 Georges Bataille, *The Accursed Share, vol 2* (New York: Zone, 1991) p90. Bataille argues that the festival is not 'a return by man to his vomit', p91.
16 Ibid at p94.
17 Ibid at p119.
18 'civilization arises in and as play': Johan Huizinga, *Homo Ludens* (London: Paladin, 1970) p198.

19 Slavoj Zizek, *The Metastases of Enjoyment* (London: Verso, 1994) p55.
20 Plato, *The Laws* (London: Penguin, 1986) 2: 674.
21 Plato, *The Republic* (London: Penguin, 1987) at 9:8:7, paras 559 d–e.
22 Plato, *Philebus* (Indiana: Hackett Publishing, 1993) at 45d–e. Also, 'The desire for a more varied and luxurious diet is . . . physically harmful and psychologically damaging to intelligence and self-discipline'. *The Republic*, ibid at 9:8:7, para 559 b.
23 Plato, *The Republic* (London: Penguin, 1987) at 9:8:9, para 571 c.
24 Ibid at 9:8:9, para 583.
25 Ibid at 9:8:7, para 558 d. In *Philebus*, op. cit., n22, Plato distinguishes between pleasures which are 'unmixed' or which have not been preceded by a sense of craving, and those which are mixed, or which satisfy the appetite.
26 Plato, *Philebus*, op. cit., n22 at 52e.
27 Lucretius, *De Rerum Natura* (Harvard: Loeb, 1995) Bk V.
28 'enjoyment as such emerges only in this surplus, because it is constitutively an excess. If we subtract surplus we lose enjoyment itself': Slavoj Zizek, *Sublime Object of Ideology* (London: Verso, 1989) p52.
29 Sigmund Freud, 'Totem and Taboo' in *The Origins of Religion* (London: Penguin, 1990) p203.
30 Plato, *The Laws* (London: Penguin, 1986) at 2: 573 d–e.
31 See for example, Waller R. Newell, *Ruling Passions: The Erotics of Statecraft in Platonic Political Philosophy* (Lanham, MD: Rowman and Littlefield, 2000). Leo Strauss, *On Tyranny* (Ithica: Cornell University Press, 1968).
32 Plato, *The Laws* (London: Penguin, 1986) 2: 575 a.
33 Foucault, op. cit., n4 at p81.
34 Pierre Legendre in Peter Goodrich (ed), *Law and the Unconscious: A Legendre Reader*, P. Goodrich, A. Pottage, and A. Schutz (trans) (London: Macmillan, 1997) p113.
35 Ibid at p127.
36 Ibid.
37 Plato, *The Laws* (London: Penguin, 1986) 3:5.
38 Ibid at 3:5: 695.
39 Tertullian, *Apologeticus de Spectaculis* (Harvard: Loeb, 1984) 9:16. See also Minucius Felix, *Octavius* (Harvard: Loeb, 1984) 31.3.
40 Plato, *The Republic* (London: Penguin, 1987) 9: 8: 561 c.
41 Ibid at 9: 9: 574 e.
42 Ibid at 9: 9: 575 b.
43 Ibid at 9: 8: 560 b.
44 Homer, *The Odyssey*, T.E. Lawrence (trans) (Oxford: Oxford University Press, 1991) Bk 9.
45 Alfred, Lord Tennyson, *The Lotos-Eaters* (Oxford: Clarendon, 1947) pp45–50.
46 Georges Didi-Huberman, 'The Molding Image: Genealogy and the Truth of resemblance' in Pliny's *Natural History*, Bk 35, 1–7. Costas Douzinas and

Lynda Nead (eds), *Law and the image: The authority of Art and the Aesthetics of Law* (Chicago: University of Chicago Press, 1999) pp71–88.

47 Pliny, *Natural History*, Bk 33, para 148 cited in Didi-Huberman, op. cit., n46 at p86.

48 Piyel Haldar, 'The Function of the Ornament in Quintilian, Alberti, and Court Architecture' in Douzinas and Nead, op. cit., n46. See also, Roland Barthes, 'The Old Rhetoric: an Aide-Memoire' in *The Semiotic Challenge* (New York: Hill and Wang, 1988) at p29.

49 On the juridical question of genealogy see generally the works of Pierre Legendre, *Law and the Unconscious*, op. cit., n34.

50 Aristotle, *Politics*, George Barker (trans) (Oxford: Oxford University Press, 1998) 1:3.

51 Ibid at 5:11.

52 Ibid.

53 Ibid at 1:6.

54 Ibid at 5:10.

55 Slavoj Zizek, *On Belief* (London: Routledge, 2001).

56 Jean-Luc Nancy, 'Human Excess' in *Being Singular Plural* (Stanford: Stanford University Press, 2000) p180.

57 On the theory of misrecognition see Jacques Lacan, 'What is a picture' in *The Four Fundamental Concepts of Psychoanalysis* (London: Hogarth Press, 1977).

58 Alain Grosrichard, *The Sultan's Court, European Fantasies of the East*, Liz Heron (trans) (London: Verso, 1998) px.

59 Ibid at pp30–31.

60 Charles de Secondat, Baron de Montesquieu, *Persian Letters* (Indiana: Hackett, 1999), Letter 103.

61 Ibid.

62 Ibid, Letter 136.

63 Ibid, Letter 102.

64 Ibid, Letter 122.

65 Ibid, Letter 24.

66 Louis Marin, *Portrait of the King*, Martha Houle (trans) (London: Macmillan, 1988) pp215–16.

67 Ibid at 219.

68 The political theology of subjectivity under absolutism is a concern of Bodin. A useful contextual discussion is to be found in Etienne Balibar, Barbara Cassin, Alain de Libera, 'Subject', David Macey (trans) in 138 *Radical Philosophy* 2006, pp15–41.

69 See Nasser Hussein, *The Jurisprudence of Emergency: Colonialism and the Rule of Law* (Ann Arbor: Michigan, 2003).

70 Edward Said, *Orientalism* (Harmondsworth: Penguin, 1995) p78.

71 Ibid at pp113–23.

72 Ibid at p21.

73 Ibid at p92.

74 Hegel, *Phenomenology of Spirit*, A.V. Miller (trans) (Oxford: Oxford University Press, 1977) para 195.
75 Ibid at para 192.
76 Ibid at para 195.
77 Anton Shutz, 'Desiring Society: Autopoesis Beyond the Paradigm of Mastership' in (1994) *Law and Critique* vol V No 2 at 149–64.
78 J.N. Findlay, 'Analysis of the Text' in Hegel, *Phenomenology of Spirit*, op. cit., n74 at p523.
79 Thomas Babington, Lord Macauley, 'Minute on Indian Education' (February 2, 1835) in Barbara Harlow and Mia Carter (eds), *Imperialism and Orientalism* (Oxford: Blackwell, 1999) pp56–62.
80 Charles Trevelyan, *On the Education of the People of India* (London: Orient Longman, 1838).
81 Karl Marx, 'The Future Results of the British Rule in India' in Marx and Engels, *On Colonialism* (London: Lawrence and Wishart, 1976) pp81–87 at 82.
82 Gayatri Chakravorty Spivak, 'Time and Timing: Law and History' in *Chronotypes; the Construction of Time* (Palo Alto, CA: Stanford University Press, 1991).
83 Georges Vigarello, 'The Upward Training of the Body from the Age of Chivalry to Courtly Civility' Ughetta Lubin (trans) in Michael Feher, Ramona Nadaff, and Nadia Tazi (eds), *Fragments for a History of the Human Body, Part 2* (New York: Zone, 1989).

3 The Sultan's Enjoyment

1 Anonymous, 'Vasco da Gama' in Samuel Purchas (ed), *Hakluytus Posthumus, or Purchas His Pilgrims Contayning a History of the World in Sea Voyages and Land Travells by Englishmen and others*, 20 vols (Glasgow: MacLehose, 1905–1907) at 2:1: 70–71.
2 One of the most extraordinary representations of the East as a dream world is Robert Irwin, *Arabian Nightmare* (Harmondsworth: Penguin, 1988).
3 Stephen Greenblatt, *Marvellous Possessions: the Wonder of the New World* (Chicago: University of Chicago Press, 1991) p20.
4 Alain Grosrichard, *The Sultan's Court: European Fantasies of the East*, Liz Heron (trans) (London: Verso, 1998).
5 'The apology for crime only pushes him to the indirect avowal of law', Jacques Lacan, 'Kant with Sade', 51 *October* 1989, at p74.
6 I am borrowing the metaphor of the frock coat from Georges Bataille's rumination on formlessness in Georges Bataille, Allan Stoekl (ed and trans), *Visions of Excess: Selected Writings 1927–1939* (Minneapolis: University of Minnesota Press, 1985) at p31.
7 Charles de Secondat, Baron de Montesquieu, in A.M. Cohler, H. Stone and B. Miller (eds), *The Spirit of the Laws* (Cambridge: Cambridge University Press, 1989) at 3:8.
8 'It is true that nature would not demand any restrictions of instinct from us,

she would let us do as we liked; but she has her own particularly effective method of restricting us. She destroys us-coldly, cruelly, relentlessly and possibly through the very things that occasioned our satisfaction. It was precisely because of these dangers with which nature threatens us that we came together and created civilization.' Sigmund Freud, *The Future of an Illusion*, James Strachey (trans) (London: Hogarth Press, 1970) p11.

9 Nicolo di Conti, R. Major (ed), *The Travels of Nicolo Conti in India in the 15th century being a collection of narratives of voyages to India* (London: Haklyut Society, 1858) p42. See also, Kate Teltscher's discussion of the reverend Edward Terry, in Kate Teltscher *India Inscribed*, pp18–20.

10 Megasthenes in John Watson McCrindle, *Ancient India as described by Ktesias the Knidian, Megasthenes and Arrian* (London: Trubner & Co, 1877) p70.

11 Thomas Roe, 'Observations collected out of the Journall of Sir Thomas Roe, Knight, Lord Ambassador from His Majestie of Great Britain, to the Great Mogul' in Samuel Purchas, *Hakluytus Posthumus*, op. cit., n 1 at 4:16:320.

12 James Forbes, *Oriental Memoirs, Selected from a Series of Familiar Letters Written During Seventeen Years Residence in India*, 2 Vols (New Dehli: Gian Publishing House, 1988) at 2:285.

13 Ibid at 2:288.

14 Ibid at 1:234.

15 Ibid at 2:245.

16 See Gerard Pommier, 'From the Gods to Monotheism, from Demons to the Devil; An Examination of Biblical Texts Concerning the Singularization of the Devil, in the Light of Freudian Metapsychology', in *Jouvert* (http://social.chass.ncsu.edu/jouvert/v3i12/pommie.htm) pp1–19.

17 Captain William Hawkins, 'His Relations' in Purchas, *Hakluytus Posthumus*, op. cit., n1 at 3:4:39.

18 Forbes, *Oriental Memoirs*, op. cit., n12 at 2:458. Forbes cites a letter from Tipoo Sultan to General Macleod justifying the cruelty 'killing and slaying, and bravery, and heroism, and holy war, and the destruction of infidels, and the arts which belong to the gallant and the brave, have descended as an hereditary right to us from our apostle' 2:257.

19 di Conti, *The Travels of Nicolo Conti*, op. cit., n9.

20 William Finch, 'Observations of William Finch, Merchant' in Purchas, *Hakluytus Posthumus*, op. cit., n1 at 4:3: 54. Compare with the following passages: 'They keepe an idoll, which they call Matta, visited yeerly by many thousands of the Indians who out of devotion cut off part of their tongues, to make a sacrifice for it.' Reverend Edward Terry, 'A relation of a Voyage to the Eastern India' in Purchas, *Hakluytus Posthumus*, op. cit., n1 at 9:6: 14. 'Idols are black and have clawes of brass with long nayles, and some ride upon peacocks and other foules which be evill-favoured with long hauke's bils . . . [their mouths are monstrous], their eares gilded, and full of jewels, their teeth and eyes of gold, silver and glasse, some having one thing in their eyes and some another'. Ralph Fitch, in William Foster (ed), *Early travels in India 1583–1619*

(Oxford: Oxford University Press, 1921) pp21–23. 'The King of Calicut and his people are given to idolatry, and serving the Devil: he hath a chapel in his palace . . . In the midst of the chapel is a seat of majesty made of copper, and also a devil of copper sitting on it: this devil hath on its head a crown, after the manner of the Bishop of Rome; but this hath overplus four horns, his mouth gaping, with four notable teeth, a deformed nose, louring and grim eyes, a threatening look, crooked hands like a flesh hook, and feet not much unlike the feet of a cock. They sacrifice a cock to him once a week.' Forbes, *Oriental Memoirs*, op. cit., n12 at 1: pp415–16.

21 Forbes, *Oriental Memoirs*, op. cit., n12 at 1:10.

22 On death and excess, see George Bataille, *Visions of Excess: Selected Writings 1927–1939* (Minneapolis: University of Minnesota Press, 1985).

23 Reverend Edward Terry, in William Foster(ed), *Early Travels in India 1583–1619* (Oxford: Oxford University Press, 1921) at pp316–17.

24 Ibid at p321.

25 Thomas Roe, in Purchas, *Hakluytus Posthumus*, op. cit., n1 at 4:16:449.

26 Ibid at 4:16:386.

27 Thomas Roe, in Purchas, *Hakluytus Posthumus*, op. cit., n1 at 4:16:453. Also 'not for any zeal he had to Christianity; but to disinherit these Children; to make these Children hatefull to all Moores, as Christians are odious in their sight'. Captain William Hawkins, 'His Relations' in Purchas, *Hakluytus Posthumus*, op. cit., n1 at 3:4:42.

28 William Finch, in *Hakluytus Posthumus*, op. cit., n1 at 4:3:39.

29 Niccolao Manucci, *Memoirs of the Mogul Court* (pub. 1708), Michael Edwards (ed) (London: Folio Society, 1958) at p178.

30 Francois Bernier, 'History of the States of the Great Moghul' in *Travels in the Moghul Empire 1656–1668* (London: Archibold Constable, 1891) 1–115 at p88.

31 Edmund Burke, *Reflections on the Revolution in France, 1790* (London: Penguin, 1968) pp97–107.

32 E.F. Oaten, *European Travellers in India* (London: Kegan Paul, 1902) at p41.

33 Plato, *The Laws* (London: Penguin, 1986) 3:4:145.

34 Forbes, *Oriental Memoirs*, op. cit., n12 at 3:419.

35 Manucci, *Memoirs of the Mogul Court*, op. cit., n29 p35.

36 Ibid at p37.

37 Ibid at p36.

38 Reverend Terry, in William Foster (ed), *Early Travels in India 1583–1619*, op. cit., n20 at p311.

39 Bernier, *Travels in the Moghul Empire*, op. cit., n30 at pp273–74.

40 Forbes, *Oriental Memoirs*, op. cit., n12 at 1:250.

41 K.S. Lal, *The Mughal Harem* (New Dehli: Aditya Prakashan, 1988) at p58.

42 Thomas Coryate, 'Certaine Observations' in *Hakluytus Posthumus*, op. cit., n1 4:17: 234.

43 Manucci, *Memoirs of the Mogul Court* op. cit., n29 at p34.

44 Ibid at p33. This theme is well analysed by Alain Grosrichard, *The Sultan's Court*, op. cit., n4 who in focusing on the Turkish seraglios notes that tyrannical power rests with the Queen Mother, or with the guardian eunuchs. See also Leslie Pierce, *The Imperial Harem: Women and Sovereignty in the Ottoman Empire* (Oxford: Oxford University Press, 1993).
45 Manucci, *Memoirs of the Mogul Court* op. cit., n29 at p62.
46 Grosrichard, *The Sultan's Court*, op. cit., n4 at p155.
47 Thomas Roe, in Purchas, *Hakluytus Posthumus*, op. cit., n1 at 4:16:332.
48 Ibid.
49 Ibid at 4:16:333.
50 de Secondat, Baron de Montesquieu, *The Spirit of the Laws*, op. cit., n6 3:8.
51 Forbes, *Oriental Memoirs*, op cit., n12 1: 234.
52 Ibid.
53 Oaten, *European Travellers in India*, op. cit., n32 at p99.
54 Alexander Dow, *The History of Hindustan* (London: Nourse, 1772) pvii.
55 Anton Schutz, 'Desiring Society: Autopoiesis Beyond the Paradigm of Mastership' (1994) *Law and Critique* Vol V No 2 149–64. Or as Zizek puts it: 'Enjoyment is provided by an awareness that people were living in a universe absolved of uncertainty, since the system possessed an answer to everything, but above all the enjoyment of the very stupidity of the system—a relish in the emptiness of the official ritual.: *The Metastases of Enjoyment* (London: Verso, 1994) p 64.
56 Thomas Roe, in Purchas, *Hakluytus Posthumus*, op. cit., n1 at 4:16:324. The obesiences, or tessilims are a feature of these rituals that are mentioned throughout Roe's chronicle. It obviously jars with his national pride that he should show a foreign monarch any sign of subservience (see 4:16: 327), and on the obligatory giving of presents 4:16:330.
57 Forbes, *Oriental Memoirs*, op. cit., n12 2:514.
58 Athanasius Nikiten, 'Travels of Athanasius Nikiten of Twer', Count Wielhorsky (trans) in R. Major (ed), *India in the Fifteenth Century being a Collection of Narratives of Voyages to India* (London: Haklyut Society, 1857) at pp14–15.
59 Reverend Edward Terry, William Foster (eds), *Early Travels in India 1583–1619*, op. cit., n20 at p312.
60 Duarte Barbarosa, in Oaten, *European Travellers in India*, op. cit., n32 at p99.
61 Grosrichard, *The Sultan's Court*, op. cit., n4 at p19.
62 William Hawkins, in Purchas, *Hakluytus Posthumus*, op. cit., n1 at 3:4:32–33.
63 Bernier, *Travels in the Moghul Empire*, op. cit., n30 at p236.
64 Ibid at p238.
65 'Animals in general, mankind in particular' is how one eighteenth century East India Company administrator and orientalist would define the 'Gentoos', or Hindus. See Nathaniel Halhed, *A code of Gentoo, or the Ordinations of the Pundits* (London: Nourse, 1776) pxiv.
66 Reverend Edward Terry, in Foster, *Early Travels in India*, op. cit., n20 p326.
67 Dow, *The History of Hindustan*, op. cit., n54 at pxvi.

68 Jean-Baptiste, Baron Tavernier, *Travels in India, 1676*, William Crook (ed) (New Dehli: Munshiram Manoharlal, 1995) at 1:125–6.
69 Bernier, *Travels in the Moghul Empire*, op. cit., n30 at pp235–36.
70 Durbars, during this period, were essentially the royal law courts presided over by the Sultan to entertain petitions and to give commands, 'where Law and Justice was administered according to the custome of the Countrey'. William Bruton, in Purchas, *Hakluytus Posthumus*, op. cit., n1 at 5:5:51.
71 Thomas Roe, in Purchas, *Hakluytus Posthumus*, op. cit., n1 at 4:16:440. Consider also his comment *'Ille mervere sed quid tu ut adesses'* 4:16:328.
72 Forbes, *Oriental Memoirs*, op. cit., n12 at 2:185.
73 William Hawkins, in Purchas, *Hakluytus Posthumus*, op. cit., n1 at 3:4:38.
74 Reverend Edward Terry, in Foster (ed), *Early Travels*, op. cit., n20 at p27.
75 Bernier, *Travels in the Moghul Empire*, op cit., n30 at p13.
76 Forbes, *Oriental Memoirs*, op. cit., n12 at 4:184.
77 Thomas Roe, in Purchas, *Hakluytus Posthumus*, op. cit., n1 at 4:16:327–28.
78 William Hawkins, in Purchas, *Hakluytus Posthumus*, op. cit., n1 at 3:4:46.
79 Thomas Roe, in Purchas, *Hakluytus Posthumus*, op. cit., n1 at 4:16:405.
80 Ibid at 4:16:325. The analogy to the theatre is used several times by Roe. The following description is contained in a letter sent to James I: 'I found him in Court, set above like a King in a Play, and all his nobles and myselfe below on stage covered with carpets; a just Theatre.' 4:16:441. More emphatically: 'And he sate in a place like a Theatre above, where the King sits in a play, and I was conducted foure steps up, just under him like a Stage, all on carpets; myselfe and all his great men were Actors, the Common people below gazing on', 4:16:444.
81 Thomas Roe, in Purchas, *Hakluytus Posthumus*, op. cit., n1 at 4:16:328.
82 Ibid at 4:16:333.
83 H. Verlest, *A View of the Rise, Progress and Present State of the English in Bengal* (London: Nourse, 1772) at p45.

4 Envy and Subjectivity in Orientalism

1 Ted Hughes 'Strong Feelings' in *Winter Pollen: Occasional Prose*, William Scammell (ed) (London: Faber and Faber, 1994) p33. Peter Ackroyd, *Albion: the Origins of the English Imagination* (New York: Doubleday, 2002) p281.
2 Charles de Secondat and Baron de Montesquieu, *Persian Letters* (Indiana: Hackett, 1999).
3 Melanie Klein's famous distinction between envy and jealousy is useful. Jealousy is directed towards achieving and possessing an object that belongs to a rival other. Envy is the desire to be the rival in order to have access to what they have. See Melanie Klein, *Envy and Gratitude and Other Works 1946–1963* (London; Vintage, 1998).
4 John Rawls, *A Theory of Justice* (Cambridge: Harvard University Press, 1971) at s25.

5 Aristotle, J.H. Freese (ed and trans), *The Art of Rhetoric* (Harvard: Loeb, 1926) 2:10.
6 Louis Marin, 'The Pleasures of Narration' in Catherine Porter (trans), *On Representation* (Stanford: Stanford University Press, 1994) p157.
7 Ibid at p158.
8 Thomas Roe, 'Observations collected out of the Journal of Sir Thomas Roe, Knight, Lord Ambassador from His Majestie of Great Britain, to the Great Mogul' in Samuel Purchas (ed), *Hakluytus Posthumus or Purchas, His Pilgrims Contayning a History of the World in Sea Voyages and Land Travells by Englishmen and others,* 20 vols (Glasgow: MacLehose 1905–1907) at 4:16:384.
9 Reverend Terry, 'A Relatione of a Voyage to the Easterne India' in Purchas, *Hakluytus Posthumus,* op. cit., n8 at 6:9:24.
10 James Forbes, *Oriental Memoirs, Selected from a Series of Familiar Letters Written During Seventeen Years Residence in India,* 2 Vols (New Delhi: Gian Publishing House, 1988), vol I, p254.
11 Ibid at 2: 240. The description of his garden is at 2:239–45.
12 Ibid at 2:239.
13 Norbert Elias, *The Civilizing Process* (Oxford: Blackwell, 2005) at p388.
14 Captain William Hawkins, 'His Relations' in Purchas, *Hakluytus Posthumus,* op. cit., n8 at 3:4:14.
15 E.F. Oaten, *European Travellers in India* (London: Kegan Paul, 1902) p142.
16 Thomas Roe, in Purchas, *Hakluytus Posthumus,* op. cit., n8 at 4:16:384.
17 Thomas Coryate, 'Certaine Observations' in *Hakluytus Posthumus,* op. cit., n8 at 4:17:478.
18 Ralph Fitch, cited in R. Masani, *Britain in India: An Account of British Rule in the Indian Subcontinent* (Oxford: Oxford University Press, 1965) p5.
19 The word 'orientalism', of course, need not be limited to a description of eighteenth and nineteenth century projections. It may be seen as a phrase in the overall long history of exoticism which has seduced the West to the point of engorged excitement. This cult of the exotic, as Phillipe Jullian notes, can be traced back to the classical Roman love of Egyptian and Persian decorative styles. In the long term it is possible to note a number of flashpoints and themes; the fetishization of Salome's dance during the middle ages, the Middle East of the Crusades, or the clothes that obsessed Watteau, Delacroix and Saint-Aubin. Twentieth century popular culture, of course, has been obsessed by stereotypical images evinced in films such as *Gunga Din, The Jungle Book, Arabian Nights, Carry On Up the Khyber,* and so on. For an overview with some analytical content, see Phillipe Jullian, *The Orientalist* (Oxford: Phaidon, 1977). Although slightly more limited in cultural scope, Gerard-Georges Lemaire, *The Orient in Western Art* (Cologne: Koneman, 2000) is a beautifully engaging survey of the influence of exoticism on Western culture.
20 Dennis Kincaid, *British Social Life in India: 1608–1937* (London: Routledge & Kegan Paul, 1973) p41.

21 'Sex . . . was only one of several forces [within the Imperial Harem] and, one of relatively little importance'. Leslie P. Pierce, *The Imperial Harem: Women and Sovereignty in the Ottoman Empire* (New York: Oxford University Press, 1993) p3.
22 Max Weber in H. Gerth and C. Wright Mills (eds), *From Max Weber: Essays in Sociology* (London: Routledge & Kegan Paul, 1974) at pp442–44.
23 Thomas Roe, in Purchas, *Hakluytus Posthumus*, op. cit., n8 4:16:375.
24 Ibid at 4:16:375–76. Contemporary analysis of the harem and seraglio is vast. On the patriarchal gaze of the colonizer and on the phantasm of the harem, see Malek Alloullah, *The Colonial Harem*, M. Godzich and W. Godzich (trans) (London: University of Minnesota Press, 1986).
25 Robert Orme, *Historical Fragments of the Mogul Empire, the Morattoes and English concerns in Indostan from 1659* (London: Nourse, 1787) p436.
26 Bernier, *Travels in the Moghul Empire, 1656–1668* (London: Archibold Constable, 1891) at pp267–68.
27 Ibid at p267.
28 James Forbes, *Oriental Memoirs, Selected from a Series of Familiar Letters Written During Seventeen Years Residence in India* (New Delhi: Gian Publishing House, 1988) at 2:258.
29 Slavoj Zizek, *The Metastases of Enjoyment* (London: Verso, 1994) p94.
30 Jacques Lacan, 'The Function of the Beautiful' in *The Ethics of Psychoanalysis: The Seminar of Jacques Lacan 1959–1960, Book VII*, Dennis Porter (trans) (London: Routledge, 1992) pp231–42 at p237.
31 Jacques Lacan, 'What is a Picture?' in *Four Fundamental Concepts of Psycho-Analysis*, Alan Sheridan (trans) (London: Hogarth Press, 1977) pp105–22 at p116.
32 Jacques Lacan, 'The Other and Psychosis' in *The Psychosis: The Seminar of Jacques Lacan, Book III 1955–1956*, Russell Grigg (trans) (London: Routledge, 1993) pp29–43 at p39.
33 Gilles Deleuze and Felix Guattari, *Anti-Oedipus: Capitalism and Schizophrenia* (Minneapolis: University of Minnesota Press, 1977) at p21.
34 Marin, 'The Pleasures of Narration' in *On Representation*, op. cit., n6 at p157.

5 *Ex Oriente Lex:* Orientalism and the Colonization of Sublime Enjoyment

1 Sir William Jones in Garland Cannon (ed), *The Letters of William Jones*, 2 vols (Oxford: OUP, 1970), letter l. 477 to John Shore, 2:785.
2 Michel Deguy, 'The Discourse of Exaltation' in Librett (ed), *Of the Sublime: Presence in Question* (New York: SUNY Press, 1993) p6.
3 See, for example, Jones, *Letters*, op. cit., n1, l. 391 to Charles Wilkins. Thomas Williamson, *The East India Vade Mecum*, 2 vols (London: J. Edwards, 1810); Phil Robinson, *In My Indian Garden* 1888 (Glasgow: MacLehose Press, 1888).

4 James Forbes, *Oriental Memoirs, Selected from a Series of Familiar Letters Written During Seventeen Years Residence in India* (New Dehli: Gian Publishing House, 1988) 1: 254.
5 Thomas Roe, 'Observations collected out of the Journall of Sir Thomas Roe, Knight, Lord Ambassador from His Majestie of Great Britain to the Great Mogul' in Samuel Purchas (ed), *Hakluytus Posthumus or Purchas, His Pilgrims Contayning a History of the World in Sea Voyages and Land Travells by Englishmen and others*, 20 vols (Glasgow: MacLehose, 1905–07) at 4:16:384. Compare the description of the same garden contained in Reverend Terry's notebooks: 'For places of pleasure they have curious gardens, planted with fruitfull Trees and delightfull Flowers, to which Nature daily lends a supply as that they never seeme to fade. In these they have pleasant Fountaynes to bathe in, and other delights by sundrie conveyances of water, whose silent murmure helps to lay their senses with the bonds of sleepe in the hot seasons of the day.' Reverend Edward Terry, 'A Relatione of a Voyage to the Easterne India' in Purchas, *Hakluytus Posthumus* at 4:6:24.
6 William Wordsworth, *The Prelude*, Bk VII, discussed in Saree Makdisi, *Romantic Imperialism* (Cambridge: Cambridge University Press, 2001).
7 Slavoj Zizek, *The Sublime Object of Ideology* (London: Verso, 1989) p202. Zizek continues in more psychoanalytic terms: 'The sublime is beyond the pleasure principle . . . it is a paradoxical pleasure procured by displeasure itself' at 203.
8 Edmund Burke, 'A Philosophical Inquiry into the Origins of Our Ideas of the Sublime and Beautiful' in *The Portable Burke* (London: Penguin, 1999) p68.
9 Jacques Lacan, 'Drives and Lures' in *The Ethics of Psychoanalysis: the Seminar of Jacques Lacan Book VII* (London: Routledge, 1992) pp87–100 at p99. Elsewhere in the same seminar Lacan summarises pithily: 'Sublimate as much as you like; you have to pay for it with something. And this something is *jouissance*.' Jacques Lacan 'In the paradoxes of Ethics, or Have you acted in conformity with your desire?' pp311–24 at p322.
10 Jones, 2 *Asiatic Researches* (1792) at p20. Cited in John Drew, *India and the Romantic Imagination* (Oxford: Oxford University Press, 1987) p 197.
11 Forbes, *Oriental Memoirs*, op. cit., n4 at 2:240. The description of his garden is at 2: 239–45.
12 Burke, 'the Sublime and Beautiful,' op. cit., n 8 at p64.
13 Ibid.
14 Ibid at p71.
15 Sue Chaplin, 'How the Sublime comes to Matter; An Irigarayan Critique of Hobbes, Locke and Burke' in 2 *Feminist Legal Studies* (2000) 119–20 at 119.
16 Edward Said, *Orientalism: Western Concepts of the Orient* (London: Penguin, 1995).
17 Nathaniel Halhed, 'Preface' in *A Code of Gentoo Laws, or the Ordinations of the Pundits* (London: Nourse, 1776).
18 John Drew, *India and the Romantic Imagination* (New Delhi: Oxford University Press, 1998) p199.

19 Jones, 'On the Divine Inspiration of the Jewish Scriptures' in John Shore (Lord Teighnmouth) *Memoirs of the Life, Writings and Correspondence of Sir William Jones* (London: Hatchard, 1804) pp280–81. See also, Jones, 'Ninth Discourse on the Origin and Families of Nations' (1792) in *The Works of Sir William Jones* in 13 Volumes 3: 176. It is interesting to note the range of eighteenth century English works suggesting the influence of brahminism on ancient religious life in Britain. For a discussion, see Drew, *India and the Romantic Imagination*, op. cit., n18 at pp50–51.
20 See Michael J. Franklin, *Sir William Jones* (Cardiff: University of Wales Press, 1995). Franklin does suggest, however, that William Jones may have also initiated the society of the 'Druids of Cardigan'.
21 Jones, *Letters*, op. cit., n1 at l. 362 to Viscount Althorp. Also, 'By rising before the sun, I allot an hour every day to Sanscrit, and am charmed with knowing so beautiful a sister of Latin and Greek', l. 449 to John Macpherson.
22 Jones, *Letters*, op. cit., n1, l. 464 to Earl Spencer. The lines are in fact Jones's translation of a stanza from a Sanskrit poem.
23 Jones, *Letters*, op. cit., n1, l. 391 to Charles Wilkins.
24 Jones, 'Second Anniversary Discourse' in 1 *Asiatic Researches* (1784) at p22.
25 Jones, *Letters*, op. cit., n1, l. 382, to Patrick Russel.
26 Jones, 'Presidential Address' in 1 *Asiatic Researches* (1784) at p221.
27 Polybius, cited in Anthony Pagden, *Lords of all the World: Ideologies of Empire in Spain, Britain and France, c.1500–c.1800* (London: Yale University Press, 1998) p19.
28 Jones, 'A Discourse on the Institution of a Society, for Inquiring into the History, Civil and Natural, the Antiquities, Arts, Sciences, Literature of Asia, by the President, 1784' in *Works*, op. cit., n19 at 3:2.
29 Jones, *The Letters*, op. cit., n1, l. 445 to Robert Orme.
30 Jones, 'Third Anniversary Discourse' in 1 *Asiatic Researches* (1784) at p41.
31 Hodges, *Travels in India During the Years 1780, 1781, 1782 and 1783* (London: J. Edwards, 1794).
32 Jones, op. cit., n26 at p221.
33 Jones, 'Hymn to Ganges' in *Works*, op. cit., n19 at 6: 383. For a different analysis of the 'Hymn to Ganges' see Tejaswini Niranjana, *Siting Translation: History, Poststructuralism, and the Colonial Context* (Berkeley: University of California Press, 1992) p19.
34 Jones, 'Ode to Surya' in *Works*, op. cit., n19 at 6: 383.
35 Jones, 'Preface to the Institutes of Hindu Law; or the Ordinances of Menu according to the Gloss of Culluca comprising the Indian System of Duties, religious and civil' in *Works*, op. cit., n19 at 2:91.
36 Jones, *Letters*, op. cit., n1, l. 93 to Henry Albert Schultens.
37 Ibid, l. 447 to C.W. Boughton Rouse.
38 Jones, 'On the Gods of Greece, Italy and India, 1784' in *Works*, op. cit., n19 at 3: 344.

39 Jones, 'Preface to the Institutes of Hindu Law; or the Ordinances of Menu according to the Gloss of Culluca comprising the Indian System of Duties, religious and civil' in *Works*, op. cit., n19 at 2:76.
40 Ibid at 2:78.
41 Ibid at 2:76–77.
42 Jones, *Letters*, op. cit., n1, l. 447 to C.W. Boughton Rouse (it is pertinent, in this context that Boughton Rouse was then secretary to the Board of Control for India).
43 See Peter Goodrich, *Reading the Law. A Critical Introduction to Legal Method and Legal Technique* (Oxford: Blackwell, 1986).
44 *Calvin's Case* 1608 7 *Coke Report* 1A. In *De Laudibus Legum Anglicae* (1773 edn), Sir John Fortesque remarks 'I am convinced that our laws of England eminently excel, beyond the laws of all other countries' cited in Peter Goodrich, *Languages of Law: From Logics of Memory to Nomadic* Masks (London: Weidenfeld and Nicolson, 1990) at p212.
45 Halhed, 'Preface' in *Code of Gentoo Laws; or Ordinations of the pundits*, op. cit., n17 at p.ix.
46 Forbes, *Oriental Memoirs*, op. cit., n4 at 2:317.
47 Jones, 'Best Practicable System of Judicature' in *Letters*, op. cit., n1, l. 387 to Edmund Burke.
48 Jones, *Letters*, op. cit., n1, l. 485 to the Marquis of Cornwall.
49 Ibid at l. 558 to 2nd Earl Spencer. Consider, too, his remark that the 'three excellent things, which the ancients feigned to be the daughters of their supreme God, a good system of laws, a just administration of them, and a long peace will render this country a source of infinite advantage to Great Britain': l. 397 to William Pitt the Younger.
50 Jones, *Letters*, op. cit., n1, l. 443 to Patrick Russell.
51 Gayatri Chakravorty Spivak, 'Translator's Preface' in Jacques Derrida, *Of Grammatology*, Gayatri Chakrovarty Spivak (trans) (Baltimore: Johns Hopkins University Press, 1976).
52 John Strawson, 'Islamic Law and English Texts' in 6 *Law and Critique* 1 (1995) pp21–38 at p33.
53 Forbes, *Oriental Memoirs*, op. cit., n 4 at 2:318.
54 Jones, 'Preface to the Institutes of Hindu Law; or the Ordinances of Menu according to the Gloss of Culluca comprising the Indian System of Duties, religious and civil' in *Works*, op. cit., n19 at 2:75.
55 Jones, *Letters*, op. cit., n1, l. 383, to Earl Spencer.
56 Jones, *Letters*, op. cit., n1, l. 440 to Patrick Russell. See also l. 464 to Earl Spencer where he describes Menu as 'the first created man, many millions of years old'.
57 Daniel J. Boorstin, *The Mysterious Science of the Law: An Essay on Blackstone's Commentaries* (Chicago: Chicago University Press, 1996) at p45.
58 Jones, *An Essay on the Law of Bailments*, 1790 (Buffalo: William S. Hein, 1998 edn) at p173.

59 Jones, *Letters*, op. cit., n1, l. 485 to Lord Cornwall.
60 Jones, 'Second Anniversary Discourse 1785' in *Works*, op. cit., n19 3:42–44.
61 Jones, 'Charge to the Grand Jury 1785' in *Works*, op. cit., n19 at 3:3, p3.
62 Jones, *Letters*, op. cit., n1, l. 516 to John Shore at p835. The text Jones refers to is 'of law there can be no less acknowledged, than that her seat is the bosom of God, her voice the harmony of the world'. Richard Hooker, *Of the Laws of Ecclesiastical Polity* cited in *Letters*, p836.
63 Burke, 'the Sublime and Beautiful', op. cit., n8 at p 69.
64 Jean-Luc Nancy, 'The Sublime Offering' in J. Librett (ed), *Of the Sublime*, op. cit., n2 at p52.
65 Burke, 'The Sublime and Beautiful,' op. cit., n8 at p 65.
66 Friedrich Nietzsche, *The Anti-Christ*, Thomas Common (trans) (London: Allen & Unwin, 1930). For a pertinent analysis, see Adam Geary, 'The Fourth Book of the Legislator: Nietzsche and John Neville Figgis' in Peter Goodrich and Mariane Valverde (eds), *Nietzsche and Legal Theory: Half Written Laws* (New York: Routledge, 2005) at pp165–84.
67 Nietzsche, *The Anti-Christ*, op. cit., n66 at s.56. For comment, see Wendy Doniger, 'Introduction' in *The Laws of Manu* (London: Penguin 1991) at pxv.
68 Jones, *Letters*, op. cit., n1, l. 93 to Henry Albert Schultens.
69 Ibid, l.268 to Viscount Althorp.
70 Jones, 'Charge to the Grand Jury 1785' in *Works*, op. cit., n19 at 3:20.
71 Ibid at 3:20.
72 Grosrichard, *The Sultan's Court, European Fantasies of the East*, Liz Heron (trans) (London: Verso, 1998) pp92–93.
73 Jones, *Letters*, op. cit., n1, l. 383, to Earl Spencer.
74 Ibid, l. 372, to Earl Spencer.
75 Ibid, l. 558, to Earl Spencer.
76 Ibid, l. 483, to Henry Dundas.
77 Jones, 'Preface to the Institutes of Hindu Law; or the Ordinances of Menu according to the Gloss of Culluca comprising the Indian System of Duties, religious and civil' in *Works*, op. cit., n19 at 2:84.
78 Jones, *Letters*, op. cit., n1, l. 409 to John Macpherson.
79 Pierre Legendre, in Peter Goodrich (ed), *Law and the Unconscious: A Legendre reader*, Peter Goodrich, Alain Pottage and Anton Schutz (trans) (London: Macmillan, 1997) p262.
80 Jones, 'Ninth Discourse on the Origin and Family of Nations, 1792' in *Works*, op. cit., n19 at 3:62.
81 James Beattie, *Treatise* (1783) cited in Chaplin, op. cit., n15 at p120.
82 According to Jones, the 'laws of the ancient legislator are obscure when detached, yet clear when connected' in *Letters*, op. cit., n1, l. 584 to Edward Hay. It is precisely this process of finding connections that rationalizes the Oriental sublime spirit of Oriental law.

6 Anglican Pleasures in the Orient: Staging the Rule of Law

1 Thompson cited James Forbes, *Oriental Memoirs, Selected from a Series of Familiar Letters Written During Seventeen Years Residence in India* (New Delhi: Gian Publishing House, 1988), 4:71.
2 Jacques Alain Miller, 'Jeremy Bentham's Panoptic Device,' 41 *October* (1997) at p6.
3 Jeremy Bentham, *Works*, Vol 11 p72, cited ibid at p20
4 Slavoj Zizek, *The Sublime Object of Ideology* (London: Verso, 1989) pp186–87.
5 John Stuart Mill, 'Letter to E. Lytton Bulwer, 1836,' cited in Eric Stokes, *The English Utilitarians in India* (Oxford: Oxford University Press, 1989) at p241.
6 Bentham, 'Sanctio, in Latin was used to signify the act of binding, and, by a common grammatical transition, anything which serves to bind a man. According to a Latin grammarian, the import of the word is derived from the word sanguis, blood: because among the Romans, with a view to inculcate into the people a persuasion that such or such a mode of conduct would be rendered obligatory upon a man certain ceremonies were contrived by priests: in the course of which the blood of victims was made use of.' Jeremy Bentham, *An Introduction to the Principles of Morals and Legislation* (Oxford: Clarendon, 1996) at 3.2.147.
7 Ibid at 1:1:125.
8 Ibid at 3.2.147.
9 John Stuart Mill, 'Utilitarianism' in H.B. Acton (ed), *Utilitarianism, On Liberty and Considerations on Representative Government* (London: Dent, 1984) at p6.
10 Ibid at p13.
11 Ibid at p15.
12 Ibid at p413.
13 Ibid at p416.
14 Ibid at p418.
15 Stokes, *English Utilitarians*, op. cit., n5 at p13.
16 'To trade with civilised men is infinitely more profitable than to govern savages', Thomas Babington, Lord Macauley, 'Speech in Parliament on the Government of India Bill, 10 July 1833' in G. Young (ed), *Prose and Poetry* (Cambridge MA: Harvard UP, 1957) at pp716 and 719.
17 Thomas Babington, Lord Macauley, 'Minute of 2 February 1835' in *Prose and Poetry*, op. cit., n16 at 724.
18 Mill, 'Memorandum of the Improvements in the Administration of India during the past thirty years' cited in Stokes, *English Utilitarians*, op. cit., n5 at p259.
19 Parliamentary Papers, Moral and Material Progress Report, 1859–60 in Stokes, *English Utilitarians*, op. cit., n5, at p263.
20 See the *Civil Procedure Rules* (London: HMSO, 1999).
21 Stokes, *English Utilitarians*, op. cit., n5 at p275. See also Sir H. Verney Lovett, 'District administration in Bengal 1818–1858' in H.H. Ddodwell (ed), *The*

Cambridge History of India Vol 6 (Delhi: S. Chand, 1964). 'The magistrate may be considered the delegate of the ruling powers of the government, the collector its agent in everything that concerns its interests and the interests of those connected with it in the land; but the two duties are intimately connected and the function materially assist and affect one another.'

22 James Fitzjames Stephen cited in Stokes, *English Utilitarians*, op. cit., n5 at p279.
23 James Fitzjames Stephen, *Liberty, Equality and Fraternity* (London: Hatchard, 1872) at pp98–99.
24 Stokes, *English Utilitarians*, op. cit., n5 at p267.
25 Max Weber, pp234–67.
26 James Mill, *The History of British India*, 6 vols (London: Baldwin, Cradock & Joss, 1826) 5:513.
27 Fitzjames Stephen, cited in Stokes, *English Utilitarians*, op. cit., n5 at pp245–46.
28 Bentham, *Introduction*, op. cit, n6 at 2.11.136–37.
29 Ibid at 2.11.137.
30 Ibid.
31 Ibid at 2.14.143.
32 Ibid at 2.11.263.
33 Mill, 'Utilitarianism' op. cit., n 9 at p8.
34 Ibid at p10.
35 Ibid at pp8–9.
36 Uday Singh Mehta, *Liberalism and Empire: a Study in Nineteenth Century British Liberal Thought* (Chicago: University Chicago Press, 1999) at p92.
37 Stokes, *English Utilitarians*, op. cit., n5 at p14.
38 Daniel Bivona, *British Imperial Literature 1870–1940: Writing and the Administration of Empire* (Cambridge: Cambridge University Press, 1998).
39 Rudyard Kipling, 'The Conversion of Aurelian McGoggin' in *Plain Tales from the Hills* (London: Penguin 1990).
40 Adam Smith, 'The Wealth of Nations', 7:3 in P. Tuck (ed), *East India Company 1600–1858* (London: Routledge, 1998) document 23.
41 The original *firman* which granted the British possession of lands in Calcutta was presented to Gabriel Broughton, a company doctor in Surat who had cured Jehanara, the favourite daughter of Sha Jahan. See F. Yeats-Brown, *Indian Pageant* (London: Eyre and Spottiswoode, 1942) at p76.
42 Anonymous, 'A Few Remarks on Certain Draft Acts, Commonly called Black Acts' *Calcutta Review* 1846.
43 Bernard Cohn, 'Representing Authority in Colonial India' in Eric Hobsbawm and Terrence Ranger (eds), *The Invention of Tradition* (Cambridge: Cambridge University Press, 1983) pp165–209. Consider too, the reasons given by Joanne Punzo Waghorne, 'How very disappointing it must have been . . . to see the likes of the raja of Pudukkottai who ruled an area measured in square miles more capable of a grand show than this dowdy queen'. See *The Raja's*

Magic Clothes: Re-Visioning Kingship and Divinity in England's India (Penn: Penn State University Press, 1994) at p8.

44 Stokes, *English Utilitarians*, op. cit., n5 at p285.

45 James Fitzjames Stephen, *History of Criminal Laws of England*, 3 vols (London: Macmillan & Co, 1883) 3:345.

46 These incidents are given fuller historical treatment in R.C. Majumdar, *British Paramountcy and Indian Resistance* (Bombay: Bharatiya Vidya Bharan, 1963) pp11–20.

47 Forbes, *Oriental Memoirs*, op. cit., n1 at 2:45.

48 Ibid at 3:419–20.

49 Lord Valenta cited in Lord Curzon of Keddleston, *British Government in India: the Story of the Viceroys and Government Houses*, 2 vols (London: Cassell & Co, 1925) 1:71, emphasis added.

50 Stokes, *English Utilitarians*, op. cit., n5 at p17.

51 Ibid.

52 James Talboy Wheeler, *History of the Imperial Assemblage at Dehli held on 1st January 1877 to celebrate the assumption of the title of Empress of India by her Majesty the Queen including Historical Sketches of India and her Princes Past and Present* (London: Longmans, Green, Reader and Dyer) at p22.

53 Elizabeth Collingham, *Imperial Bodies: The Physical Experience of the Raj, c.1800–1947* (Cambridge: Polity, 2001) at pp133–34.

54 Viceroy Lytton, 'Speech on Proclamation Day, 1st January 1872' cited in Wheeler, *History of the Imperial Assemblage*, op. cit., n 52 at p84.

55 Thomas Metcalfe, *Ideologies of the Raj* (Cambridge: Cambridge University Press, 1997) at p77.

56 Cited in Cohn, *Representing Authority in Colonial India*, op. cit., n43 at p188.

57 Michael B. Caswell, 'Are Western Societies Characterised by the Rule of Law?' *Unpublished Paper* held with author.

58 For further detailed accounts see, 'The Procession of Indian Princes' in W.F.B. Laurie, *Sketches of Some Distinguished Anglo-Indians* (London: W.H. Allen, 1888) pp301–05. Also see 'Minute by the Viceroy on State Ceremonial and Costume in India', 8 August 1879, file no. 922, l/p&j/6/16, oioc. (political and judicial dept. papers) for a fascinating account of the significance of clothes. For commentary, see Alan Trevithick 'Some Structural and Sequential Aspects of the British Imperial Assemblages at Dehli' 24 *Modern Asian Studies* 3 (1990) 561–78. See also, Bernard Cohn, *Colonialism and Its Forms of Knowledge: The British in India* (Princeton: Princeton University Press, 1996) at pp106–62.

59 Metcalfe, *Ideologies of the Raj*, op. cit., n55 at p75.

60 Lady Elizabeth Balfour, *The History of Lord Lytton's Indian Administration 1876–1880* (London: Longmans, Green & Co. 1899) at p128.

61 Cohn, *Representing Authority in Colonial India*, op. cit., n43 at p207. The decision to hold the ceremony in Delhi, and not in Calcutta the Imperial capital, was significant. Delhi, being the historic seat of the Moghul empire.

62 Balfour, op. cit. n60 at p133: 'In the opinion of the best judges in India, after some years experience, the assumption by the Queen of the title of Empress had had the results of far reaching importance. The supremacy of the British Government had of course been long admitted but in many areas the chiefs gave themselves the airs of independent powers. The twenty-one guns ceased after the Delhi assembly to be a sign of equality with the representative of the sovereign', at p133.
63 John Cotton, quoted in Charles Allen and Sharada Dwivedi, *Lives of the Indian Princes* (London: Arrow Books, 1986) at p153.
64 Wheeler, *History of the Imperial Assemblage* op. cit., n52 at p45.
65 Marquis Curzon, 'Justification of the Delhi Durbar' in H. Cladwell Lipsett, *Lord Curzon in India 1898–1903* (London: Everett & Co., 1903).
66 See Thomas Metcalfe, *Ideologies of the Raj* (Cambridge: Cambridge University Press, 1997) at p75.
67 Cohn, 'Representing Authority in Colonial India', op. cit., n43 at 188.
68 Wheeler, *History of the Imperial Assemblage* op. cit., n52 at p113.
69 For this argument I am grateful to the prompting of Anton Schutz.

7 Conclusion: Dust is Miscarried

1 George Bataille, 'Dust' in Isabelle Waldeberg (ed), *Encyclopaedia Acephalica; Comprising the Critical Dictionary* (London: Atlas Press, 1996).
2 *Bumper Development Corporation Ltd v Commissioner of Police of the Metropolis and others (Union of India and others, claimants)* [1991] 4 All ER 638–49.
3 Peter Ackroyd, 'A Note on English Melancholy' in *Albion: the Origins of the English Imagination* (London: Doubleday, 2003) at p59.
4 For what might be the most vehement assessment of Raj Nostalgia see Salman Rushdie, 'Outside the Whale', in Anne Greet, Syd Harrex and Susan Hoskin (eds), *Raj Nostalgia: Some Literary and Critical Implications* (Adelaide: CRNLE, 1992) pp111–12.
5 Mircea Eliade, *Myths, Dreams and Hysteria: the Encounter between Contemporary Faiths and Archaic Realities*, P. Marret (trans) (London: Harvill Press, 1960).

Index